BLACK & BLUE

BOB BERGHAUS

BLACK & BLUE

A SMASH-MOUTH HISTORY
OF THE NFL'S
ROUGHEST DIVISION

CLERISY PRESS

LIBRARY OF CONGRESS CATALOGING-IN-PUBLICATION DATA

Berghaus, Bob, 1954–
Black and Blue : a smash-mouth history of the NFL's roughest division
/ by Bob Berghaus.
p. cm.
ISBN-13: 978-1-57860-301-5
ISBN-10: 1-57860-301-3
1. National Football League—History.
2. Football—United States—History.
I. Title.

GV955.5.N35B44 2007
796.332'64—dc22

2007022741

EDITED BY
JACK HEFFRON

COVER AND INTERIOR DESIGNED BY
STEPHEN SULLIVAN

Photos on 13 (Moore, Barney), 45, 54, 98, 102, 109 courtesy of the Detroit Lions
Photos on 22–23, 94, 134, 171, 175, 179, 180–181 and 183 courtesy of the Minnesota Vikings
Photo on 117 courtesy of Bettmann/Corbis
All other photos courtesy of the *Green Bay Post-Gazette*

Clerisy Press
1700 Madison Road
Cincinnati, OH 45206
www.clerisypress.com

FOR LISA

THANK YOU FOR YOUR CONSTANT LOVE,
AND FOR PUTTING UP WITH A LOT OF LONG NIGHTS
AND LATE DINNERS THROUGH 25 YEARS OF MARRIAGE.

- - - - -

FOR KELLY

I STILL LOVE YOU, EVEN THOUGH YOU CALLED
FENWAY PARK A DUMP.

ACKNOWLEDGMENTS

This was an enjoyable project to work on and it brought back a lot of memories of watching Packers games with my dad during the 1960s.

First and foremost, I'd like to thank everyone who was interviewed for this book. Most of you gave me a lot more time than previously agreed upon. Some of you even thanked me for having the opportunity for sharing your stories. Believe me, the pleasure was all mine. It was fun being 12 and 13 again.

I would like to thank the public relation staffs of the Bears, Lions, Packers and Vikings for helping me with interviews and for allowing me access to your archive departments. I would also like to thank the *Green Bay Press-Gazette* for supplying the majority of the pictures in this book.

Special thanks to Jeff Ash of the *Press-Gazette* for all the time he spent searching for pictures and to Eric Goska for his research and fact checking. I'd also like to thank Don Langenkamp for his help and overall wisdom. You helped me more than you think you did.

I'd also like to thank Clerisy Press for allowing me to do this book. I had a lot of fun.

Last but not least, I'd like to offer special thanks to four former bosses who took chances on me during my career and gave me opportunities that led to where I am today: Jim Cohen, Bill Dwyre, Carol Hunter and Chuck Salituro.

ABOUT THE AUTHOR

BOB BERGHAUS was born in 1954 and raised in Milwaukee where he was a fan of the Green Bay Packers teams coached by Vince Lombardi. Berghaus went on to work for the *Milwaukee Journal* and *Milwaukee Journal Sentinel* where he covered the Milwaukee Brewers from 1991-95 and the Green Bay Packers from 1996-98, covering the Packers in Super Bowl XXXI and XXXII. He then moved to Green Bay to become sports editor of the *Green Bay Press-Gazette*. He has earned several writing awards including being named Wisconsin Sportswriter of the Year in 1991 by the National Sportscasters and Sportswriters Association. He left Green Bay in the summer of 2003 for Asheville, North Carolina, where he is currently sports editor of the *Asheville Citizen-Times*. He and his wife, Lisa, have a daughter, Kelly.

TABLE OF CONTENTS

Chicago Bears coach George Halas looks on from the sidelines during a 49-0 loss to the Packers on September 30, 1962. Behind him are guard Stan Jones, also kneeling, and assistants Sid Luckman and Phil Handler.

INTRODUCTION

The first time I remember being truly excited about the Green Bay Packers was New Year's Eve Day in 1961. I was seven years old and the Packers were going to play the New York Giants for the National Football League championship.

The Packers lost in the title game to the Philadelphia Eagles in 1960, but I don't recall that game. A year later, though, I couldn't go anywhere in Milwaukee, which is two hours south of Green Bay, without hearing some reference about the Packers. And they were just three years removed from a 1-10-1 season.

I watched that game in my family's living room with my dad and my brother David, becoming more excited each time the Packers scored that day, which was a lot. The Packers beat the Giants, 37-0, behind the play of Paul Hornung. The Golden Boy scored 19 points, setting a record for a championship game. Shortly after the game ended, Dave and I scrambled to our room, put on our football helmets and ran to the front yard where we played our own championship game.

"I'm the Packers," I shouted, taking advantage of my older brother status. Up and down the street other boys were out throwing the football, even though the weather was more suitable for sledding.

Yeah, I was a Packers fan as a kid. Every afternoon I'd rip open the paper to look for any stories involving Hornung, Bart Starr, Boyd Dowler and Herb Adderley, my favorite Packers. At an early age, I also became aware of the Packers' chief rivals: the Bears and Lions. It seemed like when the Packers lost, or played a close game, either Chicago or Detroit was involved.

I remember the 1962 Packers team, the one some football historians call one of the best ever. They barely beat the Lions in Green

Bay and then, on Thanksgiving in Detroit, they got buried by the Lions. Or more appropriately, Starr was buried, sacked 11 times in a 26-14 loss, the only defeat for Green Bay that season. To this day I can close my eyes and recall the images on our black-and-white TV showing Lions defensive tackle Alex Karras standing over the fallen Starr time and again. Karras became a villain that day.

I was heartbroken the next year when the Bears, led by Mike Ditka, Ed O'Bradovich and big Doug Atkins beat the Packers twice and won the NFL championship. I always reasoned that had Hornung not been suspended for the entire season for gambling, the Packers would have won a third straight title.

The first Packers game I attended came in August 1964, an exhibition game against the Bears at Milwaukee County Stadium, where the Packers played some of their games. I didn't know I was going until about four hours before the game, and I remember shaking with excitement when Dad told me that the neighbor down the street had invited me.

We left almost two hours early because of traffic. I had been to County Stadium twice before for Milwaukee Braves games, but this was different. I had never seen so many people in my life. The stadium was barely half-full for the Braves games I attended. On this night, people were packed like sardines in the left-field bleachers where we sat, and almost 50,000 people were in the stadium. Our seats were about forty yards behind the Packers bench, maybe halfway up the bleachers. I didn't care; it was thrilling to be there, and even more thrilling that Hornung, my hero, scored every point in a 21-7 victory in his return to the game following his suspension. Those were the days when exhibition games were taken seriously and the starters played well into the second half.

The next time I went to a Packers game in Milwaukee, I was seventeen and the Packers weren't the best team anymore. They played a Monday night game in Milwaukee against the Lions, whose players I recall were wearing black arm bands in memory of Chuck Hughes, a backup end who suffered a heart attack on the field and died eight days earlier during a game against the Bears.

By that time, the Vikings, the team that wore the funny purple pants in the 1960s, had become the dominant team in the division known as the Black and Blue for its physical style of play. Defense, always defense, is what the four teams were known for during the 1960s and '70s. Whenever those teams played, you could expect scores like 9-7, 14-10 or 13-10.

The Packers of the 1960s were led by defensive stalwarts such as defensive end Willie Davis and tackle Henry Jordan up front, safety Willie Wood and Adderley, the fleet-footed cornerback. In the middle was the bald, menacing figure of Ray Nitschke, who mauled any running back who dared to sprint toward him.

When the Vikings dominated the division, the players I remember the most are the guys up front: Jim Marshall, Carl Eller, Alan Page and Gary Larsen. They made up the smothering foursome that became known as the "Purple People Eaters."

Any final score in which the winning team had more than 21 points was considered a shootout. Big hits on the quarterback generally replaced big plays on offense.

When the Bears dominated the division in the 1980s, their famed 46 defense, led by middle linebacker Mike Singletary and defensive ends Dan Hampton and Richard Dent, was the focal point of that team.

As a sportswriter, I didn't become heavily involved in covering the Packers until the Brett Favre era. By then, football was more open. While the scores in division games were higher, the intensity never lacked. The teams have always played a style befitting the towns they represent—hard-working cities where the fans take their football seriously.

Welcome to the Black and Blue.

Clockwise from top left, Lions receiver Herman Moore; Vikings quarterback Fran Tarkenton; Bears linebacker Dick Butkus; Packers running back John Brockington; Packers quarterback Brett Favre pushing away Vikings linebacker Jeff Brady; Lions defensive back Lem Barney; Bears quarterback Jim McMahon

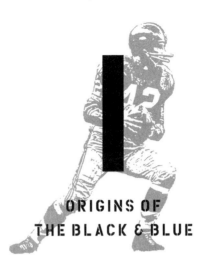

ORIGINS OF THE BLACK & BLUE

Even today, older fans vividly recall the classic images of the Black and Blue Division. Forrest Gregg's fierce countenance, his facemask caked with mud. A snarling Dick Butkus wearing a blood-stained jersey. A gleeful Alex Karras crushing quarterback Bart Starr time and again in the Lions' Thanksgiving Day massacre of the Packers. Jim Marshall and the "Purple People Eaters" devouring another defenseless quarterback.

Frozen images on the field. Frozen fans in the stands. Frozen in time in the annals of professional football. Even before the northern tier of the NFL became a division, it was segregated by its style of play. Black and Blue.

- -

Packers fullback Jim Taylor fights off Lions linebackers Carl Brettschneider (left) and Joe Schmidt during a game in Green Bay in 1962. Lions end Darris McCord approaches from the left.

Nobody really remembers when the term originated. Could Pat Summerall have used it while doing play by play of a Packers-Bears game? Could Bud Grant have uttered it while describing a late-season clash between the Vikings and Bears at Wrigley Field or against the Packers in the mud and snow at old Metropolitan Stadium?

"We used it in one of our highlight films," said Steve Sabol, president of NFL Films, which was established in 1962. "I think it was in a Bears highlight film or might have been in one of the Lions highlight films that we mentioned that it was the Black and Blue Division.

"I think we might have popularized it, but to say we created it I'm not sure. But I know we popularized that phrase when it was used in our highlight films a lot. We used it whenever we did a highlight film for anyone of those four teams. It was guaranteed 'the Black and Blue Division' was going to be in the script."

Whoever came up with the phrase as a moniker for the NFC Central Division was on target. Long before domed stadiums and artificial turf, the Chicago Bears, Detroit Lions, Green Bay Packers and Minnesota Vikings were the face of the NFL in the 1960s when the league went from an alignment of two conferences to four divisions, one of which consisted of the Bears and Packers, Lions and Vikings.

And the game they played was bare-knuckle football. Punishing running backs were met by linebackers whose names were filled with consonants: Ray Nitschke, Wally Hilgenberg, Wayne Walker. And of course, Dick Butkus.

Even before the Central Division existed, Black and Blue was the style of football those teams played. The Bears, Lions and Packers had been around the NFL almost since the league's inception. The Vikings were an expansion team that didn't join the NFL until 1961 but by the middle of the decade had built a reputation as a hard-nosed team. The fact that the Vikings played in the most frigid, unforgiving region didn't hurt their image.

The Black and Blue was about running the football and knocking the snot out of the guy on the other side of the line. It was about Butkus and Nitschke, two of the meanest, nastiest and talented individuals who ever played middle linebacker. It was about indestructible Jim Marshall, who never missed a game in 20 seasons, and the Purple People Eaters, a defensive line that made life miserable for opposing quarterbacks and running backs. It was about Thanksgiving Day football in Detroit and snow banks that ringed the Met and Wrigley Field and Lambeau Field in December.

True enough, football was indeed a rugged game on most fields in the 1960s, but it was brutal on the gridirons where the Packers and Bears, Lions and Vikings competed on Sundays.

Dave Robinson was an All-American linebacker at Penn State when he was drafted by the Packers in the first round in 1963. Early in his rookie season he realized that what he took for rough play on college fields didn't compare to the punishment dished out at the next level.

"When I was at Penn State, the games against Syracuse, Pittsburgh and West Virginia were tough, tough games," said Robinson. "When we played each other it was just unbelievable the hitting that went on in those games.

"Those were just average games in the National Football League. And then you talk about our games against Detroit, Minnesota and Chicago, well, you multiple that by four."

Robinson remembers a collision he witnessed between Lions tackle Lucian Reeberg and Packers defensive end Lionel Aldridge. The carnage was reminiscent of an Ali-Frazier fight.

"I was out there on the kickoff team and my roommate, Lionel Aldridge, said, 'I'll take this guy and try and bust the wedge.' I'm running down the field and all of a sudden I heard this hit that sounded like a minor explosion. I looked back to my left and Lionel's lying there dazed and this guy's lying there dazed also. Little specks of silver paint were all over the field, on Lionel's jersey, everywhere. They hit helmet to helmet and all the paint had popped off Reeberg's helmet and he had little white spots over his helmet where the paint had been."

"That's what it was; it was a physical division," said Mike Ditka,

Dave Robinson, a first-round draft choice out of Penn State, joined the Packers in 1963. By 1966 he was an All-Pro player and one of the best outside linebackers in the National Football League.

a Hall of Fame tight end who won a championship with the Bears as a player in 1963 and as their coach in Super Bowl XX. "It was a black and blue division. And every one of those teams was basically, I guess you have to call them blue-collar teams. That's what they were.

"Football wasn't open like it is today but those were teams that played good defense. That's what they were based on. Ran the ball effectively and they were good solid football teams that would get up in your face and knock the crap out of you. That's what I remember. The games I played as a player against the Vikings and the Packers and the Detroit Lions were the most memorable ones."

Another maniacal middle linebacker of the Butkus-Nitschke genre, Mike Lucci, played for the Lions from 1965-73 with a wild-eyed intensity that fit perfectly into what the Black and Blue was all about.

"Look at the teams involved. The Lions were number one in defense for a lot of years in the '60s; they didn't have a lot of offense," said Lucci. "The Packers, who even when they were winning, ran the football. It wasn't like they were throwing to beat teams. And they had a good enough defense, a helluva defense.

"The Bears had Butkus and they played a lot of defense, and the Vikings, by the end of the '60s, were building that great defense and front four. So when you really look through the whole thing everybody had a good defense. And so you prided yourself on the defense and the idea of hitting hard and beating them up along the way. Overall, the teams were really more defensive-minded than offensive-minded."

The Packers, who in 1967 won the first Central Division title and the last of their five NFL championships under Vince Lombardi, had a solid offense during the 1960s, led by quarterback Bart Starr and running backs Paul Hornung and Jim Taylor. Helping create holes for the running game and protecting Starr was right tackle Forrest Gregg. All four are in the Hall of Fame, but only Starr and Gregg were still around when the Packers began playing in the Central. By then, Hornung and Taylor had been replaced by Donny Anderson and Jim Grabowski.

While the offense could score more than the average NFL team, it was the Packers' defense that people remember, a unit that had a lineup featuring five Hall of Fame players.

Nitschke was the bald, menacing man in the middle, a toothless, tough-as-nails player. His snarling countenance plus a gaping hole where two front teeth once resided were enough to make most offensive linemen consider a new line of work.

Playing in front of him were Willie Davis, a gifted left end, and Henry Jordan, a talented tackle.

The Packers' secondary was led by safety Willie Wood, a quarterback in college who was undrafted but signed by the Packers after sending a letter to Lombardi asking for a tryout. He became one of the best free safeties in the history of the game, finishing his career with 48 interceptions. Herb Adderley, an All-American running back at Michigan State, became a feared cornerback in the NFL, capable of shutting down any receiver who lined up against him.

Those five were starters in a 37-0 shutout of the New York Giants in the 1961 NFL championship game, the first title won by the victory-starved Packers in 17 years. They were the core of a defense that a year later registered three shutouts and allowed just 148 points in 14 games.

"I've always said that the greatest franchise I ever got to see was the Packers under Lombardi," said Ditka, who is not known to freely hand out superlatives.

Larry Hand, a defensive end for the Lions from 1964-77, considered it an honor to have played in the same conference and division with one of the most respected teams in the history of professional football.

"To be quite honest, I still root for Green Bay a little bit mainly because they were also a class act," said Hand. "I felt stronger about—and respected—Green Bay more than any team in our division because they were a bunch of guys that were good hard-working guys and team players.

"I look back and those were some of the fonder memories in the early years because I was playing against a great team and a dynasty.

I felt fortunate because a lot of players didn't get to do that."

Hand said he didn't feel the same respect for the Vikings, who took over dominance of the Midwest teams after the Packers won their second Super Bowl under Lombardi following the 1967 season. Lombardi briefly moved to the Packers' front office and then to the Washington Redskins and retired. The Packers, who were suddenly an old football team, slipped into oblivion for the next quarter century before the foursome of Ron Wolf, Mike Holmgren, Brett Favre and Reggie White helped bring the Super Bowl trophy back to Green Bay after a 29-year absence.

The Vikings finished with a 3-8-3 record in 1967, their first with Bud Grant as coach. Ironically, his first victory in the NFL was over Lombardi's Packers, 10-7, in a game at Milwaukee County Stadium in which the Vikings held Green Bay to an unimaginable 42 yards rushing.

"One thing from my perspective that disappoints me in retrospect is that Lombardi and Grant didn't get a chance to coach against each other more. Only one year, and they split," said Lee Remmel, the official historian of the Packers.

The rematch that season was also close, although more high scoring as the Packers prevailed 30-27 in Bloomington, Minnesota. Sadly, that was the final Central Division confrontation between the two strong-willed, legendary coaches. If the rivalry had continued, who knows how much black and bluer the division would have been?

That was the highest-scoring game between division teams that year, and one of three times in 12 games in which the winning team scored more than 20 points. There were three ties and four other games decided by four points or less. The highest winning margin in a game between Black and Blue teams was 11 points.

In their six games against division teams, the Packers scored 111 points, or 18.5 a game. In the eight games outside of the division, the Packers scored 241 points, or 30.1 points a game. The Vikings scored 67 points, or 11.1 per game within the division and 166 or 20.8 per contest in other games.

Coach Bud Grant (left) and defensive tackle Jim Marshall both were instrumental in the Minnesota Vikings playing in four Super Bowls in the 1970s. Grant, who also won four Canadian League championships as a coach, is in the Hall of Fame. Marshall, who never missed a game in 20 seasons, is not.

Defense—always defense—was the core of divisional play.

"The games were classics," said Grant, who lives in suburban Minneapolis where he gets to watch his son coach high school football. "Those games against Green Bay, Detroit and Chicago were just classic Black and Blue games.

"I remember sitting at a post-game press conference after one game and some guy says, 'Why can't you score more points, you only scored 13. And I said, 'Yeah but we won, that's the way this game is played in this division.'"

The following year Minnesota won the Black and Blue with an 8-6 record for the first of four straight division titles. During that stretch the Vikings played in Super Bowl IV, losing to the Kansas City Chiefs. Green Bay ended the Minnesota streak with a division championship under coach Dan Devine in 1972, but that was an aberration. The Vikings came back and won the next six division championships and played in the Super Bowl three more times.

As great as the Vikings were, especially the defense that featured the Purple People Eaters—front four of Jim Marshall, Alan Page, Gary Larsen and Carl Eller—they really can't be mentioned in the same breath as the 1960s Packers. The Vikings were 0-4 in the Super Bowls under Grant, outscored in those games 96-34.

But they were almost unstoppable during the heyday of the Black and Blue, winning 10 of 11 championships from 1968-78 and playing in six NFC championship games.

The Vikings often won ugly, as they did during a 1971 game against the Packers when they totaled 87 yards but won the game 3-0 on a late field goal after forcing a turnover. The offense could generate points, especially outside of the Black and Blue and when Fran Tarkenton was the quarterback. But when people remember the Vikings, it's the Purple People Eaters and a secondary that included Hall of Fame safety Paul Krause, who holds the record for most interceptions in the NFL with 81.

Grant coached the Vikings from 1967-1983 and again in '85.

He was the stoic figure who wouldn't allow heaters on the sidelines of Metropolitan Stadium, a baseball park that served as the Vikings' home for 22 years before they moved indoors in '83. When asked to define Black and Blue, Grant turns philosophical.

"We all played outdoors, and Green Bay was the only football stadium we played in," said Grant, who also coached ten years in the Canadian Football League, leading the Winnipeg Blue Bombers to four Grey Cup championships.

"Detroit had a lousy stadium. When we played the Bears in the beginning it was at a ballpark, Wrigley Field. We played on baseball diamonds and nobody ever sodded the infields. We played in grimy kinds of places.

"What people remember mostly is the bad weather, but really we played most of our games in nice weather. When we started in September and October it really wasn't bad weather. November wasn't really bad until the middle of the month. But when people talk about those days all they remember is the bad weather.

"They say, 'I remember the playoff game when the wind chill was this or that and there was all of this snow.'"

"Rivalries were as geographic as any. In those days, games were televised regionally. Consequently the people in the east and west didn't see us until the playoffs and what was the playoffs? The play-offs are played on cold, miserable fields. So that's when the people on both coasts, where the majority of the people live, saw Green Bay, Minnesota and Chicago. And they were in lousy-weather games. They don't remember much about Detroit because they weren't in the playoffs that much."

Many of the teams in the National Football League in the 1960s played in baseball stadiums. The Baltimore Colts played in Memorial Stadium, home of the Orioles. The Washington Redskins played in Griffiths Stadium, later named Robert F. Kennedy. The New York Giants played at Yankee Stadium, the most famous of baseball facilities. In St. Louis the Cardinals' home was Busch Stadium and the home of the Cleveland Browns was a mammoth and hostile anachronism called Municipal Stadium that had the worst visiting lockerrooms in the NFL and Major League Baseball. When the Atlanta Falcons joined the league in 1966 they played at Fulton County Stadium, home of the Braves.

The only teams that had football stadiums were the Los Angeles Rams (Coliseum), the San Francisco 49ers (Kezar Stadium), the Philadelphia Eagles (Franklin Field), the Pittsburgh Steelers (Pitt Stadium), the Dallas Cowboys (Cotton Bowl), the New Orleans Saints (Tulane Stadium), and the Packers, who played at Lambeau Field.

The Packers had two homes. Milwaukee County Stadium was where they played three of their regular season games from 1961 until '77 and two through 1994 when they decided to play all of their games at Lambeau.

Players enjoyed playing in Green Bay because of the atmosphere. The fans knew their football and how to have a good time in the parking lot, grilling steaks and sausages. Fans made tail-gating an art form on the Lambeau Field asphalt parking lots long before it became a national craze. It was not uncommon to see them enjoying an ice-cold beer in 20-degree weather. The players also enjoyed playing in a football-only stadium where the field was smooth and level and the only bald spots might be closer to the middle of the field late in the season.

While players knew all about the special stadium in Green Bay, Lambeau itself probably didn't become as recognized nationally as it is today until the Packers beat the Cowboys in the 1967 NFL championship game, better known as the "Ice Bowl."

BIRTH OF THE DIVISION

The NFC Central was created on November 30, 1966, when the NFL split into four divisions for the first time at a league meeting in New York.

Before the meeting, it already had been decided that Chicago, Detroit and Green Bay would be in the same division. Originally, the Atlanta Falcons were designated as the fourth team. But

Baltimore Colts owner Carroll Rosenbloom lobbied hard for the Falcons to be in the same division as the Colts, Rams and 49ers. He won and the Vikings were placed in the Central, probably the most intriguing of the four divisions because three of the league's oldest teams had been lumped together. Rosenbloom's obstinence helped the NFL give birth to a division packed with tradition, old-time legends, natural rivalries and with vivid images of mud, snow and blood-and-guts football.

"Oh yeah, when you were in either Wrigley Field, or old Tigers Stadium or Lambeau Field or at the Met, there was a different feeling there because of the weather, because of the history and the tradition," said Steve Sabol. "And the fans hated each other. There's that joke about the Bear fan and the Packer fan laying sod and the Bear fan tells the Packer fan, 'Remember, it's green side up.' I always remember hearing that joke."

Historically, the Central Division was the most successful as well as the oldest. In the 44 years the NFL had been in existence when the Central Division was formed, the championship had been won by Detroit (4) Chicago (8) and Green Bay (10)—a total of 22 times. The division also had the two most recognizable coaches in George Halas and Vince Lombardi.

Halas had been around since the inception of the Bears as an owner, player and coach. To many it seemed as if no major decisions in the NFL were made without the approval of the Papa Bear.

"We were playing the Bears at Wrigley Field and there was snow all over the field and everyplace," recalled former Lions middle linebacker and Hall of Famer Joe Schmidt.

"We lost the game 3-0. We're skating around there and (Chicago halfback) Willie Galimore is running all over the place. So I tackle him one time and I just happened to look at his shoes and he had his cleats off; he just had the iron pegs. So I jumped up and called timeout and called the official over and told him this is illegal, that he can't have this. So he got up and ran off the field. I said, 'I want to show you this and he's standing behind Halas.'

"The official says, 'George, we want to see Galimore's shoes' and George says his shoes are OK. I said bullshit he's got his cleats off and he's running all over the place. I said dammit these shoes are illegal and George says, 'I want to tell you guys his shoes are OK and both of you guys better get the hell out there and get the game going out there.'

"The official says, 'Come on, kid, let's go. I'm not going to argue with him.' "

Schmidt chuckled as he told the story. "George carried so much weight that he practically could convince everybody what to do and how to do it."

Robinson, the former Packer, recalled hearing stories that Halas owned an apartment building that overlooked Wrigley and he would be up on the top floor on a Saturday before the game spying on the workout of the next day's opponent.

"There was always that rumor that George would be up there with binoculars, watching us," said Robinson with a chuckle. "Vince would put his trick plays in Saturday practice just for George. Football was fun in those days. The word was that at one time George offered one thousand dollars for one Green Bay Packers play and Vince said, 'Hell, for a thousand dollars I'd send him one.' Stuff like that went on all the time."

What also went on was a style of football loved by purists and played by people who gave every ounce of blood and sweat they had. The only thing that could get Nitschke and Butkus off the field was a stretcher. Bill Brown and Dave Osborn, the running back tandem for the Vikings, would rather run through people than around them. Joe Kapp, the quarterback on the Vikings' first Super Bowl team, was the same way. It was the mindset of that team, of the entire division.

"We had a guy by the name of Bobby Bryant who was our corner," said Wally Hilgenberg, who started in all four Super Bowls for Minnesota. "Bobby was about six-foot one and 167 pounds and I can tell you that on two different occasions after he made a tackle he came over to me and said, 'Wally, my shoulder's out, put it back in.' And his shoulder was literally dislocated and I would jerk on it, pull down and it would pop back in. He would never leave the field.

"Today these guys get a little ding and they don't want to play for two weeks."

Hilgenberg's first professional game was as a member of the College All-Star team in 1964 against the Bears. From 1934 through 1976, a team of players, most of whom were top draft choices and college All-Americans, annually played the defending NFL champion in Chicago in the first preseason game of the year.

Hilgenberg, drafted by the Lions, was an All-American linebacker. "My brother was an assistant coach at the University of Iowa when I was playing for the Hawkeyes," said Hilgenberg. "The summer of my rookie year I went to the college all-star football team. The night before the game my brother and I were talking on the telephone, talking about the all-stars, the 1964 All-Stars playing the 1963 World Champion Chicago Bears."

During the conversation Hilgenberg was told by his brother to make sure that he opened up the game with a good lick on the player lined up opposite him.

"I'm playing left linebacker and we lose the toss and we kick off and the ball is on about the 30-yard line," Hilgenberg recalled. "The Bears come out of the huddle strong to my side and number 89 (Mike Ditka) walks to the line of scrimmage. I'm this rookie linebacker and just before the snap, I kind of drop my shoulder a little bit and as soon as the ball was snapped I threw a forearm, hit him on the chin. I knocked his head right straight back, really hit him hard.

"He just stood there after I hit him and grabbed me and pulled me in and looked straight at me and said, 'You want to play rough, huh, rookie?' And I said to myself, 'Oh, no, I just made him mad.' "He kicked my butt the whole game. It had been the biggest battle ever in my life up until that time, and it was funny, I knew after the game I had got my butt kicked. After the game he came up and said, 'You did a good job, kid. I'll see you around. You'll make it in this league.'

"Well, it was just a real encouragement to me. I knew he didn't have to tell me that."

Ditka was a devastating blocker and a gifted receiver who revolutionized the tight end position immediately by catching 56 passes as a rookie, an unusually high number for a tight end at that time. While many people think Ditka epitomized what the Black and Blue was all about, he never participated in the division as a player. He was traded to Philadelphia after the 1966 season and eventually ended his playing career in Dallas.

When Ditka, the first tight end to be inducted into the Hall of Fame, returned to the Bears as a coach, the Black and Blue had already undergone a dramatic facelift.

The evolution of the passing game forced its teams to adapt to a more wide-open game.

The Bears also had a new home, Soldier Field, which they moved into in 1971. The stadium also had an artificial surface. In 1975 the Lions moved from Tiger Stadium to the Pontiac Silverdome, an indoor stadium. One of the biggest changes occurred in 1977 when the Tampa Bay Buccaneers became the fifth member of the Black and Blue. They were considered by many purists as a fifth wheel. In 1983 even the Vikings had an indoor stadium. Every stadium except Lambeau and Milwaukee County Stadium had an artificial surface.

The entire image of the division was changing.

"Professional football in general changed. We were traditionally the defensive, hard-hitting, tough, grind-it-out conference," said Gale Gillingham, a perennial All-Pro guard for the Green Bay Packers from 1966-74 and '76. "It was basic football. You either beat these guys or they beat you.

"Now, they've liberalized the holding rules, have guys 330 pounds that can't run. Have you watched those guys trying to pull? It's a joke. You watch the trap block they run over and grab the guy and try to pull him aside. They don't hit anybody to speak of. Defensive guys can't hit anybody with their helmet. Things have changed. So I think all the game has changed. You really can see it with the old Black and Blue. Green Bay and Minnesota usually lead the league in scoring. The emphasis is offense.

"It's still a good game, I still watch it. But it definitely has changed."

While the game has changed, the Black and Blue Division lives on. Eleven years after the Bears became the first Black and Blue team since the 1967 Packers to win the Super Bowl, the 1996 Packers, led by Ironman quarterback Brett Favre, won Super Bowl XXXI.

The Packers returned to the big game the following year as 11-point favorites but were upset by the Denver Broncos.

Since the turn of the century, the Bears, Vikings and Packers have all won at least one division title. Chicago, led by middle linebacker Brian Urlacher, played in Super Bowl LXI, but lost to the Indianapolis Colts, 29-17.

Football is more open than it was during the early days of the Black and Blue, but the intensity when these teams play each other is still prevalent. The scores may be higher but the competitiveness hasn't gone away. In the first seven years of the 21st century, these four teams have combined to play 40 games against each other that have been decided by seven or fewer points. That's four more than were played during the first seven years of the Black and Blue.

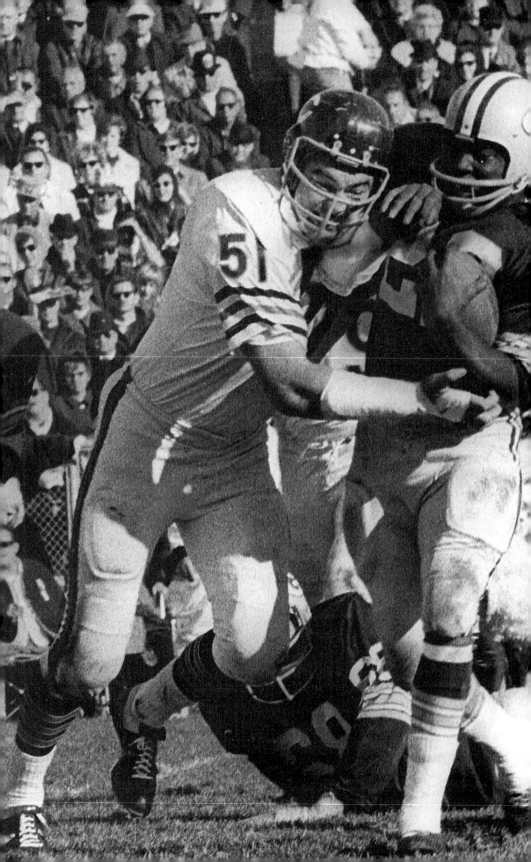

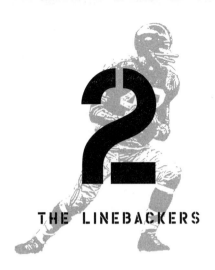

2

THE LINEBACKERS

When you think of the Black and Blue Division, images of fierce, helmet-popping tackles come to mind.

Defensive linemen such as Carl Eller and Alan Page of the Minnesota Vikings; Doug Atkins of the 1960s Bears; and Steve McMichael, a tackle on Chicago's Super Bowl XX team, could cause chaos in opposing backfields seconds after the ball was snapped.

Though smaller, Black and Blue safeties and cornerbacks have always been a tough breed. Gary Fencik and Doug Plank, who played safety together for several years with the Bears, were known as the "Bruise Brothers" for their

----

Dick Butkus delivers another vicious hit on a running back. The victim this time is Green Bay's Elijah Pitts.

physical style of play. Virgil Livers, a Bears cornerback in the late 1970s, weighed just 175 pounds but was as tough as anyone on the field. He once played a game after he ruptured a testicle, which later had to be removed.

But look into the heart and soul of the Black and Blue and you'll discover some of the best middle linebackers to ever play the game.

There are 16 linebackers in the Pro Football Hall of Fame. Ten of the 16 played middle linebacker. Five of those ten played for Black and Blue Division teams, and three of the five played for the Bears: Bill George, from 1952-65; Dick Butkus, from 1965-73; and Mike Singletary, from 1981-92.

The others were Joe Schmidt, of the Lions, and Ray Nitschke, of the Packers. During the heyday of the Black and Blue, the two meanest, biggest, hardest-hitting, most menacing linebackers to ever play the game were Butkus and Nitschke. Fittingly, both were named in 1994 to the NFL's 75th anniversary all-time team.

Both grew up in Chicago and both attended the University of Illinois. Nitschke joined the Green Bay Packers in 1958. Butkus became a Bear in 1965.

By the time Butkus joined the NFL, Nitschke was regarded as the best middle linebacker in the game, although it wasn't many years earlier that the Bears and Lions were both making the same claim for their players.

Before Butkus, the Bears had Bill George, who came into the league in 1952 as a middle guard in the 5-2 alignment, then the most popular in football. Two years later, George is credited in some circles with making history by becoming the first middle line-backer in the NFL during a game against the Philadelphia Eagles.

On passing plays, George's strategy was to make contact with the center, then drop back to help in coverage. Because the Eagles were having success completing short passes just over his head, George decided to drop back immediately. On the second play, he intercepted the first pass of his career.

George, though, didn't begin dropping back on a regular basis until a couple of years later. The actual creation of the 4-3 is credited to Tom Landry, when he was defensive coordinator of the New York Giants before making more of a name for himself as head coach of the Dallas Cowboys.

It wasn't long before other teams made the switch to the 4-3. The Lions, who by the early 1950s had become one of the best teams in the NFL, also had a player who was making a name for himself in the new position. Joe Schmidt, relatively small at six feet and maybe 210 pounds, possessed the strength to battle past an opposing blocker to abruptly end a running play. He also had incredible instincts and could made adjustments in midplay to turn into a pass defender, if necessary.

During his career, Schmidt picked off 24 passes and recovered 16 fumbles. He was a leader, and by the end of the 1950s, after helping the Lions win two of the three league championships they claimed that decade, Schmidt was regarded as the best at his position. He was named to the Pro Bowl ten straight times, beginning in 1955.

"Joe was a great football player and a great guy," said Wally Hilgenberg, who spent the first three seasons of his career with the Lions before going to Minnesota, where he played for the Vikings on four Super Bowl teams.

"(Schmidt) was probably one of the most self-disciplined players. When I got there as a rookie in 1964, there was this guy named Joe Schmidt and he was the middle linebacker. He was the guy who after practice was running wind sprints on his own, hitting (tackling) dummies, doing this and that. He was one of the hardest-working guys I'd ever seen."

Schmidt started his career in Detroit as an outside linebacker but eventually was moved to the middle, a change he said wasn't difficult because in college he was middle linebacker in a 5-2 alignment.

"Middle linebacker was not that difficult to play," Schmidt said more than forty years after his career ended. "So much is made about the position. People think you have to be a whirlwind to play it.

"You have to be a good football player, have a nose for the ball, an intuitive feeling for the ball and you have to be able to tackle people. To me, it's not that difficult to do. I played that position most of the time I played football. If you played in back of four great linemen like I did, it's really a piece of cake. I'm not trying to be humble, I'm just telling you the facts."

Schmidt is being modest. He was one of the best, and he was respected throughout the league.

Former Packers guard Jerry Kramer recalled a game during the 1960s when he was on the other side of the ball and, in amazement, watched Schmidt use an unusual motivational tactic to get defensive tackle Alex Karras more involved in the game.

"Joe was a hell of a middle linebacker, a great player. We were getting set at the line of scrimmage and Alex was down in a three-point (stance) and Joe came up behind him and just wailed him in the ass, just booted him," said Kramer, who handled most opposing tackles he played but had a difficult time with Karras.

"I go, 'Jesus Christ, Joe, don't piss him off anymore than he already is.' It stunned me that Schmidt would do that, that anybody would do that to Alex at that time.

"I guess Alex understood Joe was trying to get him excited, get him up, get him pumped, and he acted like nothing happened," Kramer continued. "When you have your captain kicking you in the ass to get you ready for a play, or a game or anything else, that's indicative of a high level of emotion to me."

In Green Bay, the Packers had an emotional leader in Nitschke, although he really didn't begin a path that led to the Hall of Fame until after Vince Lombardi became the Packers' coach in 1959.

Drafted in 1958, Nitschke, a fullback and linebacker at Illinois, played out of control, both on and off the field. He didn't start immediately for Lombardi, and there were some assistant coaches who felt he was a detriment because he was a heavy drinker who had a penchant for getting into fights.

But Lombardi saw the potential in Nitschke and never gave up on him. Nitschke also got married and settled down, which helped his disposition off the field. On the field, his considerable talent began to blossom in 1961, when the Packers won the first of five championships under Lombardi.

Nitschke played with emotion and took advantage of the Packers' incredible defensive line, which included future Hall of Famers Willie Davis and Henry Jordan, to roam the field and make play after play.

He was known for his love of hitting and for never taking a play off, even in practice. Running back Chuck Mercein joined the Packers midway through the 1967 season and found out he and the other backs had regular encounters with the Packers' linebackers, Nitschke included.

"Lombardi believed in a live blitz pickup," Mercein said. "We would protect our own quarterback and run these different pick-ups. But there was an unwritten rule that you could not cut your own linebackers, you could not go down on their knees, you had to stand up and face them. And they came.

"So I never transgressed against that rule, but for some reason Jim Grabowski decided he just maybe had enough of taking these direct hits from these big linebackers. Every one of them was bigger than our backs by a lot. He cut on Ray, took his knees out from under him. And Ray came up swinging. As a matter of fact he ripped Jim's helmet off and started pounding on him. All Lombardi did was turn around and walk away. There was no criticism. That was part of the deal, having to play offense against the Green Bay Packers' defense, and something I'll never forget because you basically had to stand there and get run over. You had to make your pickup because you didn't want to show the coach that you maybe missed an assignment."

Mercein also remembers a different side of Nitschke, who died of a heart attack in 1998 at the age of sixty-one.

"He was an interesting character," Mercein recalled. "Ray would always greet you with a hug. He was known for his hugs—that was a very warm, personable thing to do."

Nitschke was regarded as the hardest-hitting linebacker during the mid-1960s, but he lost that badge of honor when Butkus came along. Like Nitschke, Butkus was also known for wrapping

Packers middle linebacker Ray Nitschke talks with the media following a Green Bay victory in the 1960s.

his arms around people, giving bear hugs that opposing players never forgot.

"He had the ability to kind of run through you when he tackled you," Mercein said. "The hit would start and it wouldn't end until you were on the ground and often times he was driving you into the ground. He was just like a real good strong heavyweight puncher, a guy who would really hurt you. Some guys have a pull kind of a punch. Dick tackled like he was going to knock you out of the game. He's often said he would have been just as happy to knock you out of the game.

"It was crazy. He was a very, very intimidating guy.

"I saw him at the Super Bowl (XLI) and I felt like telling him that every time there's inclement weather I think about him because my knee hurts so much. There was one time when I ran the ball up the middle on a slant 34, between guard and tackle. I don't know who was supposed to block Dick, but he got a clean shot at me and he crushed me from the outside of my left knee. My left foot was in the ground, my left knee with Dick's shoulder pad firmly against it and I was standing up.

"It was like a right angle. I looked at this and thought, 'Oh My God, I must have broken my leg or some damn thing.' I've never seen anything like this. And it popped right back in but I knew it was injured because it hurt a lot and sure enough I had torn the ligaments."

Mercein's first encounter with Butkus was long before either of them played in the NFL. Butkus and Mercein both played high school football in the Chicago area, and both made the all-state team, Butkus as a linebacker and Mercein as a running back. The all-state team was honored at a dinner at the University of Illinois, which was a big deal for Mercein, who was recruited nationally before deciding to attend Yale. He was sitting at a table with some of the other players and looked up at the dais and noticed Illinois coach Pete Elliott.

"I saw coach Elliott and next to him was a big man. Looked to me like it might be Ray Nitschke because he looked like he might be a pro type of player," Mercein said. "I asked somebody, 'Is that Ray Nitschke?,' and he said, 'No, that's Dick Butkus.'

"He was a man. I'm 18, a silly young boy. I was immature looking. Dick had a 19-inch neck, probably weighed 235 and was six-foot three. I used to read in the paper about him. They used to have his rushing yardage, the number of tackles he made and the number of people who went to the hospital, the people he would hit. It was like the other team's injury report."

That reputation grew when he played at Illinois. By the time he reached the NFL, Butkus weighed close to 250 pounds. He was huge for that time but also had catlike instincts and the physical strength to maul people. Bill George was still with the Bears when Butkus came into the league. George, who could still play and would become the first linebacker inducted into the Hall of Fame, was replaced by Butkus. After sitting on the bench in 1965, he played one season with the Los Angeles Rams.

"He not only hit hard, but anything that was loose—a shoe, a kneepad, an elbow pad, a wristband—he'd rip off. He had this way of dismembering a guy," said Steve Sabol, president of NFL Films, who was often holding a camera just yards away from the spot where Butkus would drill another victim.

"Butkus was the greatest at and really the first person to strip ball carriers," Sabol said. "I never saw anyone do it until Butkus came along. He was so big he would envelope the guy and things would start flying out: his chinstrap, a knee guard, and then the ball would come out."

Sabol remembers one of the first times NFL Films used a microphone to record a pre-game coin toss.

"I think it was against the Lions," Sabol said. "The ref says, 'Captain (Dick) LeBeau, what are you going to do?' And he said, 'We'll receive.' And then the ref said, 'Captain Butkus, what are you going to do?' And he points at LeBeau and says, 'We're going to kick your ass all over the field.'

"He wouldn't even say what side he was going to defend. To me that was so typical of Butkus and the Bears. 'We don't give a shit what field we're defending, were going to kick your ass and walk off the field.'"

He joined the Bears the same year as halfback Gale Sayers, and the two rookies made an immediate impact on a team that finished with a 9-5 record in the Western Conference. The Bears ended up just behind Green Bay and Baltimore, which tied for the title with 10-3-1 records.

Sayers set an NFL record by scoring 22 touchdowns, breaking the mark of 20 set a year earlier by the Colts' Lenny Moore. Six of his touchdowns came in a late-season game in the mud against the San Francisco 49ers.

While Sayers was the most electrifying runner the league had ever seen, Butkus was perhaps the most punishing tackler. And he had a nose for the ball. During his first season, Butkus recovered seven fumbles and intercepted five passes. Coaches had never seen a linebacker like him, and they spent the next eight years building their game plans around trying to stop him.

Butkus never, ever took a play off, which added to his legend. Before he needed surgery to repair both knees, his ability to run sideline to sideline always kept him near the football. He made 22 interceptions and recovered 25 fumbles. Jim Marshall holds the career record with 29 fumble recoveries, which he did over 22 seasons. Rickey Jackson recovered 28 in 15 seasons.

Butkus' total came in just nine seasons.

Many people believe Butkus was the most intimidating player ever in the National Football League. Packers fans may dispute that because Nitschke, the heart and soul of the Packers defense during the 1960s, was also intense and wild-eyed on the field.

"I don't think there was anyone more intense than Dick," said former Packers offensive guard Gale Gillingham, who played against Butkus in college as well as the NFL. "He was always talking, cussin', chewing people out. He just played hard all the time."

Sometimes it would be his own teammate that caught the wrath of Butkus. Former Lions linebacker Mike Lucci, who developed a rivalry with Butkus during the early 1970s, once had three interceptions against the Bears at Soldier Field. The person responsible for throwing those picks, Bobby Douglass, got an earful from an angry Butkus after Lucci's second theft.

"I intercepted the second pass and I can remember Dick swearing at Douglass as he's coming off the field. 'What the fuck, he's not wearing a blue shirt, you asshole. Can't you fucking see?'" Lucci remembered. "He's just swearing at him as he's coming off the field."

By the time Lynn Dickey joined the Packers in 1976, Butkus was long retired. Dickey, though, began his career in 1971 with the Houston Oilers and played against the perennial All-Pro a couple of times.

"I remember his theatrics during the game," Dickey recalled. "You could hear him screaming and yelling, and when he got the chance he'd unload on a guy. He couldn't run nearly as well, and he was about at the end of his rope, but it was interesting to be there and think you're playing against one of the all-time best."

Charlie Sanders, a tight end for the Detroit Lions from 1968-77, had several tussles with Butkus.

"He intimidated the whole NFL," said Sanders, who was elected to the Hall of Fame the day before Super Bowl XLI. "I looked at it like he was a guard playing linebacker. He didn't have the whole lateral (movement) later on, but straight downhill and physically, certainly he intimidated you by being physical and a little dirty at times. The one thing I noticed is we used to think the referees were afraid of him.

"He intimidated everybody and got away with a lot. You looked forward to playing against him. At least you knew what was expected, what he was going to dish out. I had a lot of respect for him."

Former *Green Bay Press-Gazette* columnist Don Langenkamp recalled being mesmerized watching Butkus in the locker room after a Bears-Packers game at Lambeau Field in one of the linebacker's final seasons.

"I remember after a game, Butkus couldn't even get his jersey off," Langenkamp said. "I think he had bad ribs all year. The guy couldn't move. Two guys had to take his equipment off. I was so damn fascinated watching him I didn't feel like interviewing anybody.

"Toward the end of his career he was really banged up. Both of his knees were shot. But boy, he could still play."

Butkus and Nitschke stood out as the premier linebackers of the Black and Blue in the 1960s, but there were others.

Lucci played in just one Pro Bowl, mainly because he had the misfortune of being in the same division as the two future Hall of Famers. Lucci, who played three seasons with the Cleveland Browns before going to Detroit, was an instinctive, hard-hitting player who made 21 interceptions in nine seasons with the Lions. He returned four of those for touchdowns.

"Mike was a fighter, the type of guy you wanted in the foxhole with you," said Larry Hand, a defensive tackle who was one of Lucci's teammates in Detroit. "I think Butkus was allowed to freelance and was allowed to make a lot of great plays, and Mike wasn't a freelancing guy. He played more of a team defense.

"I'm not taking anything away from Butkus. He was definitely a great football player and the type of guy who was going to hurt you. But on the other hand, if I had to start a team, I would take Mike Lucci over Butkus because I think he would be the smarter player."

In Minnesota, Lonnie Warwick was a solid middle linebacker who was hurt by playing in the same division as Butkus and Nitschke. He was also hurt by playing behind the dominating, run-stuffing front line of Carl Eller and Jim Marshall at the ends and Alan Page and Gary Larsen in the interior.

Warwick and outside linebackers Wally Hilgenberg and Roy Winston were respected throughout the league, but they were obviously overshadowed by their defensive line when it came time for Pro Bowl selections.

"They had extremely good linebackers in Winston, Warwick and Hilgenberg," said Ken Bowman, who played center for the

Lions middle linebacker Mike Lucci was an intense competitor who played in the Black and Blue from 1965 through 1973. He participated in one playoff game and played in the Pro Bowl once.

Packers for ten seasons from 1964-73. "All three played hard and all were nearly unblockable, and they just had a great team defense concept."

Jeff Siemon replaced Warwick in the early 1970s. By that time Nitschke was retired and Butkus was in his final years. During a five-year period from 1973-77, Siemon played in the Pro Bowl four times.

Outside linebackers during the early years of the Black and Blue who became stars included Wayne Walker of the Lions and Dave Robinson of the Packers, both of whom played in three Pro Bowls. A linebacker known for his physical style of play was Doug Buffone, a man with few teeth who played with the Bears from 1967-79.

Robinson was a special player. At six-feet three-inches and 245 pounds, he had size to battle opposing linemen while trying to break down a sweep. He also was fast and adept at stopping opposing tight ends, both at the line of scrimmage and in pass coverage.

Drafted out of Penn State, Robinson broke into the NFL in 1963. By 1964 he was a starter. Two years later, Robinson was All-Pro and a Pro Bowl player. He tied for the team lead with five interceptions and, week after week, shut down opposing tight ends. One of the best plays of his career came during the 1966 NFL championship game in Dallas against the Cowboys.

The Packers' defense, which had allowed just 163 points during the season, had trouble with the Cowboys at the Cotton Bowl, and the game turned into a shootout. Led by quarterback Bart Starr, who threw four touchdown passes, Green Bay had a 34-27 lead late in the game when the Cowboys were threatening to score a tying touchdown. Dallas drove inside the Packers five-yard line and faced a fourth and goal. Quarterback Don Meredith rolled to his right and, for an instant, appeared to have a receiver open. But Robinson was in hot pursuit and grabbed Meredith, who, as he was being pulled down, threw a wobbly pass that was picked off by Tom Brown with 28 seconds left. Brown got a lot of the attention after the game, but the real hero on the play was Robinson.

"One guy who should be in the Hall of Fame is Dave Robinson," said Willie Davis, who played in front of Robinson as the Packers' left end and is one of five players from that defense in the Hall.

"Dave Robinson probably made as many big plays as any of our linebackers, and we had three great linebackers in Ray Nitschke, Dave Robinson and LeRoy Caffey," Davis said. "Dave made that big play in Dallas in the championship game, but he made a lot of big plays along the way."

After Butkus retired, the Bears were without a dominating presence at middle linebacker for almost a decade. That changed when they drafted Mike Singletary in the second round of the 1981 draft. By 1983 he was in the Pro Bowl. Two years later, in 1985, Singletary was the leader of Buddy Ryan's 46 defense that carried the Bears to an 18-1 record and a 46-10 win over New England in Super Bowl XX.

Like Butkus, Singletary covered a lot of territory. He also was durable, missing just two games during a twelve-year career. He was a terrific pass defender and was always around the ball, finishing either first or second on the Bears in tackles in his final eleven seasons. He ended his career with 1,488 tackles and 19 sacks. And his eyes were constantly moving.

"I was amazed at how fast he was, especially when he turned and sprinted back to help cover in the secondary," Dickey said. "He had a great nose for the ball, had a great feel for the game and he had all of the athletic tools that you need: speed and strength and smarts.

"He played on a good team. When you get an opportunity as a middle linebacker or a quarterback or a running back to play with really good interior linemen, boy, it makes the game so much easier."

Singletary was surrounded by excellent teammates, especially during the Super Bowl season, when Otis Wilson and Wilber Marshall flanked him and gave the Bears the best linebacking corps in the NFL. But Singletary was the leader, the one who stood out

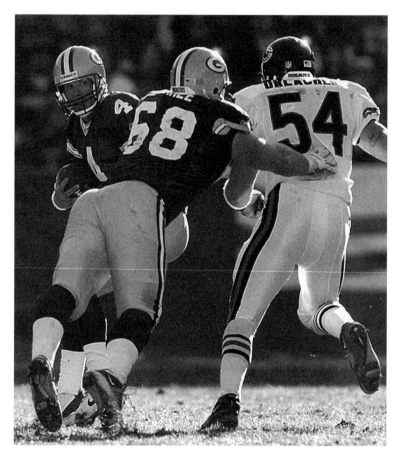

Brian Urlacher (54) closing in on Packers quarterback Brett Favre, is another outstanding middle linebacker for the Bears. He's following in the footsteps of Bill George, Dick Butkus and Mike Singletary, all of whom are in the Hall of Fame.

and played in ten straight Pro Bowls. He was inducted into the Hall of Fame in 1998.

Another inside linebacker from the 1980s and '90s who earned a lot of respect from players, coaches and front-office people in the NFL was Chris Spielman of the Lions. He proved his talent by playing in the Pro Bowl four times, all as a member of the Lions. He also possessed the play-at-all-costs mentality that would have fit in perfectly during the 1960s.

"He was as mentally tough as he was physically tough," former Lions Director of Player Personnel Ron Hughes said in a *Milwaukee Journal Sentinel* story in 2001. "Over the objection of his coaches, he once played after having a tennis ball-sized mass on his right shoulder drained. I said, 'Chris, we'd like you to sit out this week and not play,' He said, 'I'm not going to do that.' He was angry. So I said, 'Chris, at least take it easy in practice.' He finally relented, but said, 'I'm not wearing one of those (expletive) red jerseys.'"

In 2000, the Bears drafted Brian Urlacher, who played outside linebacker and free safety at New Mexico. The Bears made him a middle linebacker and, by his third game, he was in the starting lineup. He played in the Pro Bowl after each of his first five seasons and, in 2005, he was the NFL's Defensive Player of the Year, leading a defense that carried the Bears to an 11-5 record and the team's first division title since 2001. He seems to be a combination of Butkus and Singletary.

"He's evolving the definition of a middle linebacker," said Gary Fencik, a former Bears safety who played several years with Singletary. "I think Brian can continue to get better. I don't know of any middle linebacker who covers more territory than Brian does. "Sideline to sideline, pass coverage, he has tremendous skills."

There's little doubt in Fencik's mind that Urlacher would have fit perfectly with the Black and Blue mentality during the division's heydays in the 1960s and '70s.

"The thing I think that puts him into the category of being one of the better Black and Blue players is the way he goes about his business," Fencik said. "There's no antics, there's no symbols of ego. He just does a great job and acts like he's done it a million times before. I think that's what really makes him stand out; that he doesn't make a tackle and show a bicep, get into a pose, use self-congratulatory gestures that we see commonplace today in the NFL. And people are being paid a lot of money to do that."

3

1967: THE FIRST YEAR

There was a new look to the National Football League in 1967, one that included a change to the league's playoff structure.

During the course of the season, a rookie kickoff returner with blazing speed added another dimension to Green Bay's offense; an NFL icon would coach his last game; the Baltimore Colts would not make the playoffs despite beating the Packers during the season and winning two more games than they did; and Green Bay and Dallas would play a game that would be known as the "Ice Bowl."

After years of using a two-conference format, the NFL aligned into four divisions composed of four teams each.

Packers coach Vince Lombardi, left, and Chicago Bears coach George Halas shake hands after a Green Bay victory.

The Dallas Cowboys, Washington Redskins, Philadelphia Eagles and the expansion New Orleans Saints played in the Capitol Division.

The Century Division included the Cleveland Browns, New York Giants, Pittsburgh Steelers and St. Louis Cardinals. The Century and Capitol divisions made up the Eastern Conference.

The two divisions in the Western Conference were the Coastal and the Central.

The Coastal had the second-year Atlanta Falcons along with the Baltimore Colts, Los Angeles Rams and San Francisco 49ers.

The Central Division was made up of three of the NFL's oldest franchises: the Chicago Bears, Detroit Lions and Green Bay Packers, which had a combined 22 NFL championships (Packers, ten; Bears, eight; and Lions, four) among them. The Minnesota Vikings, who had been in the league since only 1961 but had shown they had the toughness and blue-collar mentality to belong with three teams known for their physical style, joined them.

Tough guy Norm Van Brocklin no longer was the Vikings' coach, having been replaced in 1967 by Bud Grant, who made a name for himself in the Canadian Football League by winning 102 games and four Grey Cup titles in his ten seasons as coach of the Winnipeg Blue Bombers.

Van Brocklin was old school, a coach who often made his team practice six hours a day during training camp. He berated and bullied players to the point where any replacement would be welcome.

Grant, who grew up in Superior, Wisconsin, across the river from Duluth, Minnesota, was considerably more even-tempered than Van Brocklin. His practices didn't last as long and he limited hitting during practice so players would have more in the tank at the end of the season.

Grant kept his distance from the players, but he was honest and he quickly earned their respect.

"It was a big difference," said former Vikings center Mick Tingelhoff, who played his first five seasons under Van Brocklin. "They really were two completely different personalities.

"Van Brocklin was an old-style, Lombardi-type of coach, very loud. And he was a rough person, where Bud is probably one of the cleanest-living people I've ever seen in my life. He hated alcohol, didn't smoke. He didn't want us swearing on the field and we had to wear a coat and tie to everything when we were on a trip. He was just a gentleman's gentleman. He still wanted you to play good football, but good, hard clean football."

The Lions also had a new coach. Joe Schmidt, a perennial All-Pro middle linebacker who had retired as a player in 1965 and joined the Lions' coaching staff as an assistant, replaced Harry Gilmer as head coach.

And of course, the Packers and Bears had coaches known throughout the league. George Halas, who had been with the Bears from their beginning as a player, coach and owner, was entering what would be his last year of coaching. In Green Bay, Vince Lombardi was beginning his ninth season as Packers coach. He already had guided the team to four NFL championships and the first Super Bowl championship the previous year when the Packers, representing the NFL, beat the American Football League champion Kansas City Chiefs, 35-10.

History was important to Lombardi, and he was fully aware that no NFL franchise had won three straight championships. He had a chance at that elusive goal following the 1962 season after the Packers repeated as NFL champions. They were denied a third championship in 1963 when the Bears beat them twice during the regular season, edging them for the Western Conference title before going on to defeat the New York Giants for the NFL title, the last by a Halas-coached team.

Lombardi's Packers entered the 1967 season with a new look in the backfield. Paul Hornung, "The Golden Boy" halfback who had been a scoring machine, and bruising Jim Taylor, who led the team in rushing the seven previous seasons, were no longer on the team. Hornung, slowed by injuries, was taken by New Orleans in the expansion draft, although he retired before playing a game. Taylor, a Louisiana native who had played out his option in 1966, signed a contract with the Saints. Donny Anderson and Jim

Joe Schmidt, a perennial All-Pro middle linebacker for the Lions, coached the team from 1967-72. Standing behind him is tight end Charlie Sanders, who was enshrined into the Hall of Fame in 2007.

Grabowski, known as the "Gold Dust Twins" for the huge contracts they signed prior to joining the Packers in the 1966 season, replaced Hornung and Taylor.

- - - - -

The Packers still had a veteran offensive line led by All-Pro guard Jerry Kramer and All-Pro tackle Forrest Gregg. Bart Starr, who threw just three interceptions in 1966 on his way to the NFL's Most Valuable Player award, was back at quarterback. He had a reliable group of receivers in Carroll Dale, Boyd Dowler and tight end Marv Fleming.

At the heart of the Packers was their defense, which boasted six players who had been consensus All-Pro the previous season in leading the team to a 12-2 regular-season record. End Willie Davis, tackle Henry Jordan, linebackers Ray Nitschke and LeRoy Caffey, safety Willie Wood and cornerback Herb Adderley all returned. All but Caffey would later be enshrined in the Pro Football Hall of Fame.

"What a defense," exclaimed Chuck Mercein, a fullback who joined the Packers midway through the 1967 season. "I know you can make cases for other teams, but when you look at Ray Nitschke in the middle, Dave Robinson on the strong side and LeRoy Caffey on the weak side, those linebackers were tremendous, and all big, all 250-pounders who could run.

"Look at that secondary with Willie Wood at free safety, Tom Brown at strong safety, Herb Adderley, just a wonderful corner and an All-Pro, and Bobby Jeter, formerly a great running back.

"And those ends: Willie Davis was as good as anybody and as quick as you could get; Lionel Aldridge, Henry Jordan, Ron Kostelnik, every one of those guys was a really top-notch player. A lot of them are in the Hall of Fame now and a lot of them were All-Pro for many, many years. So you look at that Green Bay Packers defense and that's the reason why we won a lot of games 10-7, 13-3, 16-10. Defense was the name of the game."

What made that year particularly tough for the two-time defending NFL champion Packers was that every opponent was going to give them their best shot, especially the Packers' three Black and Blue counterparts.

Defense was certainly the cornerstone of the Black and Blue Division in 1967, especially when those teams played each other. Of the 12 games within in the division, the winning team scored more than 17 points just three times. The largest margin of victory was 11 points. Four games were decided by four points or less and three games ended in ties.

The highest scoring of those kiss-your-sister outcomes occurred in the first-ever Central Division game on September 17. The Packers and Lions opened the season at Lambeau Field and played to a 17-17 tie that was really two games in one.

The first half was reminiscent of a Thanksgiving Day clash five years earlier in which the Lions sacked Starr 11 times en route to a 26-14 victory, the only time the Packers lost during the 1962 season.

In this game, he was dropped seven times, four of which came at the hands of Alex Karras, who often seemed to outplay Kramer, Green Bay's All-Pro guard. Starr threw four interceptions in the first two quarters including one to a rookie named Lem Barney who made a diving catch, rolled to his feet and ran 24 yards for the first score of the game.

But the Packers stormed back, using two big plays to help salvage the tie.

The first was in the fourth quarter. Trailing 17-7, Starr, faced with third and 39 at the Green Bay 45, called for a screen pass. As the Green Bay blockers purposely let the Lions defenders past them to chase Starr, the quarterback kept back-pedaling until he finally dumped a pass to Grabowski near the line of scrimmage. The second-year fullback followed his blockers for a 53-yard gain to the Detroit two. From there, Elijah Pitts stormed in for a touchdown that cut Detroit's lead to 17-14.

Then, with a little more than two minutes remaining, Starr

struck it big one more time. After being dumped for a nine-yard loss to his three-yard line, he called a play using a formation the Lions hadn't seen. Pitts lined up in a double-wingback formation, on the right flank of receiver Carroll Dale, who ran a deep route, hoping to take a couple of defenders with him. The Lions bit, which created an opening for the Packers.

Starr scrambled in the end zone before dumping to Pitts at about the five. Pitts put a move on Barney and was off on an 84-yard gain to the Detroit 13.

For a moment it looked like the Packers were going to fully complete the comeback, but Detroit held, and Don Chandler came on and kicked a field goal to tie the game.

The Packers kicked off, forced the Lions into a punt and got the ball back. With eight seconds on the scoreboard clock, Starr threw a short pass to Boyd Dowler, who gained 13 yards to the Detroit 38. The scoreboard showed two seconds remained.

Green Bay was certainly within range for Chandler, especially since these were the days when the goalposts were on the goal line, not ten yards back like they are today.

But before the field goal unit could come onto the field, the referee picked up the ball and signaled that the game was over because on his timepiece, which was official, the game was over.

Lombardi was upset when he talked to reporters following the game.

"I can't understand it," he growled. "That's the quickest eight seconds I've ever seen in my life. I can't understand how a pass play can take eight seconds when it went out of bounds."

Lombardi should have been grateful the game ended in a tie, which was embarrassing but not as bad as a loss.

Almost forty years later, Schmidt remembers his first game as a coach for two reasons: a chat with Lombardi and the sick feeling of letting a win slip away.

"We played a very good game and Lombardi was very complimentary to me after the game," Schmidt recalled. "I can't remember if he called me kid or what, but he said, 'You had your team ready to play, you played a good game.'

"It was a good game, but we should have really won that game. We made a mistake defensively at the end that gave them an opportunity."

The Packers had the Bears the next week, also at Lambeau, and Starr's early season woes continued. He threw an unimaginable five interceptions, giving him nine for the season and six more than he threw during the entire 1966 season.

The Packers also lost three fumbles and needed Chandler to bail them out at the end of the game.

Green Bay led 10-0 at the half, but the Bears tied the game on a field goal by Mac Percival and a 13-yard run by Gale Sayers, who otherwise was held in check by rushing for just 63 yards.

The Packers finally won the game, 13-10, when Chandler booted a 46-yard field goal with just 63 ticks remaining on the clock.

The game story in the *Chicago Tribune* almost seemed to go out of the way to taunt the Packers for their narrow win.

> *The triumph, first of the championship campaign, put them into a tie with Detroit for the lead in the Central Division of the National Football League Western Conference. But it left them little over which to gloat. They resembled anything but monarchs of all professional football, turning the ball over on eight occasions to an embattled Bear defense— five times on interceptions and three times on fumbles.*

Some sense of normalcy returned the following week when the Packers, playing a Milwaukee home game, shut out the Falcons, 23-0.

Lombardi's boys finally played their first road game, and it wasn't a walk in the park. They faced the Lions at Tiger Stadium, where the crowd always seemed hostile, especially toward the Packers when they would run on to the field.

"Fans loved to get on Vince Lombardi in Detroit," recalled former linebacker Dave Robinson. "They just hated him. Vince used to say if they thought Detroit could beat us handily they would be cheering, so all those boos mean they knew we were capable of beating them all the time. So the boos were really cheers for us. Us young kids believed that, and it would get us all fired up."

Like they had a few weeks earlier, the Lions jumped out to an early lead, this time taking advantage of a couple of interceptions thrown by Zeke Bratkowski. The backup was playing instead of Starr, who was out with an injured shoulder he initially hurt during preseason.

One of the interceptions was made by defensive end Larry Hand, who grabbed a tipped pass and scrambled four yards to give the Lions a 10-0 lead.

The Pack battled back as Bratkowski put the Packers on the scoreboard just before the half with a 19-yard scoring strike to Anderson.

After halftime, Green Bay took control. Chandler tied the game with a field goal in the third quarter and gave the Packers a 13-10 advantage with another one early in the fourth. Green Bay's defense then scored a touchdown when Robinson batted a pass thrown by Milt Plum. Nitschke snatched it out of the sky and rumbled 20 yards for a touchdown and a 20-10 Green Bay lead.

Bratkowski and Dowler hooked up on a scoring pass before the Lions ended the 27-17 loss to the Packers with a consolation touchdown.

The Packers were 3-0-1, but already banged up. In addition to Starr, several other players already were nicked up. Injuries would haunt the Packers all season.

The winless Minnesota Vikings came into Milwaukee the next week. Bratkowski played again and with the exception of one play, failed to generate any offense in a 10-7 loss to a team that would eventually finish with a 3-8-3 record.

But that one play was memorable as Bratkowski threw an 86-yard scoring pass to Carroll Dale in the first quarter.

When Lombardi was told that the play was the longest of the

receiver's career, he smiled sarcastically.

"Well isn't that just lovely," he said. "That gives us something we can really get our teeth into when we look at game films Monday."

The Minnesota defense showed glimpses of their future by limiting the Packers to 42 yards rushing. They finally won the game when Fred Cox booted a 12-yard field goal with just eight seconds remaining.

Following the outcome, the stoic Grant was predictable when asked what it meant for his first NFL win to come against Green Bay.

"The important thing about today is not that we beat the Green Bay Packers, but that we won a ball game," he said.

The Packers were still in control of the division with a 3-1-1 record. The Bears, who beat the Lions the same day, were 2-3 and Detroit, with its new coach, was in third place at 1-3-1.

"It was a very humbling job and I wasn't prepared for it," Schmidt said. "I didn't have the experience and I didn't have the knowledge, so I stumbled around for a while."

The Lions eventually finished 5-7-2 and followed that with a 4-8-2 record in 1968. But Schmidt improved as a coach and put together four straight winning seasons before retiring after the 1972 season. In six years as a head coach he compiled a 43-34-7 record and took the Lions to the playoffs in 1970.

One of the highlights for Schmidt and the Lions in 1967 was the play of Barney, an extremely athletic cornerback whom the Lions drafted in the second round out of Jackson State. Barney made ten interceptions his rookie season, returning three for touchdowns. He averaged 23.2 yards per return on his interceptions.

"He was gifted," Schmidt said. "He was able to cover people in single coverage without a problem. His gift was being able to close on a receiver, even if he was behind a step. When the ball was in the air, he could close with a burst of speed, make up the difference and make the interception.

"He was a big-play guy and that's what you need. The more big-play guys you have, the better you'll be. He could have been a hell of a receiver, too."

After wins over New York and St. Louis, the Packers were 5-1-1 at the midway point of the season. They lost in week eight, blowing a 10-0 lead to the Baltimore Colts, who rallied behind Johnny Unitas for a 13-10 victory at Baltimore's Memorial Stadium. The loss was particularly painful because Pitts and Grabowski, the team's starting backs, were both injured. Pitts was done for the season, while Grabowski would return and play some games, but he wouldn't be the same.

The Packers followed that setback with a 55-7 dismantling of the Cleveland Browns at Milwaukee in a game that was one for the history books. Rookie Travis Williams, probably the fastest player drafted by Lombardi, tied an NFL record by returning two kickoffs for touchdowns, giving him three for the season. He would bring back one more that season, establishing an NFL record at the time. Cecil Turner of the Bears tied the mark three years later.

Williams' returns of 87 and 85 yards highlighted a 35-point first period for the Packers that allowed Lombardi to clear his bench in the second half.

"Those two kick returns by Williams are something you're not going to see more than once in a lifetime on one single day," Lombardi told reporters after the game.

Before Williams, only Timmy Brown had returned two kick-offs for touchdowns in the same game. That feat has been duplicated just three times since Williams's magical day.

Donny Anderson scored four touchdowns and fullback Ben Wilson rushed for an even 100 yards filling in for Pitts and Grabowski.

The coach also was pleased with his resilient team for the way it bounced back from the last-second loss to the Colts and overcame the injuries.

"We've always risen to every challenge in the past and we did it again today," Lombardi said.

The Packers climbed to 7-2-1 the following week by pitching a 13-0 shutout against the 49ers. Starr, though, had to leave the game after injuring his shoulder again. Linebacker Ray Nitschke, the leader of the great defense, also made a rare exit to the sidelines after he was knocked woozy during one play. All Nitschke missed were four plays and he was back on the field.

The rematch against the Bears was next, and a win would clinch the division title just 11 weeks into the season. Talk had been heating up in Chicago that maybe Halas, now seventy-two, was too old to coach. Maybe that's why Lombardi almost went out of his way to praise Halas, whom he deeply respected, following a hard-fought 17-13 win at Wrigley Field.

"The Bears played a tremendous game, and I just have to tell you, that old man is a great old man," Lombardi said of his counterpart.

"I don't want to see any of you guys misquoting me about Halas," he added. "I said he's a great man, a great coach and that's the way I want to see it in the papers."

Grabowski, who had returned to the lineup, was injured again in a tough, bare-knuckle game that was still in doubt before Starr chewed time off the clock with a 55-yard drive inside the Bears' 30. When the drive stalled, Chandler attempted a field goal, which was blocked by the Bears. But they only had 31 seconds to work with, and after a couple of plays the game ended with Green Bay claiming the first Central Division championship.

"They come up for us—every team comes up for the big one," Lombardi said. "It's been a tough season and we've had some guys hurting. Now maybe we can get them rested up."

Three weeks later, the Bears ended the season with a win and a 7-6-1 record in what would be Halas's last game as their coach. He retired during the off-season, ending his career with a regular-season record of 318 wins, 148 losses, 31 ties.

Sayers rushed for 880 yards and scored 12 touchdowns, three on kickoff returns. He made the Pro Bowl along with Butkus and defensive back Richie Petitbon, who tied for the team lead in interceptions with five. The Bears finished second in the 16-team NFL in total defense that season, allowing 3,406 yards, behind only the Packers, who gave up a league-low 3,300. Chicago's problems were on offense. The Bears scored just 239 points, thirteenth in the league, and rushed and passed for 3,293 yards, which ranked fifteenth, or second last.

The Vikings had comparable offensive numbers (233 points and 3,478 yards) but they showed improvement throughout the season. Running back Dave Osborn rushed for a division-high 972 yards and made the Pro Bowl. The Minnesota defense also finished sixth in overall defense (3,856 yards) and seventh in points (294). They also played the Packers extremely tough for a second time later in the season.

The Vikings put up another great fight in the highest scoring game between division rivals that season. The Packers had a seemingly safe 27-17 lead before the Vikings erupted for ten fourth-quarter points to tie the game.

At the end of the game, Minnesota had the ball but the Packers caught a break when Joe Kapp bobbled a snap. The ball was slapped around until Green Bay safety Tom Brown pounced on it at the Minnesota 28.

With time slipping away, Starr took his team to the 12 before Chandler came out and booted a 19-yard field goal with just eight seconds remaining for the winning points.

Next up for the Packers were the Rams, who trailed Baltimore by a game in the Coastal Division. It was a must-win for Los Angeles and a game that the Packers didn't need. Regardless, they played hard and appeared to be on their way to victory with a 24-20 lead with a minute to play. But on fourth down, linebacker Tom Guillory blocked a punt by Anderson, and Claud Crabb recovered at the Packers' five. Roman Gabriel passed to Bernie Casey a couple of plays later for the win, setting up a showdown the following week with the Colts, whom the Rams tied earlier in the season.

Baltimore entered the final game with an 11-0-2 record, and since the teams tied earlier in the season they were playing for a playoff berth.

On December 17 in Los Angeles, the Rams were too strong, powering to a 34-10 win, one that was so dominating, many around

Chuck Mercein was cut by the New York Giants midway through the 1967 season. He was signed by the Packers and played a prominent role in the 21-17 victory over the Dallas Cowboys in the NFL championship game.

----

the NFL believed they were suddenly the favorites to win the championship.

The Packers finished 9-4-1 after losing to the Pittsburgh Steelers, giving them a two-game losing streak for the first time since 1965 and for just the fourth time since the 1960 season.

The Western Conference championship game was held December 23 in Milwaukee, the Packers' second home. Green Bay's running attack was in shambles. Starters Pitts and Grabowski were out for the year and Anderson and Wilson also were banged up. Williams and Mercein appeared to be the starters going against the Rams' famed Fearsome Foursome defensive line.

"We're in real bad shape all right," Lombardi told the media a couple of days before the game. "This is the worst shape we've been in for a postseason game since I've been here. The backfield outside of Bart Starr is uncertain."

Mercein lost a fumble on the Packers' first series, one of four Packers turnovers that day. The Rams took an early 7-0 lead, but then Green Bay, looking comfortable in the twenty-degree weather, started to dominate.

Williams scored on runs of 46 and two yards, Mercein scored on a six-yard run and Starr and Dale connected on a 17-yard scoring play that gave the Packers the lead for good in their 28-7 win.

The Green Bay defense, led by Henry Jordan, who had three sacks, got to Rams quarterback Roman Gabriel five times.

Some say the Rams couldn't handle the cold conditions, but coach George Allen thought differently.

"The Packers played like the champions they are," Allen told the press after the game. "If they continue to play the way they did against us this afternoon, there's no doubt that the Packers will remain as champions of the world. They out-hit us and deserved to win."

THE ICE BOWL

Two days before the NFL championship game, the Dallas Cowboys arrived in Green Bay, where the temperature was in the twenties.

Jerry Kramer (both gloved hands on the ground) clears out Jethro Pugh and leads Bart Starr into the end zone with 13 seconds remaining for a 21-17 victory over the Dallas Cowboys in the game known as the "Ice Bowl."

It was cold, but not unbearable.

"I don't expect the cold to bother us," Cowboys coach Tom Landry told reporters. "All I want is a good field to play on."

The next day, Lombardi took reporters to a control room where he displayed a bunch of flashing bulbs that, in his mind, guaranteed the field would be extremely playable, regardless of how cold it got.

That year, Lombardi paid approximately $80,000 to have a heating system installed under the Lambeau Field turf. The system was comparable to an electric blanket, made up of 14 miles of heating coils that would keep the field from freezing.

Game day arrived, along with a front that brought in the coldest New Year's Eve in Green Bay history.

The temperature was recorded at minus-13 degrees. The wind chill factor was at minus-46.

Lombardi's blanket failed, turning much of the field into a skating rink. All of this made for elements previously unseen during an NFL game and added to the intrigue of a game regarded as one of the best in NFL history. Maybe if the temperature was above zero and the heat coils had worked, the game wouldn't have captured the public's imagination the way it has through the years.

"To me, it's the greatest game ever played," said NFL Films President Steve Sabol, who was a cameraman at the Ice Bowl.

"Not only was it competitive between two great teams, you take the conditions under which it was played and that final drive on that frozen field against the Doomsday Defense; the character of that drive and what it took to do it almost surpassed the actual achievement itself."

Early on, it looked as though the Packers were going to win without a fight. The Cowboys were affected by the biting cold and trailed 14-0 after Starr threw a 43-yard touchdown pass to Dowler early in the second quarter. It was the second touchdown reception of the game for Dowler, who always seemed to be at his best in big games.

"The guy who should be in Canton and who's not is Boyd

Dowler," recalled Dowler's teammate, center Ken Bowman. "Boyd Dowler won more football games for us than you could shake a stick at, but he'll never get in because we weren't a passing team.

"We only passed when we had to or when we set it up with the run. We had a play called a 36 delay or something like that, where we'd run it with Jimmy Taylor. He'd run it when it was third and one and, bang, he'd run it for three yards. The next time it's third and one and, bang, he'd run it for three yards.

"And the next time it's third and one, we'd fake the 36 and Boyd Dowler is streaking down the middle of the field. Bart would sit there and fake the handoff to Taylor, take a few steps back and let her sail. Boyd tells stories about one Dallas game. Cornell Green was their safety and Boyd said he was coming up to stop Jimmy Taylor as Boyd was zipping past him, and he sees (Green's) eyes and they're the size of silver dollars and he suddenly realizes, 'Oops. That's my man that just went by me.'"

Dallas recovered from the early deficit, rallying behind its brilliant defense that took over and turned two Packers mistakes into ten points.

The first was a sack of Starr, who was forced into a fumble by defensive end Willie Townes. George Andrie, the Cowboys' other end, scooped up the ball and ran seven yards for a touchdown that cut Green Bay's lead in half.

Before halftime, Packers safety Willie Wood fumbled while handling a punt. The Cowboys recovered and turned the miscue into a field goal by Danny Villanueva that sliced the Packers' lead to 14-10.

Both offenses struggled as conditions worsened in the second half. The Cowboys finally took the lead when halfback Dan Reeves took a handoff from quarterback Don Meredith on the first play of the fourth quarter and threw a 50-yard touchdown pass to Lance Rentzel that gave Dallas the lead, 17-14.

Between Dowler's second score and Reeves' touchdown toss, the Packers' offense had not been productive. In 23 plays, the team had been held to minus-18 yards.

The team gained little on its first two drives of the fourth quarter as well before a punt gave them the ball on their own 32, with 4:50 remaining in the game.

"Bart looked at everyone in the huddle and he didn't say anything," recalled Bowman. "We knew this was it, that it was make or break time, that it was probably the last time we were going to see the ball and nobody had to say anything. We broke the huddle and went to work."

What happened during the next 12 plays was a group of men, future Hall of Famers and journeymen alike, working together for the ultimate reward. They had been badly outplayed for more than two quarters by the Cowboys, but now it was time to march toward their special place in history.

A player who had been cut at midseason by the Giants provided two of the more remarkable plays.

Chuck Mercein, a high school star in Illinois who had gone on to Yale and later to the Giants, was signed to the Washington Redskins' taxi squad but later acquired by Lombardi when fullback Jim Grabowski suffered a severe knee injury.

Mercein scored a touchdown a week earlier in the victory over the Rams. Here he was again in the Packers' backfield. On first-and-ten from the Dallas 30, Starr hit Mercein on a 19-yard pass down to the 11. And it was Mercein who told his quarterback that he was not being covered when running out to the flat.

"I'd never done that before, but I knew I was open in the flat and I knew that the linebacker (Dave Edwards) was taking kind of a steep drop back," Mercein recalled thirty-nine years later. "So sure enough, I said to Bart, 'If you need me, I'll be open over on the left after I check for a blitz pickup.' That was your first responsibility as a back, to check for the blitz. If they didn't come, you go out on a pattern.

"So when (Edwards) dropped straight back again, I just did a little flare and Bart laid it out there. I was so open I think he kind of pulled the string on it a little bit, that the ball actually kind of drifted to my outside shoulder instead of catching it on my inside shoulder, which would have been easier. So I had to turn a little bit and snatched it with my hands, which is what I tried to do all the time. I've got pretty big hands and can catch the football. It wasn't a problem catch, but it looked a little more difficult."

Mercein made the catch and proceeded to turn the play into a huge gain before slipping out of bounds at the 11.

The very next play, Starr called Mercein's number again, this time on a sucker, or "influence," play, as Starr called it. The play was designed to take Cowboys tackle Bob Lilly away from the spot where the ball carrier would run.

"We decided to use Lilly's tremendous quickness and anticipation to our advantage," Starr recalled in *Game of My Life*, a book about big games in Packers history. "We pulled our guard, Gale Gillingham, to the right, hoping that Lilly would try to beat him to the point of attack. This would take Lilly out of the play, which was going to be run in the spot where he originally lined up. This was a risky call, but I believed the time had come to try it, as the adrenaline was running full tilt and Lilly would likely try to make a decisive play for their defense, which he had done so many times."

The play also was dependent on Packers left tackle Bob Skoronski blocking Andrie, whom Starr anticipated would try to cover the area once Lilly was taken out. Skoronski made the block and Mercein ran eight yards to the three. Starr has said the play was the best he's ever called.

Starr then handed off to Donny Anderson, who picked up two yards for a first down at the one.

Lambeau Field was alive and the human vapor from the 50,861 fans yelling their team on created a fog-like thickness.

Starr called for Anderson again and the young halfback, at least to Bowman, appeared to have crossed the goal line. But the ball was spotted about a foot away. After a timeout, Starr went right back to Anderson, but from the start, it didn't look good.

"Bart turned around and Donny was like a young colt, his legs were going all over the place," Bowman said. "He didn't even make it to the line of scrimmage. We might have actually lost some ground on that one."

Starr called his last time out. Sixteen seconds remained. The easy decision would have been to send out the field goal unit for a kick that would tie the game and send it into overtime. Starr and Lombardi talked about the 31 wedge, a play in which Mercein would get the ball and run behind Bowman and Jerry Kramer, who would double-team Cowboys tackle Jethro Pugh. During the week while watching film, Kramer noticed that Pugh was standing high on goal-line plays, which would make it easier to take him out.

The play was called and Starr came back to the huddle. The quarterback who had led Green Bay to four previous championships again made a key decision. He didn't tell anyone he was going to keep the ball rather than risk a handoff and have Mercein slip like Anderson had on the previous play.

Bowman snapped the ball, went to double-team Pugh as Starr sneaked in for one of the most famous touchdowns in NFL history.

The following day, these were words that columnist Blackie Sherrod wrote in the *Dallas Times Herald*:

It was the epic Arctic struggle between the Cowboys and Green Bays, an impossible ballet that somehow retained the heat of a jungle trench war

The last half especially was jammed with dramatic pivotal plays that turned Lambeau Stadium into a glacial teeter. But when the title game is finally thawed and brought back for rehash, the play that will leap from the mass of climaxes will be the winning touchdown. It covered a mere two feet and its simplicity was matched only by its almighty audacity. This was the quarterback sneak by Bart Starr, a gamble that may be argued by football brains for years to come but one thing won't enter the debate—its success.

Following the game, Lombardi, standing in the warmth of the Packers' locker room, praised his team.

Ken Bowman was the center for the Packers when they beat the Dallas Cowboys in the Ice Bowl. He helped clear out Jethro Pugh, enabling Bart Starr to score the wining touchdown in the closing seconds of the game.

"This is what the Green Bay Packers are all about, that we can come back and win it in the last two minutes," he said. "They don't do it for individual glory. They do it because they respect each other and have a feeling for the other fellow."

As the years have passed, reporters who have talked to the Packers who played in the Ice Bowl have identified a rift between Kramer and Bowman about that play. Bowman believes his teammate hasn't adequately shared the credit. Kramer doesn't deny this.

"After the game we're sitting there and Lombardi (who was being interviewed on TV) called Jerry up," Bowman said in early 2007. "Jerry was his boy. Jerry was one of the players he liked. As he's passing, I said, 'Don't forget to tell him it was a double-team.' He said, 'Bow, you have ten more years to make another block like that. Give an old man his day.' And he went up there and took all the accolades."

To this day, Kramer says he simply told it as it was.

"It's obvious that Kenny was supposed to double-team with me on that play, that's what happened," Kramer recalled. "I think it's also obvious if you look at the play closely that Kenny could have gone and got a hot dog and we still would have been successful on the play. He was part of the play, part of the effort. There's no question about that. That's the way the play was designed, that's what he was there for.

"He did ask me after the game, 'Tell them about me, Jerry, tell them about me.' I knew that my career was coming to an end. I knew that I wasn't going to play much longer and that it was a nice moment. But quite frankly, I just don't see Bow being that critical in that play. That may be a little harsh, but that's the way it is if you analyze it."

Kramer also never imagined the Ice Bowl would become the defining moment of a franchise that has been around since 1919.

"We had been in a hell of a lot of big games, a lot of big plays, a lot of big moments over the course of all those years," Kramer said. "It was just a quarterback sneak. It wasn't a flea flicker or anything dramatic. It was Bart stumbling over the one-yard line, and to me it was a play that was going to be talked about for a while; maybe a year or two tops, and then it would figure into the midst of time like everything does and that would be the end of it.

"I'm stunned at the fascination of it so many years later. It was a great ballgame, no question about it, I understand that. But five championships, six conference championship games that determined titles, we had a lot of great ballgames, really. But it just didn't seem to me that a quarterback sneak would be one of the all-time big plays in the history of the universe. I think you have to be a little silly to believe that at that time. I sure didn't."

But that's exactly what it became—probably the most unforgettable quarterback sneak in the long history of the NFL.

"That drive was, to me, the most romantic moment in the history of the game and it solidified in the public's mind and in all of our minds, all of the observers there, that this team that Lombardi had created was truly a team of legend," Sabol said.

"That this was their third consecutive NFL championship, and it was won by an example of all the things Lombardi had preached. Fatigue makes cowards of us all. Self-denial. Teamwork. You never quit. All the things that Lombardi talked about can be found not only in that drive but in each one of the players who were a part of that drive."

- -

1967 DIVISION SCORES

September 17	Packers 17, Lions 17	Lambeau Field
September 24	Packers 13, Bears 10	Lambeau Field
October 1	Bears 17, Vikings 7	Metropolitan Stadium
October 8	Packers 27, Lions 17	Tiger Stadium
October 15	Vikings 10, Packers 7	Milwaukee County Stadium
October 15	Bears 14, Lions 3	Wrigley Field
November 5	Bears 27, Lions 17	Tiger Stadium
November 12	Lions 10, Vikings 10	Metropolitan Stadium
November 26	Packers 17, Bears 13	Wrigley Field
December 3	Packers 30, Vikings 27	Metropolitan Stadium
December 10	Bears 10, Vikings 10 (tie)	Wrigley Field
December 17	Lions 14, Vikings 3	Tiger Stadium

4

THE CHICAGO BEARS

During the early years of the Black and Blue, the Chicago Bears had two of the NFL's most recognizable and talented players, but little else.

Running back Gale Sayers and linebacker Dick Butkus, both of whom began their pro careers in 1965, quickly became stars. Sayers scored six touchdowns in one game and set a league record with 22 during his rookie season. Butkus was an intense competitor who combined remarkable quickness with an innate feel for the game that helped make him one of the greatest middle linebackers in the history of pro football.

Chicago Bears running back Gale Sayers (40) follows guard George Seals into the heart of the Packers' defense during a 17-0 loss to the Packers in the season opener on September 21, 1969. Defensive end Willie Davis (87) and linebacker Dave Robinson (89) try to stop Sayers.

The Bears won the NFL title in 1963, ending the Green Bay Packers' two-year run as NFL champs. But the championship proved to be the last for legendary coach George Halas, who had losing records in two of his next three seasons. He eventually retired following the 1967 season, when the Bears finished the first year of the Central Division with a 7-6-1 record.

Sayers was running circles around the other teams and Butkus was manhandling any quarterback and running back he could find, but few others made significant contributions for the Bears. In 1968, Sayers suffered a ruptured cartilage and two torn ligaments in his right knee in a game against the San Francisco 49ers. He was out for the season and would never be the same again.

The Bears finished 7-7 that season. Sayers came back and won a rushing title in 1969, but the Bears slipped to 1-13, the worst record in football. Butkus had nine sacks and made three interceptions, but with the exception of outside linebacker Doug Buffone and defensive end Ed O'Bradovich, who was at the end of his career, the Bears' defense had many holes.

The offense also lacked efficiency. Journeyman Jack Concannon split time at quarterback with Bobby Douglass, a six-foot-four left-hander out of Kansas who preferred to run rather than pass. When Douglass ran, he was tough to bring down because of his size and his determination to get as much as he could. He averaged eight yards a carry and finished second on the team in rushing behind Sayers, with 408 yards. He wasn't as effective as a passer, completing just 45.9 percent of his attempts.

Douglass never became a good passer, and his decision-making drove his coaches and teammates crazy. There was a time during the 1971 season when coach Jim Dooley moved in with Douglass to help him better understand what the Bears were trying to accomplish on offense. It helped for a while, but not long term.

There was no disputing that Douglass could run. In 1972, he set an NFL record for quarterbacks by rushing for 968 yards. As a passer he completed just 37.9 percent of his attempts and accounted for less than 100 yards a game.

During Butkus's final six seasons, from 1968-73, the Bears won just 22 games. Despite the losing records, the Bears were still one of the meanest teams to deal with, mainly because of the men who played linebacker.

Buffone played 14 seasons and never made the Pro Bowl. He was overshadowed by Butkus but played twice as long as his teammate. He was not a linebacker to mess with.

"Buffone was the classic strong-side linebacker," said Don Pierson, the longtime pro football writer for the *Chicago Tribune*. "He could take on tight ends and, although he didn't have great speed, nobody got outside on him." One year before sacks were an official statistic, he had something like 22 sacks when Jim Dooley was turning him loose.

Sayers suffered another major knee injury in 1970. He played in 1971 but retired following the season.

THE WALTER PAYTON ERA

The Bears had trouble winning, but their fortunes would eventually change. Jim Finks, who helped build the Vikings into the Black and Blue's dominant team, was hired by the Bears two days before the start of the 1974 season. Finks spent that season evaluating all phases of the Bears' operation. After finishing with a 4-10 record, Abe Gibron, a rotund, colorful character who during one cold Sunday in Minneapolis was rumored to have poured a bottle of bourbon into a pot of chicken soup during halftime, was fired. As his replacement, Finks tabbed Jack Pardee, who was an All-Pro linebacker as a player.

Finks also did what he did best: draft quality players. His first pick for Chicago wound up being what he's most remembered for. He selected Walter Payton out of Jackson State University, although it took Bears fans a little while to understand just how good of a pick Payton would turn out to be.

He had modest success in 1975, when the Bears, with a lot of new players, finished 4-10. The following year Payton exploded, rushing for 1,390 yards and scoring 13 touchdowns as the Bears improved to 7-7, sweeping the season series with division rivals Detroit and Green Bay and splitting with Minnesota.

By 1977, Payton was a household name in the NFL and the Bears were a playoff contender again. Payton flirted with 2,000 yards before finishing with 1,852 in helping the Bears to a 9-5 record and a spot in the playoffs. Payton combined speed and toughness to eventually become the NFL's all-time leading ground gainer before he retired.

"I always gave the scouting report when we played him. That was my job," said Paul Wiggin, who was an assistant coach with the Vikings and later moved into their front office. "I said, 'We have to machine gun him,' meaning don't think that the first guy that hits him is going to stop him, not because you aren't a good tackler, but because whatever it is about him he probably wants not to be tackled more than you want to tackle him and because he can back it up with skill. Walter Payton was a great football player in every way. He was truly a great player on the field; he got every ounce out of his talent."

The Bears made an early exit in the 1977 playoffs with a 37-7 loss to the Dallas Cowboys, who would go on to win the Super Bowl. But as he did with the Vikings, Finks methodically built a dynasty in Chicago.

Payton was the star, but other players from Finks's first three drafts—defensive end Mike Hartenstine; cornerbacks Virgil Livers and Doug Plank; linebacker Tom Hicks; offensive tackle Dennis Lick; and quarterback Bob Avellini—were among the starters. Also in the lineup was Gary Fencik, a wide receiver at Yale whose athletic ability impressed Finks. He signed with the Bears as a free agent, came to camp in 1976 and made the team as a safety. He was starting by 1977.

Pardee left to coach the Washington Redskins following the 1977 season and was replaced by Neill Armstrong, who suffered through an eight-game losing streak after the Bears opened the season 3-0. The Bears did win four of their last five and beat the

Packers in the second-to-last week of the season to help keep Green Bay from making the playoffs, which was some consolation.

The Bears were back in the playoffs in 1979, when Payton scored 16 touchdowns and rushed for 1,610 yards to help his team to a 10-6 record, the same as Tampa Bay, which won the division. Joining the Bears that year was a rookie defensive end named Dan Hampton, giving Finks another number-one draft pick who would become a Hall of Fame player. Hampton, Fencik and Plank were part of a defense that posted two shutouts and held four other teams to seven points or less. The Bears were beaten by Philadelphia in the playoffs, 27-17, but the team was getting closer to becoming special, especially on defense where the players exhibited classic Black and Blue toughness.

The problem was at quarterback. Avellini eventually gave way to Mike Phipps, who was replaced in 1980 by Vince Evans, who also started in 1981. But Evans threw a total of 22 touchdown passes during those two seasons compared to 36 interceptions.

Armstrong was fired partly because he believed too much in Evans. Mike Ditka, one of the stars of the 1963 NFL title team, was hired by management as the new coach, and one of the first things he wanted to do was find the right quarterback to lead his team.

"We would have never gotten over the hump with what they were doing at quarterback," Ditka said. "I saw that the first year I came there, and the people tried to tell me how good this guy was or how good that guy was. Yeah, yeah, but you weren't going to win with them. So you had to get a guy in there you could win with, and that was Jim McMahon."

Finks left after the 1981 season. His last two drafts, in 1980 and '81, brought the Bears more pieces to the eventual Super Bowl puzzle. Linebacker Otis Wilson and fullback Matt Suhey were the big names in 1980, and offensive tackle Keith Van Horne and linebacker Mike Singletary led the class of 1981.

During the next couple of years Ditka and Jerry Vainisi, the new Bears' general manager, continued building the team. Tackle Jim Covert, wide receiver Willie Gault and cornerback Mike

Bears running back Walter Payton dives over the line for a first down during the third quarter of Chicago's 9-7 victory over the Packers on September 16, 1984. Packers safety Mark Murphy moves in at left to try to make the stop.

Richardson were drafted in 1983. Linebackers Wilber Marshall and Ron Rivera came in 1984, the year the Bears went back to the playoffs, although by Ditka's second season in 1983 they were showing signs of being a formidable football team again.

"We were getting ready to play them the second time in '83 and they were starting to look good," said former Packers quarterback Lynn Dickey. "I was watching them on film and I just thought, 'Boy, that defensive team is really getting better.'"

The Bears were a lot better in 1984, winning the Black and Blue with a 10-6 record, but not without some tough games with their division rivals. They won the first meeting with the Vikings at home, 16-7, and routed them the second time, 34-14. They also beat the Lions in a down-to-the-wire game, 16-14. Against the Packers, Chicago won at Green Bay, 9-7, on three Bob Thomas field goals, but lost the rematch in Chicago when Rich Campbell, who had four forgettable years in Green Bay, threw a badly underthrown pass to Phillip Epps for a 43-yard touchdown pass that beat the Bears at Soldier Field, 20-14. Terry Schmidt, a backup cornerback for the Bears, slipped and lost track of Epps.

"Terry Schmidt got beat," Fencik recalled. "Oh my God, that was a terrible thing. I remember that. Schmitty got canned after that. I remember that really well. I was a free safety going over (to help) and I went, 'Oh God, touchdown.'"

What Fencik also remembers about that season is going into RFK Stadium in Washington, D.C., in the first round of the playoffs. The Redskins were the defending Super Bowl champs, but the Bears weren't intimidated and won their first playoff game since 1963 with a 23-19 victory. The following week, Chicago lost in the NFC title game to San Francisco, 23-0. The win over the Redskins showed the Bears that they were close to being a championship team.

"Washington had Joe Theismann at quarterback and they had the Hogs and the old RFK Stadium was an intimidating place. It generated a lot of noise, "Fencik said. "To win the game, and particularly the defense, the way we played in the fourth quarter. As I recall, we walked on the field on our side of the 50-yard line three times in that quarter and I don't think they got a first down.

"I think coming back from that game I felt the defense had come of age. Now we got blanked 23-0 the next week in San Francisco, but I think it was really important to win a game on the road, and we had been playing particularly well in the second half of that season. Then we got into the '85 season and I think there was a focus and a commitment from the entire team."

THE SUPER BOWL SEASON

Kevin Butler saw that focus in his first meeting with the Bears. He was an All-American kicker from the University of Georgia and joined the team after being selected in the 1985 draft. It didn't take long for him to realize he was walking into a special atmosphere.

"I'll tell you one little story that'll sum up what the camaraderie was like," said Butler. "I was drafted in the fourth round and came up two or three days after for minicamp and went into that first meeting.

"Saturday in the meeting, Walter Payton got up and made an emotional speech. Mike Singletary got up and made an emotional speech. Mike Ditka, Jim McMahon, people were mad, frustrated and hungry. And this was minicamp. They talked about winning a Super Bowl and not settling for anything else.

"I walked out of there, called my fiancée in Georgia and said, 'Listen, Kathy, we've got to change our wedding date.' She was like, 'Oh, my God. You've been up there four hours and you've met somebody.'"

I said, 'No. I just got out of the first meeting and I'm going to make the Bears and we're going to the Super Bowl and we can't get married on the weekend we have planned because that's Super Bowl Saturday.'"

Butler's future wife needed more convincing, but the date was changed, which was good because on January 26, the day after Butler's originally scheduled nuptials, the Bears completed one of the greatest seasons in the history of the NFL's oldest franchise

Bears defensive tackle William "The Refrigerator" Perry hauls in a short touchdown pass during the second quarter of Chicago's 16-10 victory over the Packers on November 3, 1985.

with a 46-10 whipping of the New England Patriots in Super Bowl XX. And Butler, who kicked 31 field goals during the regular season, was on the field at the Louisiana Superdome often that day, booting three field goals and five extra points.

The 1985 Bears were a classic Black and Blue team. The offensive line dominated the line of scrimmage and created enough room for Payton to run. The defense smothered the opposition.

Hampton and Richard Dent were the ends. Steve McMichael played left tackle and William Perry, a 330-pound rookie, was the other tackle, although he gained more notoriety as a part-time running back. Singletary, his eyes always moving, was the middle linebacker. He was flanked by Wilber Marshall and Otis Wilson.

The cornerbacks were Leslie Frazier and Mike Richardson.

Fencik was the free safety and Dave Duerson the strong safety. They played the defense known as the 46, which caused as much havoc as any defense in the history of the game.

"That '85 defense of the Bears was the best I'd ever seen," said Dickey, who played quarterback for the Packers from 1976 until 1985. "I would match that defense against any in the history of the game. If you thought you could work on anything, any part of it, their corners, I thought we could probably work on those guys. But it didn't matter.

"The corners were the only ones, if we had some time, we thought we could work on these guys, but therein lies the whole problem. The front seven guys—maybe Fridge wasn't the best all-around defensive tackle, but say six of the seven were the six best players in the whole league, on one team.

"Those six guys—Marshall, Singletary and Wilson at line-backers and Hampton, Richard Dent and Steve McMichael—I thought were the six best players at their position in the whole league. If you ever could snap your fingers and just get the flu and you couldn't play that week, that was the week to get it."

What's ironic is that the Bears went into training camp with some turmoil. Todd Bell, a starting cornerback, held out, as did line-backer Al Harris. It didn't matter. Ditka and defensive coordinator Buddy Ryan plugged in Duerson, who made All-Pro, and Marshall.

"He made a name for himself the moment he walked on the field," Fencik said. "It was a combination of good, experienced players, good young players including a rookie, William Perry, and having Buddy Ryan.

"I think one of the geniuses that Buddy brought to defense, yes he had a variety of fronts, he did a great job on matchups, but Buddy gave a little bit to each part of the defense, a little flexibility to make some changes on the field, gave you some options on how to run his defenses. I really think that brought ownership for all the players to the game plan. It made you aware much more when you were watching film and when you were in practices what defenses were going to be run against which offensive set."

Dickey remembers being stunned by the speed of Singletary.

"Mike Singletary was the first and only (middle linebacker) I've ever seen to play a double zone where he played the safety on the weak side of the field," the ex-Packers quarterback said. "He started out about four to five yards out from the line of scrimmage so at the snap of the ball the corner on that side would come up and jam and Mike would turn around and sprint to the far corner of the end zone to play in the double zone. I thought, 'Wow, what's that about?' But I was amazed at how fast he was when he turned and sprinted back there. He had a great nose for the ball, had a great feel for the game."

The Bears' defense really blossomed in the last eleven games, posting two shutouts, holding two other teams to just field goals and three others to ten points or less. The only bad game came when the Bears were 12-0 and talk was heating up about an unbeaten season. They went into Miami to play the Dolphins, whose 1972 team finished the season 17-0. The Dolphins jumped on the Bears early and scored a 38-24 victory, the only blemish on the team's record that season.

On offense, Payton rushed for 1,551 yards. When the Bears passed, wide receivers Willie Gault and Dennis McKinnon and tight end Emory Moorehead proved to be able targets. The line was led by tackles Jimbo Covert and Keith Van Horne. The other starters were guards Mark Bortz and Tom Thayer. The center was Jay Hilgenberg, who signed with the Bears in 1981 after he went undrafted following a solid career at the University of Iowa. That group helped the Bears lead the NFL in rushing four straight years, from 1983-86. Hilgenberg said former offensive line coach Dick Stanfel helped the line become successful.

"The guy should be in the Hall of Fame," Hilgenberg said. "It's a shame he's not. He's the best. Just the technique that he worked on with us was endless. Every single day on the field he was on us about technique, the proper technique. It's kind of funny. I did some radio work this past year and started watching a lot of tape and stuff of games and talking to coaches and their philosophies of offensive line play, and these offensive line coaches nowadays, they're just terrible."

The Bears dominated on the field and had fun off. They were colorful and had a coach who was a good quote and wore his heart on his sleeve. When he was upset, like he was when he threw a wad of gum at a boisterous fan during a game against San Francisco, the whole world knew it.

"We had a lot of fun," recalled Fencik. "We just had a lot of personalities, a lot of unique characters. If not by design, I think Mike as a head coach who was a former player and probably a pretty good character himself, Mike was pretty tolerant. As long as you came to practice and played well in the games, what you did in your off time, he didn't really think that should be a distraction.

"When he threw gum into the stands at halftime at San Francisco, it was a lot of fun to be a part of that. Even though that was kind of a sideshow, it provided a lot of levity to the team. I think we were at the beginning of the NFL moving towards celebrating not just the people on the field but recognizing that you can capture more fans, the peripheral fans, by emphasizing the personalities of the players behind the face mask."

By the time the Bears got to the playoffs, there seemed to be little doubt about how the season would finish. After a first-round bye the Bears played host to the Giants in 14-degree weather at Soldier Field. McMahon broke open a close game with a pair of touchdown passes to McKinnon in the third quarter as the Bears won, 21-0. The defense held New York to ten first downs, 32 yards rushing and didn't allow the Giants a third-down conversion in 12 attempts.

The following week in the NFC championship game against the Los Angeles Rams, the Bears treated the home crowd to another shutout. McMahon scored the team's first touchdown on a 16-yard run and Marshall put the finishing touches on the 24-0 victory by returning a fumble 52 yards for a score in the fourth quarter.

Two weeks later in New Orleans, the Bears put the finishing touches on their superb season with a 36-point blowout of the AFC champion Patriots. Perry scored a touchdown, capping a season that would make him millions in endorsements. Payton, the team's heart and soul, did not score and Ditka would later say that's the one regret he has—not finding an opportunity for Payton to score.

Overall, though, Ditka has fond memories about bringing a championship back to the city where George Halas became a coaching legend. Halas died in 1983, missing out on seeing the NFL title return to Chicago.

"I remember the players," Ditka said twenty years after that championship. "I remember everything about Jerry Vainisi and myself putting the team together. I remember that my goal was to go back to Chicago to coach and win the Super Bowl. That was my payback to coach Halas, who had enough confidence in me and gave me a chance to do it. I was in the mold of him, and he knew I would bring a certain amount of toughness back to the Bears and we would play the game the way he would have liked to seen it played and the way he would have coached it himself.

"To me, that's where the satisfaction comes. It's for nothing else. We won it because we had good players. It wasn't because I was a great coach, we had good players. But we put those players in place and we put them in a position to play the best football they could and they did, and you know what? When we did it we had fun, too. It wasn't life and death every week, and people got to see that these people were individuals with personalities and character. We let that shine through so it became fun."

NO MORE SUPER BOWLS FOR DITKA

The Bears won the Central with a 14-2 record in 1986, but McMahon was sidelined with a shoulder injury late in the season, creating havoc at quarterback. The Bears played the Redskins at home in the second round and Doug Flutie, signed during the season, started at quarterback. He threw a 50-yard pass to Gault in the first half and the Bears held a 13-7 lead. But they faltered in the final two quarters and fell, 27-13. The same thing happened the next year. McMahon played but the Redskins beat the Bears in Chicago again, this time 21-17.

In 1988, the year after Payton retired, the Bears advanced to the NFC title game but lost to the 49ers in Chicago, 28-3.

The Bears won 52 regular season games from 1985-88, more than any other team in the NFL in that four-year period. Despite that dominance, they played in the Super Bowl just once.

"It was just an awesome defense but it's one of those things that when you sit back and reflect upon things you say to yourself, 'Why didn't this team win more than one Super Bowl or why didn't it go to more than one Super Bowl,'" former Packers general manager Ron Wolf said. "That Bear team with that defense was one of those teams."

"We all played together for a long time," Hilgenberg said. "We had a lot of talent for a lot of years there. The biggest negative of the whole career in Chicago is that we didn't win more Super Bowls.

"That's the big thing about us; it's something that we have to live with. We had opportunities to win more Super Bowls and we just didn't get it done. You know, we could say we had injuries at quarterback and stuff like that, which we did, but we still should have won. We were talented enough to win Super Bowls."

Ditka coached the Bears through the 1992 season, winning two more division titles but not reaching the NFC championship game after the 1988 season.

Dave Wannstedt replaced Ditka but had just two winning seasons (both 9-7) in six seasons before being fired after a 4-12 record in 1998. Much of the problem with the Bears' decline was that when the last of the players from the Super Bowl team retired or moved on, they weren't replaced by talented players. During Wannstedt's final four seasons as coach, the Bears did not have one Pro Bowl player.

Wannstedt was replaced by Dick Jauron, who led the Bears to a 13-3 record in 2000, but the Bears were eliminated in the play-offs at home by Philadelphia.

He coached two more seasons before being fired and replaced

Chicago Bears coach Mike Ditka shouts at his team during its 25-12 victory over the Packers on September 22, 1986.

----

by Lovie Smith, the former defensive coordinator of the St. Louis Rams.

In 2005, his second season, the Bears played good old-fashioned Black and Blue football, sweeping both the Packers and Lions and splitting with the Vikings in winning the NFC North. The defense, led by Brian Urlacher, whose play brought back memories of Butkus and Singletary, dominated at times like the famed 46 group twenty years earlier. But the Bears' offense didn't have anyone like Payton, and after receiving a first-round bye, they exited the playoffs with a loss at home to the Carolina Panthers.

The 2006 season brought more improvement and more glory back to Chicago. The Bears cruised to the Black and Blue title again and won a nailbiter in overtime in the divisional playoffs against

Seattle. The following week, they returned to the Super Bowl for the first time in 21 seasons by whipping the New Orleans Saints at Solider Field, 39-14.

The Bears went to the Super Bowl but the Vince Lombardi trophy did not return with them. Instead, it went to Indianapolis after the Colts rallied to beat the Bears, 29-17.

Of all the original Black and Blue teams, the Bears have carried on a strong defensive tradition throughout the years.

"I think defensively, at least, anybody who comes into the Chicago Bears organization recognizes that when you play defense for the Chicago Bears that there's a very rich heritage at many different positions," Fencik said. "You do feel that obligation to live up to what is a very well-deserved reputation of being very tough defenses. I know I felt it, and Hampton and Singletary and everybody else I played with did. You recognize that there were a lot of players before you and you're part of a heritage that is very strong and has very deep roots in the NFL."

SPOTLIGHT: JIM FINKS AND THE HILGENBERGS

Before free agency, teams were built through the draft, by trades and with players picked up on the waiver wire. There may not have been anyone better in the history of the National Football League at build-ing teams from the ground up than Jim Finks.

He did it twice with teams in the Black and Blue. Finks, a former player in the NFL and a general man-ager in the Canadian Football League, became the

Jim Finks

Vikings' general manager in 1964, their fourth year in the league. By 1968, the Vikings had enough talent to compete for the Black and Blue title, which they won for the first time, start-ing a streak of ten division titles in 11 seasons.

When Finks went to the Bears in 1974, Chicago had gone through seven straight seasons with a non-winning record. By 1977, the Bears were back in the postseason. He left the Bears in 1982 because owner George Halas did not consult him in hiring Mike Ditka as coach. Ditka won a Super Bowl after the 1985 season with many players acquired during Finks's tenure in Chicago.

The first draft picks Finks made for both teams were special. With the Vikings, he selected Carl Eller, a defensive end from the University of Minnesota, with the sixth overall pick in the draft. Eller went on to be a perennial All-Pro who eventually was enshrined in the Hall of Fame.

With the Bears, Finks's first pick was Walter Payton, who played his college ball at Jackson State. It took Bears fans a little while to realize that Finks knew what he was doing. By 1977, Payton was on his path to greatness after rushing for a Bears record 1,852 yards during a 14-game season.

With both teams, Finks had an eye more on building the team around the defense. That was especially the case with the Vikings. When Eller was drafted, he joined veteran end Jim Marshall, who had been acquired in a trade in 1961, the team's first season. In 1965, Finks traded for defensive tackle Gary Larsen. In 1967, Alan Page, an All-American with Notre Dame, was obtained with one of the Vikings' three picks in the first round of the draft. The foursome of Marshall, Eller, Larsen and Page would become known as the Purple People Eaters, one of the most feared front fours in NFL history.

Along the way Finks also acquired safety Paul Krause in a trade with Washington. That was one of his better deals because Krause eventually was enshrined in the Hall of Fame after swiping 81 passes, a record that still stands.

His prize moves with the Vikings included drafting Eller, Page and offensive tackle Ron Yary, all of whom are in the Hall of Fame; trading for Krause; and hiring coach Bud Grant, another Hall of Famer who guided the

Vikings to four Super Bowl appearances.

In addition to drafting Payton, other Hall of Fame players Finks drafted in Chicago were defensive end Dan Hampton and middle linebacker Mike Singletary.

Finks also was a master of watching the waiver wire and signing undrafted free agents. One family is particularly grateful to Finks.

On the waiver wire, Finks picked up Wally Hilgenberg, a former high draft pick of the Lions who was traded to the Steelers, and eventually cut in 1968. Later that summer, Hilgenberg, coming off a knee injury, thought his career may have been over.

Finks gave him a second chance and Hilgenberg delivered. He was the starting linebacker in four Super Bowls for the Vikings.

Finks knew about Hilgenberg. So did Vikings assistant coach Jerry Burns, who was the head coach at Iowa when Hilgenberg played. So did Grant, who tried to sign Hilgenberg when he coached in the CFL. They all felt he could contribute, and they were correct. Hilgenberg started for most of the next 11 seasons.

"I had tremendous respect for him as a man," Hilgenberg said of Finks, who died from lung cancer in 1995. "But he also knew the game of football. He was a very direct and straightforward guy, fair and honest. The reason Pittsburgh cut me was I asked for more money to leave Detroit and come to Pittsburgh. They weren't willing to do it and we got into a hassle and they cut me. I went to Minnesota and Jim Finks gave me about 20 percent more than what I was asking for in Pittsburgh."

After Finks went to Chicago, he made another move that was beneficial to the Hilgenberg family. Jay Hilgenberg, Wally's nephew, and a starting center at Iowa, wasn't drafted in 1981. Wally Hilgenberg called Finks.

"I told him that he was a player and that he should

take a look at him," Wally Hilgenberg recalled.

Jay Hilgenberg had a good career at Iowa but was told by one of his coaches that he probably wasn't going to get drafted. When he was contacted by Bill McGrane, an assistant to Finks, Jay initially told him he wasn't interested.

"(McGrane) said, 'Well, just take a couple days and think about it and call me back,'" Jay Hilgenberg recalled.

"I got over it. My pride was the thing that was hurt. But, you know, my uncle told me going to a camp is all attitude. So I went there and the story goes, Bill McGrane later told me the first day of practice when I was out there, Finks told McGrane that they're going to have a hard time running me out of here."

Jay Hilgenberg broke into the starting lineup in 1983, won a Super Bowl ring two years later and played in seven Pro Bowls.

Finks wasn't through with the Hilgenbergs. He became general manager of the New Orleans Saints in 1986. Two years later, the Saints had a 12-4 record. Joel Hilgenberg, Jay's brother, also played his college ball at Iowa. Like Jay, he was not drafted.

"I called Jim Finks up and said, 'Jim, I've got another one for you,'" Wally Hilgenberg said. "He said, 'Have him call me,' and he signs Joel Hilgenberg and Joel plays eleven years for the Saints. So Jim Finks signed all three of the Hilgenbergs that played football for the teams where we spent the significant amount of our careers."

5

THE DETROIT LIONS

During the Lions' first twenty-four years in Detroit, they played in the National Football League championship game five times and won four titles. They were at their best in the 1950s, winning three titles during a six-year stretch from 1952-57.

The Lions also came close a couple of other times in the fabulous '50s. They reached the championship game in 1954, but lost to Cleveland. Two years later, the Lions played the Bears in the final week of the season in what amounted to a winner-take-all game for the Western Division title. The Lions lost that game, but they

----

Lions tackle Alex Karras pressures 49ers quarterback John Brodie during a game in 1970. During the 1960s, the Lions' defense was one of the best in the NFL, due in large part to the play of Karras.

99

were back in the championship the following year, winning their fourth overall championship with a 59-14 pasting of the Browns, whose running game was led by rookie and future Hall of Fame fullback Jim Brown.

Bobby Layne, who played as hard off the field as he did on it, was Detroit's quarterback in three of the four championship games they played in during the '50s. Tobin Rote, acquired from Green Bay in a trade in July 1957, directed the Lions to their 45-point rout of the Browns. He and Layne shared the quarterbacking duties until Layne broke his leg late in the year. Against Cleveland, Rote completed 12 of 19 passes for 280 yards and four touchdowns (146.4 passer rating) as Detroit became the first team to beat the Browns by more than 28 points. Halfback Doak Walker, fullback John Henry Johnson, linebacker Joe Schmidt, defensive back Yale Lary, tackle Lou Creekmur and center Frank Gatski are among the Hall of Fame players who spent at least a season with the Lions during the decade.

Things haven't been so fabulous in Detroit since the glory years of the '50s. In the 49 seasons from 1958 through 2006, the Lions had just 16 winning seasons and never reached the Super Bowl, although they played in the NFC title game in 1991, losing to Washington, 41-10.

Since the Lions' last NFL title, the sports fans in the Motor City have watched the Detroit Red Wings win three NHL Stanley Cup titles, the Detroit Tigers win two World Series and the Detroit Pistons garner three NBA championships.

While Detroit's other professional teams have had their golden moments, the Lions have experienced many miserable seasons during their time in the Black and Blue.

The Packers have won two Super Bowls and lost another during the history of the division. The Bears won Super Bowl XX and lost Super Bowl XLI. The Vikings played in four Super Bowls during an eight-season span from 1969-76 and won 16 division titles while experiencing just eight losing seasons during the first forty years of the Black and Blue.

The Lions have had the most coaches (13) and the fewest division titles (three) of the original four Black and Blue teams since the division was officially formed in 1967. They've also had just three players since 1967 go on to the Hall of Fame: cornerback Lem Barney, running back Barry Sanders and tight end Charlie Sanders, who was elected into the Hall the day before Super Bowl XLI.

Barney played 11 seasons and had 56 interceptions, seven of which he returned for touchdowns. He averaged 19.2 yards per interception and is first on the Lions' all-time list with 1,077 return yards.

Barry Sanders was on his way to being the NFL's all-time leading rusher when he inexplicably retired following the 1998 season. He had just rushed for more than 1,000 yards for a tenth straight season and won his second league MVP award. Charlie Sanders made the Pro Bowl seven times.

While Barney and the Sanderses never won a championship, the Lions experienced most of their success in Black and Blue during the time those three played. When Barney and Charlie Sanders were in their prime, the Lions had four straight winning seasons from 1969-72. During Barry Sanders's career, the Lions had five winning seasons in a seven-year span from 1991-97, making the playoffs all five times, although the only postseason game they won was in 1991.

That leaves just seven other winning seasons, clearly a sign that the Lions have had the least amount of success of all the Black and Blue teams. But in the formative years of the Black and Blue, they were awfully close to being a great team on a couple of occasions.

The Lions were 9-4-1 in 1969, the same record the Packers had two years earlier when they won Super Bowl II. But 1969 was the same year when the Vikings joined the NFL's elite.

Led by coach Bud Grant and his smothering defense, Minnesota beat the Lions twice, won the division with a 12-2 record and went to the Super Bowl. That was the year before the NFL merged with the AFL.

The NFL was in its third year of having four divisions. During

Lem Barney began his NFL career in 1967 by returning an interception for a touchdown in the first game he played, against the Green Bay Packers. Barney is in the Hall of Fame.

the season the Lions beat Cleveland, which won the Century Division with a 10-3-1 record and went on to lose the league title to the Vikings. The Lions also shut out the Los Angeles Rams, who won the Coastal Division with an 11-3 record. The Rams lost in the first round of the playoffs to the Vikings, 23-20.

In those days only division winners advanced to the playoffs, which kept the Lions out. When the leagues merged the following year, old-guard NFL teams Baltimore, Cleveland and Pittsburgh were moved to the American Football Conference, joining teams from the AFL.

Under the new format, the six division winners in the two conferences advanced to the playoffs along with the team with the best record among the non-division winners in each conference.

In 1970, the Vikings once again won the Central with a 12-2 record and beat Detroit twice, 30-17 in Detroit on November 1 and 24-20 two weeks later at the Met in Minnesota. In between those losses to the Vikings, the Lions dropped a 19-17 decision to the New Orleans Saints when Tom Dempsey kicked an NFL record 63-yard field goal with no time remaining.

"We're 5-4 after that game and it looks like we're out of the playoffs," said Mike Lucci, who played middle linebacker for the Lions from 1965 until 1973. "To make the playoffs, it looked like we had to win the rest of our games.

"Well, we win out. We go to LA and come back in that game and beat the Rams. The next week we beat the Packers 20-0 in the last game and we finish 10-4. The fans come on the field and take the goal posts down."

Another team the Lions beat down the stretch to make the playoffs was the San Francisco 49ers, who eventually made it to the NFL championship game. The 49ers were regarded as one of the NFC's better teams, but the Lions beat them easily, 28-7.

By the time the Lions finished the season, they were confident going into the playoffs on the road against Dallas.

Other than that poor stretch at midseason, the Lions were nearly unbeatable. In the second week of the season Detroit crushed Cincinnati, the eventual AFC Central champs, 38-3.

Later in the season after they beat San Francisco, the Lions hosted old AFL power Oakland in the traditional Thanksgiving Day game. The Raiders, who won the AFC West that season, jumped out to a 14-0 lead before Detroit rallied for a 28-14 victory.

The victory was the first on Thanksgiving for the Lions since 1962, when they beat the 11-0 Green Bay Packers, 26-14, in a game in which they sacked Packers quarterback Bart Starr 11 times.

The Thanksgiving game tradition in Detroit started in 1934. There were two perks to the game: playing on national television and the ten-day break before the next game.

"I kind of liked it," Lucci said. "We looked at it as a chance to go on national TV and then we got three or four days off. It was like, 'Let's go out there and show them what we're made of.'

"It was kind of a rush and also a little bit of that these guys (opponents) are not tough enough to play on Sunday and again four days later, so let's show them how to do it."

The Lions had a defense that was at times nearly invincible, posting two shutouts, holding two other teams to just a field goal and four others to 14 points or less.

The line was anchored by tackle Alex Karras, who had slowed down by that point in his career but was still capable of instilling fear into opposing offensive linemen. During the early 1960s, Karras was one of the most feared tackles in the NFL and made the Pro Bowl three straight times (1960-62). In 1963 he was suspended for gambling on NFL games and missed the entire season. He returned in 1964 but made the Pro Bowl just one more time, in 1965.

His quick hands and feet made it incredibly difficult for opposing offensive linemen.

"He was the best. He should be in the Hall of Fame," said former Lions middle linebacker Joe Schmidt, who was a teammate of Karras's and later coached him. "He was very difficult to block because of the way he was built and because of his strength and quickness. He was just so damn good on the football field."

Tackle Jerry Rush and defensive end Larry Hand were others who made it hard for teams to run on Detroit. Wayne Walker, Lucci and Paul Naumoff were the linebackers, and the secondary was led by cornerbacks Dick LeBeau and Barney, who had nine and seven of the 28 interceptions grabbed by Detroit that year. Barney ran back two of his thefts for touchdowns.

"We had a helluva football team," said Lucci, who played on a defense that gave up 202 points. That tied for second lowest in the NFL with the Rams, behind the Vikings' total of 143.

The offense was led by running back Mel Farr, who rushed for 717 yards and nine touchdowns while scoring two more on pass receptions.

Charlie Sanders, a third-year veteran, was a Pro Bowl tight end who led the team with 40 receptions and 544 receiving yards. Ed Flanagan, a Pro Bowl center in 1970, was the leader of the offensive line.

The coach was Schmidt, an All-Pro middle linebacker and a classic Black and Blue player who retired in 1965 and took over as coach in 1967. After a couple of lean years, the Lions played better in 1969, then had the great finish in 1970 to make the playoffs for the first time in thirteen years.

The playoff game was held the day after Christmas in Dallas. Dallas rushed for 209 yards but couldn't get in the end zone. The Lions held Dallas on fourth and goal early in the final quarter, but quarterback Greg Landry, whose fumble in the first quarter set up a Dallas field goal, was tackled for a safety that gave the Cowboys a 5-0 lead.

Schmidt eventually pulled Landry in favor of Bill Munson, who played better but couldn't get the Lions into the end zone. Late in the game, though, the Lions appeared to be ready to sneak off with the victory. Munson threw deep and Earl McCullough was open. The ball bounced off his hands and was intercepted by cornerback Mel Renfro.

"If he would have caught that," Schmidt said thirty-five years later, his voice trailing off. "If he would have caught it maybe we would have won the game 7-5.

"Maybe I should have changed quarterbacks sooner. I put Munson in, gave Landry another series of downs in the second half. We didn't do anything so I changed quarterbacks at the end of the game.

"I think we had a good enough team to go to the Super Bowl. We beat the 49ers a couple times. We would have played those guys next because they beat the Minnesota Vikings."

Everybody remembers that the 49ers would have been easy pickings had they just beat the Cowboys.

"I remember half those players like it was yesterday," said Lucci, who played middle linebacker with an intensity befitting of the Black and Blue. "The next game we would have played the 49ers, who we had beaten three or four times in a row if you go back and look."

Lucci was close. The Lions had won three of the four previous meetings against San Francisco, including one that season by 21 points.

"They couldn't beat us back then and that's the team we could have beat I think, and that would have been our chance to go to the Super Bowl," Lucci continued. "We all believed we could have been there and should have been there."

"I totally agree with that," said Jerry Green, a former Lions beat writer for the *Detroit News*. "My feeling was at end of the '70 season, the Lions won their last five games and in the process beat the 49ers, beat the Cardinals, they beat the Rams, beat the Oakland Raiders. Four of those teams at the time the Lions beat them were in first place in their division. The only team that wasn't was the Packers, and the Lions beat them in the last game.

"That was probably the Lions' best chance of ever going to the Super Bowl. They had the best team in pro football at the time, I felt, but they did not have a mature offense. They lost that playoff game and Greg Landry, who was not a very mature quarterback at the time, had a bad game."

The Lions' problems on offense weren't all at quarterback on that day. Steve Owens, who had carried the team down the stretch, was hurt. So was Farr. But to get shut out and give up a safety still hurts to this day.

"The memories I have of that game is I felt the coaches were more nervous than the players," said defensive end and tackle Larry Hand, who played with the Lions from 1964 until 1977. "Steve Owens got us to the playoffs. Mel Farr had been hurt, hurt his shoulder. I remember we started that game throwing some swing passes to Mel Farr and thinking, 'Here's a guy who has a bad shoulder and we're throwing swing passes to him.'

"I guess the biggest thing I felt about that game was that we could have won it. It came right down to the last couple minutes of the game."

"I think we had a good enough football team to go to the Super Bowl," recalled Schmidt, who was elected to the Hall of Fame in 1972. "We had a pretty good football team. It took us a couple of years to get going, but we had some good players and it was fun."

There is almost a sadness in Schmidt's voice as he talks about that year. The Cowboys went on to beat the 49ers, the team that couldn't beat Detroit, and Dallas advanced to the Super Bowl. There, they lost on a last-second field goal to the Colts, 16-13.

But there's always next year, and for the Lions, 1971 was a year when the city of Detroit was optimistic about its football team. Newspaper stories leading up to training camp frequently mentioned the Super Bowl and the Lions in the same sentence.

The Lions hadn't lost much talent from the previous season. There may have been some concern about the overall depth on the offensive line, but with Flanagan at center and offensive tackle Rocky Freitas, things seemed OK. On defense, most of the players who had limited teams to 200 points the previous season were back.

Schmidt, though, wasn't sure how effective Karras could be. Once one of the most dominant and nastiest tackles in the NFL, injuries had caught up to him. There also was the feeling by some in the organization that his heart no longer was in the game. Karras also may have been a player motivated to play only part of the time and against certain teams.

"The top two guys I played against were Merlin Olsen and Alex," former Packers offensive guard Jerry Kramer recalled. "I spent extra time on those boys. They kept me awake at night and they put me asleep at night thinking about them, worrying about them and trying to figure out how badly I would harm them the next day, what I was going to do, imagining what you would go through."

Kramer shared a story of how years later he told a reporter who was doing a historical piece on the Packers and Lions how he felt Karras would always play a great game against the Packers but then have a lackluster effort the following week against an inferior opponent.

The reporter Art Daley, who covered the Packers for the *Green Bay Press-Gazette*, eventually talked to Karras and told him what Kramer had said.

"I assume Alex is going to be pissed, dispute it, call me a son of a bitch and a few other things," Kramer said. "And Art says to me that Alex said, 'I think Jerry's right about that.'"

Knowing that Karras was near the end of his career, the Lions drafted defensive tackle Bobby Bell out of the University of Cincinnati. Bell was projected to be an impact player but once he got to training camp, the Lions feared they had made a mistake. He wasn't ready to replace Karras, whom the Lions didn't think could play effectively anymore. On September 1, they made a trade for Dick Evey, a journeyman tackle for the Rams.

Almost two weeks later and five days before the Lions would open the season on Monday night against Minnesota, the Lions cut Karras, a story that stayed in the papers for the next several weeks.

Karras had been a media darling, a guy who could say anything he wanted and was rarely challenged because he was good copy. He played a starring role in the movie *Paper Lion*, which was filmed in early 1968 and released later that year. The movie was based on the book by George Plimpton in which the writer spent a training camp as a quarterback with the Lions.

Other Lions, including Schmidt, were in the movie. Karras,

though, had a bigger role and he was good, which turned his life in a different direction. Football no longer was his main focus and maybe hadn't been for a while, according to some of his former teammates.

Schmidt decided to cut Karras, which created a stir in Detroit.

"He had got involved in this movie thing," Schmidt said. "We were dearly in need of defensive linemen. We were struggling. I talked to him about trying to increase his productivity and be more

Lions tackle Alex Karras holds off Dan Grimm of the Atlanta Falcons during a game in the late 1960s. Karras played with the Lions through the 1970 season but was cut shortly before the 1971 season opener.

aggressive, so to speak, but he had other things on his mind and I had to make some choices."

Hand recalled that the Lions could have brought in Mike Tilleman, a defensive tackle from New Orleans, but the move wasn't made because Tilleman's salary was higher than what the Lions were willing to pay. At least that's how Hand remembers it. Tilleman eventually went to Houston where he had 15 sacks in 1972. He wound up starting for most of his 11 seasons in the NFL.

"The thing I guess that disappoints you is that you see other teams making moves by bringing in players that you know will help them," Hand said. "You're saying, 'We know there's a couple of positions where we're weak, but we don't see any attempts to fill them with solid players.' That was disappointing."

Green also remembered the Lions' pursuit of Tilleman.

"They wanted to cut Karras, they wanted another pass rushing defensive lineman and they tried getting Mike Tilleman," Green recalled. "Joe Schmidt wanted Tilleman but he had a battle with Russ Thomas, the general manager, and they didn't get him."

The Lions had a void on the line but were still a better-than-average team. The press, though, couldn't stop writing about Karras.

When the season finally began, Frank Gifford, Don Meredith and Howard Cosell were in Detroit to open the second season of Monday Night Football with a game between the Black and Blue's two best teams, the Vikings and the Lions. The Lions jumped out to a 13-0 lead, but the Vikings, who had come back to win several games between the teams in the previous years, did it again.

The Vikings clawed back and took a 16-13 lead behind the kicking of Fred Cox, whose third field goal broke a 13-13 tie.

On the other side, Lions kicker Errol Mann was also having a significant impact on the game. He missed five field goals, the fifth from 33 yards out that would have tied the score. It was the continuation of bad things always happening for the Lions versus Minnesota.

Two years earlier, the Lions lost the ball near the goal line when it appeared they were going in to the score the winning touchdown at the end of the game. In 1970, Gary Cuozzo and Bill Brown hooked up on a touchdown near the end of the game as the Vikings rallied for a victory. From 1968-74, the Lions could always find a way to lose to Minnesota.

"That streak was there but you have to work around it, hopefully get it out of your mind so you don't carry it with you," Lucci said. "You were always cognizant of the fact that those things are there, but hopefully you don't get in that position. It just was a matter of somebody making a mistake, that's what it amounts to. It wasn't necessarily some kind of voodoo or some kind of mystic spell they have on you. It was somebody making a mistake at a crucial time in the game."

The Lions bounced back to win their next four games, taking a 4-1 record into a game against the Chicago Bears on October 24. That's the game where Chuck Hughes (see "spotlight on page 116) died of a heart attack in the fourth quarter when the Lions were driving for the winning touchdown. They lost the game, 28-23.

The Lions were 7-3-1 going into the final three weeks of the season but lost all three games, partly due to the emotional toll of dealing with a teammate who died on the field.

The following year, the Vikings finished 7-7 and didn't win the Black and Blue for the first time since 1967. But they did beat the Lions twice. One of those games was a 16-14 victory when Mann had a chip-shot field goal attempt blocked by Minnesota's Bobby Bryant in the closing seconds.

Detroit, which had gone 4-0-2 in the previous six games against Green Bay, was swept by the Packers, who finished 10-4 and won the division. Detroit, 8-1-1 against the rest of its schedule but 0-4 versus the Packers and Vikings, finished 8-5-1.

Schmidt quit at the end of the season and was replaced by Don McCafferty, who had guided the Baltimore Colts to victory in Super Bowl V. The Lions finished with a 6-7-1 record in McCafferty's only season. He died of a heart attack several weeks before the beginning of training camp in 1974.

"We went on strike that summer and Raymond Berry, who had

played with the Colts, walks into a players' meeting and says, 'Guys, I just want to let you know, coach McCafferty just died,'" recalled Hand. "You're going, 'No, no, that can't be.'"

The Lions finished 7-7 in each of Rick Forzano's first two seasons and started 1-3 in 1976 when he was fired and replaced by Tommy Hudspeth. The Lions went on to four straight losing seasons, bottoming out at 2-14 in 1979.

Finishing so poorly allowed the Lions to obtain Billy Sims, the All-American running back from Oklahoma. He quickly became a crowd favorite by rushing for 1,303 yards and scoring 16 touchdowns as a rookie to lead Detroit to a 9-7 record. That was one of the Lions' two winning records in the 1980s. Sims's career came to an end with a knee injury midway through the 1984 season when he was well on his way to another 1,000-yard season. He played three full seasons and partial seasons in '82 because of a players' strike and in 1984. Despite his short career, he still rushed for 5,106 yards, second-highest in team history behind Barry Sanders.

"God, he was a good back," former Bears safety Gary Fencik said. "He had outside moves, power inside, he was very dangerous. It's just a shame Billy's career was cut so short by knee injuries. He was a tremendous back."

The Lions had seven straight losing seasons from 1984-90, winning seven games just twice. Monte Clark, who guided the Lions to a division title in 1983, was fired after the 1984 season. He was replaced by Daryl Rogers, a fairly successful college coach who didn't make it with the Lions. He was cut loose during the 1988 season, after winning a total of 18 games. Jerry Ball, a nose tackle on that team, wrote a column for the *Detroit News* in 1991 when he remembered one day that Rogers wasn't paying attention at practice.

"You never know what a head coach is thinking," Ball wrote. "Maybe it's strategy or something. Daryl turned to somebody and said, 'Hey guys, did you know there were thirty-eight pigeons on that roof?' And we were all just stunned. What kind of mind frame is this guy in when we're practicing and he's counting pigeons?"

Wayne Fontes replaced Rogers and the misery continued until

Barry Sanders rushed for 15,269 yards in 10 seasons before retiring following the 1998 season. He never rushed for fewer than 1,115 yards in one season.

1991. The Lions began that season by losing a Sunday night game to Washington, 45-0. They had been embarrassed and looked totally confused on national television, showing signs that another losing season was in store. Instead, Detroit did an about-face and won five games in a row.

The Lions' winning streaked ended with a loss at San Francisco but they came back with a win at home over Dallas, although quarterback Rodney Peete was lost for the season in that game when he tore his Achilles tendon. Erik Kramer, once cut by the Lions and a player whose only previous pass in the NFL was in a replacement game in the 1987 season, took over and threw two touchdown passes.

The Lions dropped their next two games to fall to 6-4.

In their eleventh game, Detroit was at home against the Rams when offensive guard Mike Utley suffered a paralyzing neck injury that silenced the Silverdome crowd. Utley lay motionless for several minutes and was eventually carried off the field. As he left, he flashed a thumbs-up sign that lifted the crowd's spirits and gave his teammates inspiration.

The Lions went on to win, 21-10, but the next day reality set in as the players realized their teammate would probably never walk again.

"We're sitting in there trying to watch film, we're kidding ourselves," linebacker Chris Spielman said in a newspaper story a couple of days after the accident. "It's like staring at a blank wall. I could only think of one thing: Mike. Everybody's thinking of one person who's struggling, who's really struggling to walk again."

The Lions didn't lose again during the regular season, finishing with six straight victories, a 12-4 record and their first Black and Blue Division title since 1983.

After receiving an opening-round bye in the playoffs, Detroit blew past the visiting Cowboys, 38-6, as Erik Kramer passed for 341 yards and three touchdowns. Barry Sanders ended the scoring with a 47-yard touchdown run in the fourth quarter.

"I think we had been waiting on that team to show up for the first couple of years, and in '91, it finally came together," Sanders wrote in his autobiography, *Barry Sanders Now You See Him....* "We dedicated our season to Mike. We used his thumbs-up signal as our rallying point and went on to win the NFC Central Division title. We hosted and won our first playoff game in years by blasting the talented but rebuilding Dallas Cowboys, 38-6. I don't think we realized that we were capable of such a game. If we did realize it, we certainly had never witnessed it. We ran the ball, we passed the ball and the defense dominated."

The victory moved the Lions into the NFC title game, their first championship game since 1957. But the road to the Super Bowl went through Washington, and the Redskins, who had humiliated Detroit in the season opener, were on their way to another Super Bowl title. The Lions hung tough, trailing 17-10 at the half, before the Redskins exploded for 24 unanswered points and a 41-10 win.

The Lions slipped to 5-11 in 1992, won the division with a 10-6 record in 1993 but lost at home in the opening round of the playoffs when Brett Favre threw a 40-yard touchdown pass with fifty-five seconds left to give the Packers a 28-24 win. The Lions went to the playoffs four more times in the '90s but never won another playoff game nor a division title.

Utley's injury was one of three tragedies involving the Lions in the 1990s. In 1992, linebacker Eric Andolsek was killed when a driver fell asleep in his truck, which jumped into Andolsek's yard and killed him. In 1997, linebacker Reggie Brown suffered a paralyzing injury during a game.

The beginning of the new century hasn't been kind to the Lions, who have had five different head coaches. After a 9-7 record in 2000, they won a total of 24 games the next five seasons.

Poor drafts and lack of quality free agents have accounted for the Lions' failures on the field. From 2000 through 2006, only six Lions have played in the Pro Bowl. Defensive tackle Shaun Rogers (2004 and 2005) and cornerback Dre' Bly (2003 and 2004) are the only players who have participated more than once.

SPOTLIGHT: THE DARKEST MOMENT

On October 24, 1971, more than 50,000 fans at Tiger Stadium in Detroit saw a football player die on the field.

With 62 seconds left in a highly entertaining game between the Bears and Lions, Chuck Hughes, a twenty-eight-year-old backup receiver for the Lions who moments earlier had caught his first pass of the season, collapsed with the Bears leading 28-23.

Hughes caught a 32-yard pass from Greg Landry that moved the ball to the Bears' 36 with 1:38 play. Hughes was hit by both Bob Jeter and Garry Lyle but bounced up and went to the huddle.

Landry then threw three straight incomplete passes. After the third, Hughes was heading back to the huddle when he dropped to the ground.

Bears linebacker Dick Butkus was one of the first to notice and frantically waved to the sidelines for help.

"I saw his eyes rolling around in his head and I called for a doctor," Butkus was quoted as saying in a story that appeared the next day in the *Chicago Tribune*.

Don Pierson, then a twenty-seven-year-old reporter covering the game for the *Tribune*, may have been one of the first reporters to find out that Hughes was probably not alive.

"I remember getting a call in the press box from back

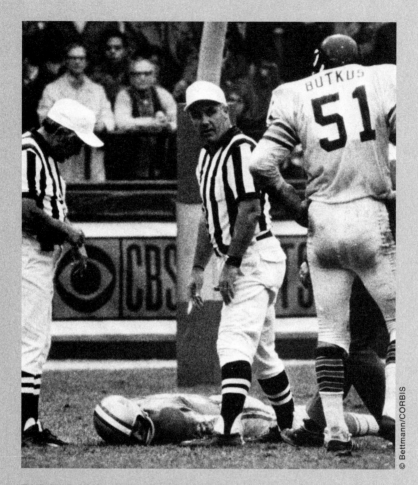

© Bettmann/CORBIS

Dick Butkus (51) looks on as two officials tend to Lions receiver Chuck Hughes, who dropped to the ground after suffering a heart attack near the end of a game on October 24, 1971. Hughes was pronounced dead 41 minutes later.

---

in Chicago. John Husar was working the desk at the time," Pierson said of his colleague. "He was a former medic and he said, 'The guy is dead.' I said, 'How do you know?' He said because the bladder had given out on him. He could see that his pants were all wet and when they picked him up on the stretcher his arm plopped over so you had a pretty good idea."

Lions linebacker Mike Lucci was on the sideline watching as the Lions' offense moved into Bears' territory, trying to score a touchdown that would improve Detroit's record to 5-1 and keep them tied for the Central Division lead with the Vikings.

Hughes entered the game in the fourth quarter after Lions receiver Larry Walton was injured.

"He went down kind of funny," Lucci said. "You watch football and play football all your life; people get knocked down and people get tripped. When you see a guy fall down without being hit it's humorous because he tripped over the yard marker, some would say.

"He went down, it looked he was shot. He just went down and hit flat. There was something wrong with the way he went down. I didn't know if anybody had hit him. Butkus was pointing at him and they came out on the field and were working on him. They were out there forever. It seemed like they were out there for an hour. They were probably out there for 15 or 20 minutes.

"They took him off and he wasn't moving. It was like the rest of that game there were rumors he was dead, he wasn't dead, this and that. When we got into the locker room, they told us he had died."

Team physicians performed CPR on Hughes, who eventually was transported to Henry Ford Hospital, where he was pronounced dead at 4:41 p.m.

An autopsy the next day revealed that Hughes suffered an acute coronary thrombosis, which caused his death. Doctors said Hughes had diseased arteries.

"We knew it by the time we started writing our stories, but I wrote the story with the reaction of the players before they knew," Pierson said.

Asked if it was difficult to write about a death on a

football field, Pierson replied, "Yeah, it was pretty challenging, I remember. I'd never seen anything like that."

Hughes was the first player to die on the field. Stan Mauldin of the Chicago Cardinals died in the locker room after a game against the Philadelphia Eagles in 1948. He complained of dizziness coming out of the shower and collapsed. Dave Sparks of the Washington Redskins died in a friend's apartment two hours after a game against Cleveland in 1954. An autopsy revealed he had the heart of a sixty-year-old.

"The interesting thing about it was the Bears were not that good, but it was probably the best game they had played," Pierson said. "I can't remember the standings or if anything was at stake, but it was such a good game and Bobby Douglass played such a good game, and to have that happen sort of complicated things as far as writing the story.

"It wasn't like the guy was a star or a great player. It was sort of a freak occurrence in more ways than one.

"The main thing was a concern for him. The players all suspected the worst. It was pretty hard to get them to talk about the game."

In Detroit, nobody talked about the game. The daily papers were full of stories during the next week about Hughes and his heart problem and about his infant and his wife, Sharon. There was a Mass in Detroit for Hughes in the middle of the week. Then the Lions left for Abilene, Texas, for his funeral. Hughes played college football at Texas-El Paso and was drafted by the Philadelphia Eagles in 1967. The Lions obtained him in a trade from the Eagles prior to the 1970 season.

Before the Lions went back to Detroit to try to prepare for a Monday night game against the Packers, Hughes's widow, Sharon, spoke to the team.

"His wife urged us to beat the Packers," Greg Landry

said in a story that appeared October 29 in the *Detroit News*. "I think we were in a stronger frame of mind because of Sharon. She was so strong, she said, 'Don't let Chuck's death ruin your season.'"

On November 1, eight days after Hughes's death, the Packers and Lions played to a 14-14 tie in a steady rain on a muddy field at Milwaukee's County Stadium.

Thirty-four years later, Lucci still marveled at the fact that his team didn't lose.

"It's a miracle we tied that game," he said. "I don't think anybody could believe what had transpired. And you almost start feeling your own mortality. At that age and you're playing football, you don't think you can be hurt, let alone die.

"It had some distraction. We went up there, and it was almost like sleepwalking. Here's a teammate that had been running around. Chuck would run patterns before practice, after practice. Of all the guys you would think would have some sort of heart problem, he never got tired. Here's a guy that drops dead on the field. It was a shock, and I think there was a distraction that existed after that."

Charlie Sanders, the Lions' tight end from 1968-77, concurred with Lucci that there was a lot of soul searching among the players.

"I think right after that it was a mental thing, the fear factor, the unknowing" said Sanders, who in 2005 was the Lions' assistant director of pro personnel. "The one thing you ask yourself is, how did this happen? You found yourself in a situation that it was very hard to concentrate on what you were doing and it almost became a personal thing where you were looking back and looking at yourself because this was unheard of.

"This thing doesn't happen, so you had a fear factor in there, too, and then the type of situation where you throw your entire trust to the NFL, the doctors this and that and the other, and go out there and do your thing until you're hurt, not dead. It was a mental thing we had to deal with. Maybe something in the back of our minds we had to deal with."

After tying the Packers, the Lions won three of their next four games and were still in the playoff hunt with a 7-3-1 record entering the final three games. But following a 32-21 victory on Thanksgiving over Kansas City, the Lions were beaten at home ten days later by Philadelphia, 23-20.

The Lions then went to Minnesota and suffered a 29-10 setback to the Vikings, who beat the Lions for the eighth straight game. That loss eliminated Detroit from the playoffs. The Lions closed the season with a 31-27 loss at San Francisco to finish with a 7-6-1 record a year after they had made the playoffs for the first time since 1957.

"It was always there, it was something you couldn't get away from," said Joe Schmidt, a Hall of Fame linebacker for the Lions who was coaching the team the day Hughes died.

"It was difficult for the remainder of the season."

6

THE RIVALRIES

Jerry Kramer, the Green Bay
Packers' great guard from the
Lombardi era, was a raw, unsus-
pecting rookie in 1958. He had only a
vague notion that the Chicago Bears were
the team's rival 200 miles to the south.
But Kramer, fresh off the University of
Idaho campus in Moscow, had no inkling
how all-consuming this rivalry of all
National Football League rivalries was to
Packers and Bears fans alike.

So a happenstance meeting nearly
fifty years ago with "a prim little lady,"
as Kramer describes her, remains vivid
because it was like a slap in the face. It

**Bears outside linebacker Doug Buffone (55)
pursues Packers halfback Donny Anderson
during a game at Lambeau Field.**

brought into sharp focus the depth and breadth of the clashes between the two teams.

Indeed, this oldest of NFL rivalries, this hallowed twice-a-year bloodletting, lies at the very core of what would become the Black and Blue Division.

"I didn't know shit about (the rivalry)," Kramer recalled. "Back in Moscow, Idaho, we didn't get the Bears very much. We didn't get anything very much. So I'm pretty ignorant about everything."

Kramer was aware the Bears were the upcoming opponent. But he was totally unprepared for a chance encounter that elevated the game to the status of a holy war.

"I go into a news shop and come out with a cigar or something and a little lady was walking by," he said. "She was a prim little lady, and then she says to me, 'Are you ready for them sons of bitches Bears?'

"I look at her and I'm stunned. I say, 'Yes, ma'am. Yes, ma'am.' That kind of got you going a little bit. You'd like to think in a rivalry, there's a certain amount of gentleman's game. But (the fans) didn't give a shit about that. All I heard was, 'Kill the Bears. Maim the sons of bitches.'"

In this present-day era of round-the-clock sports on cable television, the Internet, endless sports babble on radio talk shows and an inexhaustible flood of print media coverage, it seems virtually every contest is a rivalry of some sort.

"Backyard brawls" and "border wars" abound. Teams invariably "don't like each other very much." There is never "any love lost when these two get together." And, of course, "you can always throw out the records when these two teams meet."

Ratings and readership need rivalries. Hence, nearly every game is a rivalry, no matter how superficial the circumstances.

But the Packers-Bears rivalry is that rare jewel in the world of sports, certainly comparable to college rivalries such as Army-Navy, Harvard-Yale, North Carolina-Duke. It is one without a need for clichés. It stands at the zenith of the NFL in terms of longevity and competitiveness. Even in today's Madison Avenue-influenced NFL with its slick marketing and endless hyperbole, the game retains the same primeval nature it did back in 1921 when the Chicago Staleys (the Bears two years hence) defeated the Packers, 20-0.

The stark numbers speak to the game's competitive level: Bears, 87 wins; Packers, 79 wins. Six ties, where everyone walked off the field miserable.

But the numbers are but a façade. The essence of this rivalry lies in the strong personalities of the coaches, the reverent tones former players use when they reminisce and the utter disdain fans hold toward the other side, raw emotions nurtured and handed down from generation to generation as priceless as family heirlooms.

Tickets to a Bears-Packers game are a scalper's delight. Walk into men's bathrooms in some of Green Bay's watering holes and you'll notice Bears logos in the urinals so rabid Packers fans can relieve themselves and "piss on the Bears" at the same time. Those snarling visages of Dick Butkus and Ray Nitschke never seem to fade. Neither does the sting from a hail of snowballs directed at the visiting Packers in the days when the games were played at Wrigley Field.

"I never felt more like a gladiator than when I played at Wrigley Field," former Packers linebacker Dave Robinson said. "The fans were vicious when the snow was falling. They must have put those snowballs in a freezer or something. When you were down at one end of the field, they'd snowball you. But those were ice balls they were throwing."

Bears center Jay Hilgenberg remembers the fence-like partitions put in place at Lambeau Field to keep the fans back as visiting players walked from the locker room to the playing-field entrance. "You knew the crowd would be right on those gates and try to taunt you and yell at you," he said. "We'd come through there at about ten o'clock in the morning (for warm-ups) and the smell of alcohol was unbelievable. Green Bay fans—they liked to have a few drinks before games."

There are those who feel the rivalry's intensity has dimmed over time. They cite the increased player movement from free agency and

Halfback Paul Hornung (5) heads upfield during a 49-0 victory over the Chicago Bears on September 30, 1962. Packers lineman Fuzzy Thurston blocks Bears defensive back J.C. Caroline (25), and guard Jerry Kramer (64) stops Bears defensive tackle Maury Youmans (82).

coaching turnover. Many in Chicago felt that when Dave Wannstedt, an assistant coach with the Dallas Cowboys, replaced Mike Ditka as coach, he didn't have a true appreciation for the rivalry. He said all the right things leading up to the game, but some players didn't think he really understood what the rivalry was about.

"In fact he came in and made the statement that it's just like every other game," recalled former Bears kicker Kevin Butler. "He lost me as a player. He got rid of me as a player, but he had also lost me as a player.

"I truly believe when he came in he had that Dallas mentality that, you know, this isn't real football. Real football is what we've been doing in Dallas. And you know that was a mistake. I think the public, the fans in Chicago, sure picked up on it. Did he try to right the wrong? I think he did, because he started stressing the importance. He learned the wrong way, but first impressions sometimes are the worst."

Wannstedt split the first two games against Green Bay during his first season in 1992. He never beat the Packers after that, as the Bears were swept in each of Wannstedt's final five years before he was fired.

When Lovie Smith was named the Bears' coach in 2004, he announced at his introductory press conference that one of his immediate goals was to regain the upper hand after years of Packers dominance with Brett Favre at quarterback.

At least Smith was civil when he revealed those intentions. Even larger-than-life personalities such as George Halas, Curly Lambeau and Vince Lombardi showed some restraint. But when Forrest Gregg coached the Packers in the mid-1980s and Ditka was guiding the then-superior Bears, the rivalry turned bitter and was marred by several ugly incidents. Players on both teams say Gregg was obsessed with beating the Bears to the point of losing all reason. That was never more evident than in 1984, Gregg's first season.

The Packers' Hall of Fame offensive tackle fully appreciated the importance of beating the Bears. But with Gregg, beating the Bears didn't merely fit into his scheme of things; it was the entire

Forrest Gregg was a Hall of Fame offensive tackle during his
playing days for the Green Bay Packers, helping them to five
NFL titles and to victory in the first two Super Bowls in the 1960s.
He returned as a coach in 1984 but never posted a winning record
in four seasons. He was intensely disliked by many members of
the Chicago Bears during his tenure as coach.

----

scheme, even in a meaningless preseason game.

The backdrop of Milwaukee County Stadium, with both team benches on the same side of the field, seemed tailor-made for potential mayhem. From the beginning, Gregg acted as though his entire coaching future hinged on this one game. Then-quarterback Lynn Dickey remembers it well.

"We were ahead in the game and Forrest kind of took it like a Super Bowl," Dickey said. "Forrest was calling timeouts with about a minute to go right before the half and Ditka was like, 'What are you doing down there? Let's get this thing over with.' Well, something was said and Gregg and Ditka got into this big shouting match. Then we went into halftime and Forrest had this great big scowl on his face. He said, 'You guys worry about them (the Bears) and I'll take care of Ditka.'

"I just rolled my eyes, thinking Ditka would whip your ass so bad."

For the record, the Packers won 17-10, but Gregg was just getting warmed up. "He'd have those guys whipped into a frenzy," Hilgenberg said.

Following that game, the Packers and Bears agreed to discontinue playing each other during the exhibition season.

The teams split during the regular season in 1984, which was the only time under Gregg when the Packers won a game that counted. The Bears swept the Packers during their Super Bowl season in 1985, using a Monday night game to kick more sand in the Packers' faces by inserting massive defensive tackle William (The Refrigerator) Perry as a fullback for five plays. He scored a touchdown and created a path that Walter Payton followed into the end zone for two other scores. In the rematch in Green Bay, he caught a touchdown pass in a 16-10 win.

One ugly scene in Lambeau Field on that day saw Packers safety Kenny Stills (whom Gregg once referred to as "a heat-seeking missile") drill fullback Matt Suhey so long after a play had ended that Suhey actually was walking back to the huddle.

The following year it got worse. On a day when several

Packers were wearing towels with the numbers of some Bears players on them, Packers nose tackle Charlie Martin picked up quarterback Jim McMahon several full counts after a play had ended and attempted to turn him into a human accordion by body-slamming McMahon head-first to the turf.

"It was so late after the play that I didn't realize he'd done that until that night when I saw the replay on TV," Hilgenberg said. "And I remember Martin had that towel with the numbers on it. I was just thankful he had my number on there. It would have been real embarrassing if they didn't consider me one of the guys they had to take out to win the game."

Perhaps Bears defensive back Gary Fencik sums it up best: "You try to knock the snot out of someone. You don't really think about injuring someone."

After Gregg left, civility returned to the rivalry, according to Ditka.

"When I took over coaching, Bart (Starr) was coaching up there and it was a class operation," he said. "It got out of hand in the mid-'80s there with Forrest Gregg. There was some bad blood, some bad times. They did some things they shouldn't have done, and it took the respect out of the game and it took a lot out of the rivalry, I thought. After he left, when (Packers coach) Lindy Infante and those guys came in, the rivalry was great. It was just good football based on them trying to beat us and us trying to beat them. It wasn't based on somebody trying to hurt somebody."

Packers president Bob Harlan, to this day, said Gregg is responsible for what happened during some of those games.

"There were some embarrassing moments, and that was too bad," he said. "I felt badly about it. I thought it tarnished the rivalry, but more importantly I thought it tarnished the Green Bay Packers and I said so publicly.

"It was embarrassing that it came to this. But it was almost a bitter, bitter relationship between the two head coaches, and I almost think it was more so on Forrest's part. He was desperate to get this guy."

Coaches usually become agitated with players when they talk trash about the opponent prior to a game, but that didn't seem to matter with Ditka and Gregg.

"Mike was saying things during the week that would get you up, and Forrest Gregg was doing the same," Fencik said. "Usually players are smart enough or are encouraged not to say a lot that ends up as bulletin-board material, but those rules for a short window of time really seemed to go out the window."

Through the years Gregg has denied he hated the Bears or ordered players to go out and hurt opposing players. But some people don't buy that.

"I didn't like what was going on there when he coached," said Gale Gillingham, a former guard who was a teammate of Gregg's in the 1960s. "I became a Bears fan for a couple of years."

At times, some ill will would spill over into the stands, but generally, fans seemed to have a grudging respect for the other side. Seven Chicagoans, in fact, became legendary in Green Bay in the 1970s and 1980s when they made their annual pilgrimage north.

They were known as "The Magnificent Seven" and all wore white cowboy hats as they embarked on a weeklong tour of Green Bay's bars before Sunday's game. They commandeered a motel suite a block from Lambeau Field and hosted a nonstop party after bar hours. And one memorable Sunday, even the "Mag Seven" outdid themselves.

Overcome by open-armed acceptance from Packers fans (and a week of drink and debauchery), the guys in the white hats reportedly decided to buy a beer for everybody in their row at Lambeau Field. Their row, that is, all the way around the stadium.

Now what rivalry can top that?

THE OTHER RIVALRIES

There are some who believe that the Packers-Vikings rivalry became just as important as the Bears rivalry to the Packers players. While the Packers and Bears have played twice as many games,

Green Bay's rivalry with Minnesota has consistently been more intense since the 1970s.

For Gillingham, who played with the Packers from 1966-74 and in 1976, the Vikings game was always important to him, partly because Minnesota was the team to beat for a long time. Also, he and his family moved from Wisconsin to Minnesota after his sophomore year in high school. He later attended the University of Minnesota before being drafted by the Packers.

"They were a major rivalry with us," Gillingham said. "They always brought out our best and we brought out their best. That whole Black and Blue, every game was tough but the Vikings were just a lot better team. They could score more points than us.

"I've always felt that it was a big game. You always had Bear week when I got here, but I always felt the Vikings was a big game, always thought they were a major, major rival."

Before pro football arrived in Minnesota, the Packers were the closest NFL team. Because of that, they were adopted by Minnesotans as their team. When the Vikings joined the NFL in 1961, many of their new fans cheered for the Packers when the teams played each other.

"When we came there in 1963, my rookie year, the Vikings were only three years old and we got a bigger ovation than the Vikings when we came out on the field," former Packers linebacker Dave Robinson recalled. "This didn't do anything to help the relationship between us and the Minnesota Vikings. The Vikings players were so upset that they played us tough as dogs. It was 'The Game' for them, so if they lost every game but beat Green Bay, especially at home, it was a successful season for them.

"There were a lot of dogfights."

Former Vikings center Mick Tingelhoff, who spent his entire seventeen-year career with the Vikings beginning in 1962, does remember the Packers game always being one the Vikings looked forward to, especially during the early years when the Packers were the best team in the NFL.

"Green Bay really had a good team with all of the great

Mick Tingelhoff made the Minnesota Vikings' roster as a free agent in 1962. The durable center never missed a game in his 17 seasons with the team. He played in four Super Bowls.

players they had," he said. "I don't think it was just another game. It was always a big game and the fans really got into it. There were a lot of Green Bay fans from Minnesota and a lot of Viking fans from Wisconsin. It did get a lot of attention because we were so close to each other. It was a great rivalry and really a lot of fun."

Jerry Kramer remembers the Vikings always being a tough out from the start, even though the Packers were the class of the NFL.

"We were supposed to kick the hell out of them and we'd really get into a dogfight," the former All-Pro guard said. "Every time we went to play over there it was a dogfight, a knock-down, drag-out right to the last minute, it seemed like. I never really understood that, but it was anything but a stroll in the park. It was a long day. Bring your hat, bring your light, because it's going to be a full day of work. We're going to be here for a while."

The Vikings picked up lots of fans from Wisconsin because of coach Bud Grant, who grew up in Superior, Wisconsin, just across the river from Duluth. He played in the NFL and the NBA before becoming a coaching legend in the Canadian Football League. He became the Vikings' coach in 1967 and led them through the greatest era in the history of that franchise.

Through the years the rivalry has almost always been competitive. From 1961 through the 2006 season, the Packers held a 46-44 advantage with one game ending in a tie. In the lone playoff meeting between the teams, the Vikings won 31-17 following the 2004 season.

Of those 91 regular season meetings between the teams, 36 have been decided by seven points or less, with 17 of those being settled by three or fewer points. Both sides have had long stretches where they dominated, but all of those games decided by a touchdown are a true indication that many of the contests were intense battles, regardless of the teams' records.

Part of the charm of the rivalry, especially before free agency, was that rosters didn't change very much and the players got to know who was lining up on the other side of the ball.

"You built a certain amount of respect for each other as well as a certain amount of animosity for each other," said Scott Studwell, who joined the Vikings' front office after a fourteen-year career as a player from 1977 until 1990. "As players, I think you had a lot of familiarity with players, schemes, systems. And with Green Bay, you always had that border rivalry. There was one year when we played in Milwaukee in that baseball stadium, and it was like playing at home for us because it was the same type of setting, same type of field."

The rivalry took on added luster in 1992 when both teams hired coaches who were protégés of San Francisco 49ers coach Bill Walsh. Mike Holmgren was hired by the Packers and Dennis Green by the Vikings. Green had the upper hand early on, winning the first four meetings. Holmgren's Packers won five of the next ten before Holmgren left Green Bay for the Seattle Seahawks following the 1998 season. Holmgren had trouble at the Metrodome, the bubble-shaped indoor home of the Vikings, winning just once in seven tries with Brett Favre as quarterback.

Holmgren talked about the rivalry at a press conference during the 2004 season.

"It was a tremendous rivalry," he said. "It was going before I got there and then Denny Green and I were both hired in 1992. We had some great games with them. When we started, they were a little bit ahead of us, they were a better football team than we were. Then we got to where we could play them. We would usually win the game at Lambeau and they would win the game at the dome. It was a heck of a deal. It's a great rivalry in sports."

Favre, a three-time MVP of the NFL, did struggle in Minnesota and twice was injured and didn't finish games during the Holmgren era. One of those was in 1995, when the Packers were on their way to a win before backup T.J. Rubley threw an ill-advised pass that cost the Packers the game.

"The games over there, I thought were cursed, that building," Holmgren remembered. "I had a quarterback that had the game won. He audibled out of a quarterback sneak into a pass, threw an

The Vikings have always been a thorn in the side of Brett Favre.
Here the Packers quarterback tries fending off Wayne Rudd when the
teams met in a playoff game in January of 2005 at Lambeau Field.

interception and they won. Our linemen were going to kill him on the field in front of a million people. That was just one of the things that happened. It was wild over there."

The next-closest rivalry for the teams in the Black and Blue may involve the Vikings versus the other three teams, for similar reasons. When the Packers' dynasty ended after the 1967 season, the Vikings took over as the team to beat. The fact that their run of domination lasted longer than the Packers' intensified the desire of the other three teams to pull off the memorable upset.

Under Bud Grant, the Vikings won 10 of 11 division titles from 1968 until 1978 and played in the Super Bowl four times. During that stretch they completely dominated the Black and Blue, compiling a 53-12-1 record against their other rivalries. The only year they failed to win the division was in 1972, when the Packers split with the Vikings, swept both the Bears and Lions and won the Black and Blue with a 10-4 record. The Vikings dropped three of their last four games and finished with a surprising 7-7 record.

But Minnesota's overall domination of the other teams made them a team to beat during that stretch. In the forty years of division play, the Vikings own winning records over all three of the other teams. They were 41-37-1 against the Packers, 45-33-1 against the Bears and an astounding 57-21-1 versus Detroit.

There also were other reasons, and some were personal.

Some reporters who covered the Bears swear that Ditka wanted to beat the Vikings almost as badly as the Packers, mainly because the first game he ever played in the NFL left a bitter taste that never left his mouth. On September 17, 1961, the Minnesota Vikings, a new franchise, opened the season by pounding the Bears 37-13 at Metropolitan Stadium in Bloomington, Minnesota. Ditka was so irate and embarrassed that he got into a fight on the sidelines with teammate Ted Karras, whom Ditka didn't think was playing hard enough.

"With Ditka as head coach, everybody was the biggest rival but Ditka didn't care for the Vikings," Jay Hilgenberg said. "I think the Vikings beat the Bears quite often before we became good."

For Hilgenberg, the Vikings' game was always a big one. He grew up in Iowa as a Minnesota fan, mainly because his uncle, linebacker Wally Hilgenberg, was with the Vikings during their dominating days and participated in all four Super Bowl games Minnesota played. At an early age, Jay Hilgenberg spent time with many of the Vikings, including future Hall of Famers such as coach Bud Grant and defensive tackle Alan Page.

"That was always my dream," he said. "I wanted to play for the Vikings. When I was a kid, I used to go hunting with Bud Grant and Roy Winston and Lonnie Warwick, a lot of the Viking players. We used to go to training camp. I remember seeing Bill Brown at a Pizza Hut, sitting there having pizza with him.

"In fact, when I was a sophomore in high school, my father took my older brother and myself down to New Orleans for the Super Bowl between the Steelers and the Vikings. And I went up to the room, my uncle's room, to talk to him and he wasn't there but his roommate was Alan Page. I sat in the room and talked to Alan Page for like 20 minutes. And then it ended up my rookie year (1981) was Alan Page's last year in the NFL.

"He played for the Bears. So being a sophomore in high school talking to Alan Page and all of a sudden being a rookie in the NFL and here's the guy you practice against every day. That guy helped me so much. Every day in practice he helped me. He taught me so much about how to attack a defensive lineman."

Sometimes, personality clashes between key players heightened a rivalry in the locker room and in the stands. When Dick Butkus was playing middle linebacker for the Bears, he dominated most of the centers he played. But he probably had his most intense battles with opposing centers in division games. Lions center Ed Flanagan and Butkus simply didn't like each other.

"There was a situation before a game in Chicago when Dick Butkus and Ed Flanagan nearly got into a fight," former *Detroit News* reporter Jerry Green recalled. "They had many battles through the years, and this time they started jawing at one another and it almost turned into a melee."

Former Lions middle linebacker Mike Lucci and Butkus went through a period where they didn't talk to each other over something Lucci had said, half in jest.

"I remember Butkus had written a book, and sportswriters asked me what I thought of him writing a book," recalled Lucci, who played with the Lions during the same years Butkus was with the Bears, from 1965 through 1973. "I said, 'He wrote a book? Hell, I didn't know he could even read.' Just a comment like that. He comes to Detroit to play us. We had beaten them eleven out of thirteen times, something like that, just like the Vikings were doing to us. We go out there and instead of shaking hands with me he steps back. So we don't shake hands."

That just added fuel to the rivalry between the Bears and Lions, which was intense in the 1950s, '60s and early '70s.

"So three weeks later we go to Chicago and it's all over the papers this and that and he blasted me or something," Lucci said. "Not even blasted. You know how you say something and the sportswriter writes it and it writes itself? We got to Chicago and these people are booing and throwing shit and we win the game. I've got my helmet off and (teammate) Bob Kowalkowski told me I better keep my helmet on. I put my helmet on and here comes a full Coke can. Bam, hits my shoulder pads. I'm walking off and people are yelling and screaming. I'm going down to the dugout and some guy takes an apple and hits me in the top of the helmet with the apple.

"I try to grab the guy, pull him in the dugout and he jumps back. They had this wire mesh on the steps going into the locker room. They're just shaking the mesh like they were a bunch of animals. They were so into the game, so into the rivalry that it made it bigger than it really was.

"We loved playing the Bears because we played them all the time and it was a rivalry, but the fans made it even more rabid. There was a mentality that existed: We're going into Chicago, we might beat the shit out of them, we might beat them on the score. But you better get ready because you're going to have to fight your ass off."

Through 2006, the Lions played the Bears 152 times and the Packers 153. For whatever reason, the Packers-Lions rivalry is not talked about with such passion as that of the Packers-Bears or the Packers-Vikings. Green Bay is two hours from the Michigan border, where there may be more Packer fans than Lion fans.

To be sure, there has been an intensity between the teams at times, particularly during the 1960s. But the rivalry has never reached the sometimes-frenzied level as the yearly battles between Green Bay and their two other Black and Blue rivals.

"Every game is important," said Larry McCarren, who played center for the Packers from 1973 until 1984 and has been the team's longtime radio voice. "The Lions are not only third on the Packers' batting order, but a distant third as far as rivalries go. Why? I don't know. They were tough games, physical games, all that good stuff. But I don't have a lot to add on that."

7

THE GREEN BAY PACKERS

L ong before the Dallas Cowboys made the claim, the Packers of the 1960s were America's team.

Vince Lombardi was the coach. His stars included several future Hall of Fame players. Bart Starr was the cool and efficient quarterback. Jim Taylor was the punishing fullback. Paul Hornung was the gifted and versatile halfback. They ran behind a solid line led by right tackle Forrest Gregg, whom Lombardi called "the finest player I ever coached."

The defense was led by Ray Nitschke, among the hardest hitting linebackers in NFL history. Defensive end Willie Davis

----

Quarterback Bart Starr (15) confers with coach Vince Lombardi on the sidelines during a 9-7 victory over the Detroit Lions on October 7, 1962.

and tackle Henry Jordan were the stalwarts of a line that frequently got to quarterbacks and stopped the opponent's running game. Willie Wood, undrafted out of college, became one of the game's great safeties. Herb Adderley was a star running back at Michigan State but became a great cornerback for the Packers.

That was the core of a team that won five NFL titles from 1961-67 and the first two Super Bowls.

By 1970, all but Starr, Nitschke and Wood were gone. Starr and Wood retired after the 1971 season; Nitschke retired a year later. Teams get old and have to rebuild. It's common. But for the Packers, the wait for the return to greatness was uncommonly long.

Before Mike Holmgren was hired in 1992, five coaches failed to bring back the winning tradition after Lombardi left.

Phil Bengtson: three seasons, 20-21-1 record, one winning season, no playoffs.

Dan Devine: four seasons, 25-28-4 record, one winning season, one division title, one playoff berth.

Bart Starr: nine seasons, 53-77-3, two winning seasons, one playoff berth.

Forrest Gregg: four seasons, 25-37-1, no winning seasons, no playoff berth.

Lindy Infante: four seasons, 24-40, one winning season, no playoff appearance.

Lombardi coached for nine seasons, compiling a winning record each season and winning five championships. The five coaches who followed combined for five winning seasons and just two trips to the playoffs in twenty-four years.

Bengtson was Lombardi's defensive coordinator. He was a good football man hamstrung with an aging team. Devine was a successful college coach at Arizona State and Missouri before he came to the Packers. After he left Green Bay, he guided Notre Dame to a national championship. His decision-making haunted the Packers for several years after he departed.

Devine was a terrible judge of talent who traded away high draft picks for players who largely did not make meaningful contributions. He struck gold with his first pick, though. John Brockington, an All-American fullback at Ohio State, came to Green Bay in 1971 and rushed for more than 1,000 yards in each of his first three seasons.

In 1972, the Packers literally ran to the Black and Blue title, ending Minnesota's four-year dominance of the division. Brockington rushed for 1,027 yards. Halfback MacArthur Lane, acquired before the season, rushed for 821 yards. The Packers clinched the division title in the thirteenth week with a 23-7 victory over the Vikings at Metropolitan Stadium.

The trouble with the Green Bay offense was that it didn't have much of a passing game. That plagued the Packers throughout most of the 1970s, otherwise known among some Packer fans as "The Crummy Quarterback Era."

The quarterback was Scott Hunter, who like Starr had attended the University of Alabama. That was the only similarity between Starr and Hunter, who had replaced the Packers legend the previous year. Hunter completed 46 percent of his passes in 1971 and just 43.2 percent in 1972, when the Packers averaged 110 yards passing and scored just seven touchdowns through the air.

In the playoffs, the Washington Redskins knew exactly what the Packers would do. They used a five-man defensive front and held Brockington to nine yards on 13 carries in a 16-3 victory at RFK Stadium.

In 1973, things returned to normal in the Central. The Vikings bounced back from a 7-7 season and finished 12-2. The Packers dropped to 5-7-2.

Brockington rushed for 1,144 yards but scored only three touchdowns. Lane's production dropped to 528 yards and he averaged just 3.1 yards per carry.

The quarterback situation worsened. Hunter lost the job to Jim Del Gaizo, got it back for a couple of games, then lost it to Jerry Tagge, a hometown product who guided Nebraska to a couple of national college championships. The passing production dropped from the previous year and the Packers' pass-catchers again had just seven touchdowns. Combined, Hunter, Del Gaizo and Tagge completed fewer than 47 percent of their passes.

"We didn't have very good leadership at the top," said Gale Gillingham, who was one of the best guards in the league. "No knock on anybody there, but after Bart was done, we had nobody who could throw the ball. We literally ran our way to any victory. We could not throw the ball."

Gillingham started on Lombardi's last two championship teams. He became a Pro Bowl player. Some believe he's the best guard in Packers history, better even than Jerry Kramer, a perennial All-Pro during the Lombardi era.

"The Hall of Fame ought to be reserved for unique players, not just guys who were All-Pros," said Larry McCarren, a former Packers center who played with Gillingham for three seasons and with the Packers for 12.

"If there's ever been a better collision blocker and a blocker who could hit people and could hit people in devastating fashion, if there's ever been one, I've never seen him. Gale Gillingham should be in the Hall of Fame."

Devine panicked in 1974. Wanting badly to win again, he eventually made a trade that ruined the Packers for the next several years.

Before that move, though, Devine began the season with Tagge as his starting quarterback. But after a 10-9 loss to the Bears dropped Green Bay's record to 3-3, Devine yanked him in favor of journeyman Jack Concannon, a former Bear who went 0-2 in two starts. Those included a 19-17 loss to the Lions in Detroit when Errol Mann kicked a field goal that just cleared the crossbar.

With the Packers at 3-5, Devine was desperate. He traded the team's first-, second- and third-round picks in the 1975 draft and the first- and second-round picks in 1976 to the Los Angeles Rams for quarterback John Hadl, who had been the National Football Conference Player of the Year in 1973. The move ruined the Packers for the next several years.

Hadl was 34.

Offensive guard Gale Gillingham broke into the Packers' lineup as a rookie in 1966 and was a starter in the first two Super Bowls. He played in the Pro Bowl five times during a 10-year career.

In the locker room, the arrival of Hadl gave the players a sense of hope.

"You gotta remember, guys aren't thinking big picture," McCarren said when reminded that the trade for Hadl cost the Packers a lot of potentially high picks in two drafts. "For the most part, guys are thinking, 'How is this going to affect me personally?'

"That's the way guys are. People may find that hard to believe. But unless you were a quarterback on that team and you realized you were either headed to the bench or further down the pecking order, you're thinking 'John Hadl. He was just the Most Valuable Player a season or two ago. This might put us over the top.'

"History might say one thing, but at the moment I don't remember anyone going, 'Oh, my God. We just mortgaged the future.'"

With Hadl at quarterback, the Packers won three straight games to claw back into the playoff picture with a 6-5 record, but that hope was fleeting. The Packers scored two touchdowns and a total of 23 points in their last three games, all losses, and fell to 6-8.

Devine left town before he was fired and landed on his feet as head coach at Notre Dame.

The Packers were headed toward more misery. With their top draft picks gone for the next two years, team president Dominic Olejniczak tried bringing back some of the Lombardi magic by hiring Starr as the team's coach.

Starr was inexperienced, working just one season as the Packers' quarterbacks coach after retiring as a player in 1971, and the cupboard was bare. His first three teams finished 4-10, 5-9 and 4-10. Hadl was the starting quarterback in Starr's first year, but he threw just six touchdown passes and 21 interceptions. He was involved in a trade before the 1976 season that sent him to Houston and brought Lynn Dickey to Green Bay.

"Three things happened when Starr took over," said Gillingham, who lives in Little Falls, Minnesota. "One, he wasn't experienced. Two, the Hadl trade, and three, he brought in some assistants back then that didn't do him a lot of good. But that trade held the Packers back. For how many years I don't know, but it was really bad."

The Packers won six of their first seven games in 1978 with David Whitehurst as the quarterback, scoring 24 or more points in five of those wins. But the offense sputtered down the stretch, scoring just 77 points over the final nine games.

They tied for the division title with Minnesota with an 8-7-1 record, but lost the tiebreaker because they lost to the Vikings at the Met in October and played them to a 10-10 tie at Lambeau a month later, when a win would have put the Packers in control of the division.

The Packers followed that tie with a 17-7 win at Tampa Bay and could have won the division by splitting their final two games. But the offense performed horribly in losing 14-0 at a half-empty Soldier Field. The Packers lost to the Rams 31-14 in the season finale at the Los Angeles Coliseum.

The Packers won just ten games over the next two seasons, then climbed to 8-8 in 1981. They were building an offense capable of scoring a lot of points, becoming the first Black and Blue team to move away from a run-the-ball, control-the-clock offense.

Dickey had turned into a decent quarterback after missing almost two seasons with a broken leg sustained in 1977. His favorite targets were tight end Paul Coffman, who became a Pro Bowl player, and James Lofton, who wound up in the Pro Football Hall of Fame. Dickey brought stability to the position. Before he took over in 1980, he was one of eleven quarterbacks who had started for the Packers during the 1970s after Starr was replaced going into the 1971 season.

Lofton, an All-American at Stanford, was Green Bay's first pick in the 1978 draft. He stood six-foot-three and could run 40 yards in 4.3 seconds.

"If you hang around the league long enough, you obviously get to know talent when it shows up in camp," Dickey said. "Every now and then, somebody would show up—you know, guys who just stuck out. When I was in Houston, I got to play with Charlie Joiner a couple of years and he was just different, at that early age,

Wide receiver James Lofton leaps above Lions defensive back
Duane Galloway to score a touchdown during the second quarter
of the Packers' 21-14 loss to Detroit on October 12, 1986.

----

still pretty fast and his cuts were really sharp.

"When I got to Green Bay, of course, James came along, and I thought, 'Wow, he's not like the rest of the guys that come through here.' Just a little something extra special: six-foot-four, 195 pounds, really strong, could bench close to 370. Physically fit, fast, tough guy. When he showed up in camp, I just kind of turned around and said, 'Who is that guy?' He was a little better than everyone else."

Lofton caught 71 passes in 1980 and again in 1981. In 1982, a players' strike wiped out seven games, but Lofton averaged 19.9 yards per catch and helped Green Bay to a 5-3-1 record and the team's first playoff appearance in ten years.

The Packers hosted the St. Louis Cardinals and Dickey threw four touchdown passes—one to Lofton—in a 41-16 victory. The following week, the Packers were eliminated by Dallas, but Lofton scored two touchdowns, one on a 71-yard run, in the 37-26 loss.

"He is and still remains the most accurate deep thrower I've ever seen," McCarren said of Dickey. "I played in Pro Bowls with (Joe) Theismann and (Joe) Montana. When we had good offenses in the early '80s, we were going for home runs, we weren't hitting singles. There wasn't any of this West Coast stuff. We were going for home runs."

In 1983, there were high hopes for the Packers because of their firepower. Through the first six games, they scored 161 points, but the defense allowed 166. The Packers split those games. In the seventh game, the Packers won a 48-47 shootout against Washington in a game that was the highest scoring in *Monday Night Football* history.

The Packers' defense couldn't stop anyone. By the end of the season, the offense had stagnated. Even so, the Packers could have earned a playoff berth in the final game of the season with a win over the Bears at Soldier Field.

The Packers held a 21-20 lead, but the defense failed once more, allowing the Bears to drive down the field in 90 seconds before Bob Thomas kicked a 22-yard field goal to beat the Packers, 23-21.

"I can tell you one thing that will not work," said Dickey, who threw for 4,458 yards and 32 touchdowns in 1983. "You cannot outscore people. You might do it half the time and you'll end up 8-8, which we were. You have to be able to stop people. I always wanted to play on a team that was a running team instead of having to go out where, if I wasn't 30 out of 35 with four touchdowns and no picks, it was tough to win. It's just a lot easier to play on a team that can run the football and you throw when you want to, not when you have to."

The day after the loss to the Bears, Starr was fired. He compiled a 53-77-3 record in nine seasons as coach.

Shortly after Starr was fired, Judge Robert Parins, the Packers' president, turned to another former Lombardi player, Forrest Gregg, who in 1981 had led the Cincinnati Bengals to the Super Bowl, where they lost to the San Francisco 49ers.

Gregg, like Starr, was beloved in Green Bay as a player. He was a perennial All-Pro right tackle. As a coach, he had success at Cleveland, and then at Cincinnati.

But under Gregg, the Packers developed a reputation as cheap-shot artists, mainly because of some ugly incidents with the Bears, coached by Mike Ditka.

The Packers won their first game under Gregg in 1984, then lost seven straight. They played better during the second half of the year, beating their three Black and Blue rivals one time each in going 7-1 to finish 8-8 and give Packer fans hopes for 1985.

But that was the year the Bears went 15-1. The Packers never won more than two games in a row and stumbled to another 8-8 record. Gregg won a total of nine games over his last two seasons before he took a job as athletic director at Southern Methodist University, his alma mater, before he could be fired.

Lindy Infante replaced Gregg in 1988. His first team went 4-12 and lost to the Bears twice. The following year, the Packers went 10-6, winning four games by one point behind quarterback Don Makjowski. The Packers didn't make the playoffs, but appeared to be knocking on the door.

But reality again set in. The Packers went 6-10 in 1990 and 4-12 in 1991.

WOLF, FAVRE AND THE SUPER BOWL

Bob Harlan just couldn't wait any longer.

Restless all day before Super Bowl XXXI, the Green Bay Packers' president left his New Orleans hotel 90 minutes before the team buses departed for the game. He walked more than a mile to the Louisiana Superdome, where the Packers were hoping to win the Super Bowl for the first time in 29 years.

Harlan, who began his Packers career as assistant general manager in 1971, was present to watch two other teams play for the NFL championship at most of the 28 Super Bowls played before the Packers returned to the title game on January 26, 1997.

"I'd always go over early and I'd watch them blow up these helmets before the pregame introduction, and I used to think, 'Do you think Green Bay will ever be here?'" Harlan said.

"Well, I get to the Superdome about three and a half hours before the game and the place is pretty quiet, just a few maintenance people, and here's the Packer helmet blown up."

That day, the Packers were two-touchdown favorites over the New England Patriots. It was reminiscent of the first two Super Bowls, in which Green Bay was heavily favored against Kansas City in 1967 and Oakland in 1968. In the more than two decades that followed the Packers' second Super Bowl win, they were underdogs in the majority of their games.

Harlan was 34, the publicity director for baseball's St. Louis Cardinals, when he accepted an offer to join the Packers in 1971. That was less than four years after Vince Lombardi coached his last game for Green Bay, a 33-14 victory over the Oakland Raiders in the second Super Bowl.

Harlan took over as Packers president in 1989. By October 1991, he decided that he needed to make some changes, beginning with general manager Tom Braatz. In the twenty-four years since the second Super Bowl win, the Packers had compiled just five winning seasons and qualified for the playoffs twice.

Ironically, Braatz got the job in Green Bay in 1987 because Ron

Wolf, who also had interviewed, took himself out of the running. Harlan said Wolf wasn't sure how much power he'd have. The Packers have long had an executive committee involved in many major decisions and a large board of directors.

"I think what bothered him is that if you don't know this organization very well, if you're on the outside looking in and you see a 45-person board of directors, this place could be a nightmare," Harlan said. "I got the impression that bothered Ron. He wanted to go to the airport right away and get out of town. He withdrew his name the next morning, that first time we talked with him."

The second time around, Harlan knew he had to get an aggressive person.

The first person he thought of was Wolf, who was scouting for the New York Jets.

"We had to find a strong guy to come in and take the franchise with full authority and find a way to turn it around," Harlan said. "I felt if I found the right guy, I could do that. And the right person to me was Ron Wolf."

Harlan didn't want to wait until the end of the 1991 season. He wanted the new man in place for at least the final four weeks so he could be around the team, go to practice, travel to road games and get a strong feel for the organization before making any major decisions.

Harlan wanted to talk to Wolf again and got the Jets' permission to do so.

"This was a huge break for me because this was November," said Harlan, who was ready to strike quickly.

He told Wolf the new general manager would have the authority to fire and hire the head coach.

Wolf wanted that in writing.

"I faxed that to him Friday afternoon." Harlan said. "He called me Saturday morning and said, "I think we have a deal.""

So why did Wolf say yes when he'd said no just four years earlier?

"I didn't think there was any direction there, it just seemed to be a bit chaotic in 1987," Wolf said.

And the reason for Wolf's change of heart in 1991?

"There was a direction," he said. "Bob had certain parameters he established, what he wanted done, how he wanted it done. It was an easy decision on my part."

In Wolf's nine-plus seasons in Green Bay, the Packers won four division titles, went to the Super Bowl twice and never had a losing season. He retired shortly after the 2000 season.

The Packers' first game with Wolf in charge was on December 1, 1991, against the Falcons in Atlanta. Never a man to waste time, Wolf was ready to work when he arrived at the stadium.

"Ron came up, put his briefcase next to me and said, 'I'm going to go down on the field and watch Atlanta's backup quarterback and see if his arm is still as strong as it was coming out of college,'" Harlan said.

Harlan was a little more than curious.

"I can't wait to get my flip card out to see who this is," Harlan said. "The last four days of the draft (preparations), I always make it a point to go back to the draft room and see what are we really talking about. One day, they're watching this quarterback and I think his name is Favor.

"So I watch the kid Ron tells me he's going to go and see, and I turn the flip card, I see the name and realize I know this kid. Ron comes back 45 minutes later, sits down next to me, and said, 'We're going to make a trade for Brett Favre. Are you OK with that?' I said, 'Absolutely. I told you it's your football team to run.'"

Favre had captured Wolf's interest when he was scouting for the Jets.

In July 1990, before his senior year at Southern Mississippi, Favre was injured in a car accident and had 30 inches of intestines removed. When he returned to the field, his play wasn't as good as before and his stock dropped.

But Wolf had seen enough tape from Favre's junior season to see that the kid was special. The Jets didn't have a first-round pick in the 1991 draft and Wolf tried convincing them to make a deal to move up. The Falcons took Favre in the second round, with the thirty-third overall pick, one spot ahead of the Jets.

The irony of Wolf's pursuit of Favre is that he never made it down to the field in Atlanta that day. He was besieged by cameras from Wisconsin TV stations trying to follow every move of the Packers' new general manager.

Wolf didn't need to see Favre. He'd seen Favre dominate a scrimmage between the Falcons and Seattle Seahawks earlier that summer in Portland, Oregon, strengthening his belief that the kid was going to be a star.

So Wolf returned to Green Bay with the Packers and continued to operate in a manner that validated Harlan's decision to hire him.

"The next day he goes down to practice," Harlan said. "He comes in my office and says, 'You've got a problem on your practice field. It's a country club atmosphere.' He said, 'You guys are 4-10. They're walking around like they're 10-4. We're going to make changes.'"

Harlan shook his head at the memory of Wolf's analysis.

"He grasped the situation so quickly," Harlan said. "The thing I liked about it, he did what I thought he would do. Rather than coming in January and look at everything on videotape, he's with the team and seeing it.

"The entire football operation, equipment, video, training, jumped up leaps and bounds in class. Ron brought in new people, changed the attitude. It was a marvelous change that we went through."

Wolf was definitely in charge, probably the most authoritative figure in Green Bay since Lombardi.

Larry McCarren played center for the Packers for twelve seasons: two under Dan Devine, nine under Bart Starr and one under Forrest Gregg. He experienced two winning seasons as a player. After his playing days, he remained in Green Bay as a sportscaster and watched as Gregg and Lindy Infante failed as coaches, mustering just one winning season between them before Wolf's arrival.

"One of the secrets about Ron is he is not just a personnel guy.

He is a leader," McCarren said. "I could see he was a leader very early on with the way he went about the business, just the way he made his own contribution to the cause.

"I remember covering practice on Christmas Day one year. Now the head of the football operation doesn't have to be at practice on Christmas Day, but Ron was there. And I thought, 'This guy gets it. This guy knows what it's about. He's not just a personnel expert. He's a leader.' And this guy was a leader."

Among the changes Wolf made was firing Infante on the day after the Packers beat the Vikings to finish the 1991 season with four wins and 12 losses. It was the Packers' eighth non-winning season in nine years.

The Packers initially tried to persuade Bill Parcells, who had guided the New York Giants to a pair of Super Bowl titles, to come to Green Bay. When Parcells turned him down, Wolf went on with his search.

He had his eye on Mike Holmgren, the offensive coordinator with the San Francisco 49ers and a man known for his ability to develop quarterbacks.

Holmgren had been the quarterbacks coach at pass-happy Brigham Young University when Bill Walsh brought him to the 49ers in the mid-1980s. Joe Montana learned from Holmgren. Steve Young, whom Holmgren coached at BYU, was the 49ers' backup but was ready to take over when Montana departed in 1990 because Holmgren had tutored him.

Two weeks after the 49ers' season ended, the Packers hired Holmgren as the eleventh coach in team history and the sixth since Lombardi.

Wolf had his coach.

A month later, he got his quarterback.

On February 10, 1992, Wolf acquired Favre from Atlanta for a first-round draft pick, the seventeenth overall selection in that year's draft. The deal was the culmination of a long give-and-take with Atlanta, which didn't like Favre but didn't want to give him away, either.

Holding two first-round picks in the 1992 draft, the fifth and seventeenth overall picks, Wolf always was prepared to give up a number-one pick for Favre, but the Falcons never asked until the end.

Years later, asked whether he would have traded away the fifth pick for Favre, Wolf said: "You know what? I can't answer that, but I probably would have because I still thought he was the best player in that (1991) draft."

With that number-five pick, Wolf selected Terrell Buckley, an undersized cornerback from Florida State. Wolf came under fire for his selection of Buckley, who underachieved in his three seasons with Green Bay. Packers fans also were skeptical of Wolf for using a first-round pick on a third-string quarterback who'd been a second-round pick.

Wolf made a mistake with Buckley, but not with Favre.

Other picks from Wolf's first draft were wide receiver Robert Brooks (third round), running back Edgar Bennett (fourth) and tight end Mark Chmura (sixth). All three became starters for the Packers during their rise to the top of the NFL.

When the 1992 season started, Holmgren went with Don Majkowski at quarterback. Three years earlier, Majkowski had guided the Packers to a 10-6 record, winning four games with late drives.

The Packers lost the 1992 opener, beaten 23-20 by the Vikings at Lambeau Field, then were trounced a week later, 31-3 at Tampa Bay. Favre made his Packers debut against the Buccaneers, relieving Majkowski, whose time was just about up.

The following week, Holmgren started Majkowski at home against Cincinnati, but when the veteran injured his ankle in the first quarter, he became football's version of Wally Pipp, the New York Yankees first baseman never heard from again after being replaced by Lou Gehrig.

Favre completed 22 of 39 passes against the Bengals, saving the best for last, a 35-yard touchdown pass to Kitrick Taylor with just 13 seconds remaining, giving the Packers a 24-23 win, their first under Holmgren.

What many remember about that game is the touchdown pass and Favre running toward midfield in celebration. What they forget are Favre's four fumbles. It was this type of erratic play that would drive Holmgren crazy during his first three seasons with the young gunslinger.

Favre started his first game the next week, completing 14 of 19 passes for 210 yards and a pair of touchdowns in a 17-3 win over the Pittsburgh Steelers at Lambeau Field. The Packers then dropped three straight, falling to 2-5 even though Favre played better than average in those games.

The Packers took off in the second half, winning seven of eight games, including six in a row for the first time since 1965. During that streak, Favre directed the Packers to a 27-24 victory over the Philadelphia Eagles in Milwaukee after sustaining a separated shoulder in the first half. As Packers fans would find out over the years, nothing could keep Favre from playing.

After the game, Eagles defensive end Reggie White said of Favre, "He's the best young quarterback I've seen."

The Packers took a 9-6 record into the final game of the 1992 season against Minnesota. A win would have meant a playoff berth. Instead, the Packers lost 27-7 as Favre threw three interceptions.

But the Packers finished above .500. For the first time in at least a decade, there was legitimate reason to believe the Packers were ready to have consecutive winning seasons for the first time since the Lombardi era.

Favre, who played in the Pro Bowl, finished his first year in Green Bay by completing 62.1 percent of his passes (302 of 471) for 3,227 yards with 18 touchdown passes and 13 interceptions. His favorite target, receiver Sterling Sharpe, had 108 receptions, then an NFL single-season record.

In 1993 Favre fluctuated between being brilliant and terrible, finishing with 19 touchdown passes and 24 interceptions. He opened the season by throwing two touchdown passes in a 36-6 win over the Los Angeles Rams in Milwaukee. He completed 19 of 29 passes for 264 yards and had a passer rating of 103.2. But over

Green Bay quarterback Brett Favre uses a stiff arm to keep Chicago's Shawn Lee away from him during a game at Lambeau Field. Through 2006, the Bears and Packers have played each other during the regular season 172 times.

the next four games, his highest rating was 69.1 as he threw three touchdown passes and seven interceptions.

The Packers made the playoffs with a 9-7 record, and in his first playoff game, Favre had one of those plays that is still talked about in Green Bay.

With less than a minute remaining and his team trailing the Detroit Lions 24-21 at the Silverdome, Favre rolled out of the pocket to his left, then hurled a pass across his body to the far right to a wide-open Sharpe, who hauled in the 40-yard pass to give the Packers a 28-24 win. They'd won a playoff game for the first time since the 1982 season.

The next week, the Packers lost at Dallas in the second round, but progress had been made.

Favre played better in 1994, but the defense was prone to giving up a lot of points. A 29-20 loss at Buffalo dropped their record to 6-5. The Packers scored 31 points each in the next two games against Dallas and Detroit, but the Cowboys and Lions countered with 42 and 34 and the Packers were 6-7 with three games remaining.

They began the final stretch with a 40-3 win over the Bears in Green Bay, completing a season sweep of their archrivals.

The next week, Favre executed a play that made for a great picture for any photographer paying attention. He dove fully extended for a touchdown in the closing seconds to rally his team to a 21-17 win over the Falcons in the last game the Packers played in Milwaukee, their part-time home for more than 40 years.

The Packers then went to Tampa, where they earned a trip to the postseason with a 34-19 victory over the Buccaneers. The game was bittersweet because it was the last game for Sharpe, who had sustained a neck injury that ended his career, although nobody knew it at the time.

The Vikings won the NFC Central title, but the Bears, Packers and Lions all earned wild-card berths, the first time four teams from one division had accomplished that.

The Packers and Lions met again in the playoffs, this time at Lambeau, the perfect battleground for two division rivals. Rain and snow before the New Year's Eve game had turned the field into a mud pit.

The previous year's victory, delivered on Favre's remarkable pass to Sharpe, came despite a 169-yard rushing effort from Detroit's Barry Sanders. This time, the Packers built a game plan to stop Sanders. Boy, did they ever.

The Packers played eight men near the line of scrimmage for the entire game, watching Sanders's every move. He carried 13 times and was held to a career-low minus-one yard. Other runners didn't do any better. Detroit finished with minus-four yards, a play-off record for fewest rushing yards.

Despite that defensive dominance, the Packers held a tenuous 16-10 lead when the Lions drove to the Packers' 11 in the final moments. But the defense rose to the challenge one more time and got the ball back four plays later, holding the Lions on downs. Green Bay took a safety rather than punt in the final seconds and won, 16-12.

Players were covered in mud and the defenses dominated, giving the fans a game that was throwback Black and Blue.

"Our defense, holding Barry Sanders, who I have the utmost respect for, has to be one of the greatest runners in the history of the game, among the top five, I think," Packers historian Lee Remmel said. "To hold him to minus-one yard in 13 rushes is an unbelievable accomplishment. (Defensive coordinator) Fritz Shurmur designed an unbelievable game plan in that game. It was one of the most memorable performances in Packers history."

The Packers' season ended a week later with a 35-9 loss in Dallas.

Wolf, though, said the third consecutive 9-7 regular-season record wasn't disheartening.

"We were getting better and better," he said. "The first 9-7 was a miracle, the second 9-7 was probably accurate and the third 9-7, we were a better team than the 9-7 record. That was '94. We had a couple of games that I kind of felt were taken away from us, taken out of our hands. I felt we were a better team than we were in '93 and '92."

The Packers took a large step toward the Super Bowl in 1995 by going 11-5. They were 6-4 after back-to-back losses to Detroit and Minnesota, both coming indoors, where the Packers often played poorly.

Against the Vikings, Favre so badly sprained an ankle that it at first appeared to be broken. He hadn't missed a game since taking over for Majkowski in 1992, but he didn't practice in the week that followed. Going into the next game, against the Bears, it appeared Favre wasn't going to play.

But when game day came, Favre felt better. He took the field and showed what a tough competitor he was. By the end of the day, Favre completed 25 of 33 passes for 336 yards and threw five touchdown passes in a 35-28 win over the Bears at Lambeau. It was one of those games Packers fans don't get tired of remembering.

"One of the gutsiest performances I've ever seen," McCarren said. "You want to talk about tough. That was it right there."

The win completed another season sweep of the Bears and propelled the Packers to a 6-1 finish, an 11-5 record and the team's first NFC Central title in seventeen years. Favre capped his finest season by being named the NFL's Most Valuable Player, the first of his three straight MVP awards.

He was certainly a different quarterback than the one who came to Green Bay in 1992 when it seemed only Ron Wolf thought he'd be something special.

"When he first came into camp in '92, I wasn't very impressed at all," Majkowski recalled many years later. "I mean, Brett was very green and he was very erratic. His mechanics weren't very good.

"You know, he was very young at that time and he wasn't taking the game as seriously as he obviously does now and he wasn't professional. He was just a fun kid to be around. And he could throw it a hundred miles an hour. I never saw anybody with a stronger arm, but he just wasn't really that accurate.

"I had a hard time believing, early on like the first couple of weeks, that the Packers traded a number-one pick for this kid. I just didn't see it. If you would have asked me, did you ever see him turning into the quarterback that he turned into, back then I would have said absolutely not."

The Packers beat Atlanta at home in the first round of the playoffs, then traveled to San Francisco to meet the favored 49ers.

Shurmur designed another brilliant plan that smothered the 49ers. The tone was set early when linebacker Wayne Simmons's vicious hit on fullback Adam Walker forced a fumble that was scooped up by cornerback Craig Newsome and returned 31 yards for a touchdown. Favre then led touchdown drives of 62 and 72 yards as the Packers took a 21-point lead on the way to a 27-17 win, vaulting them into the NFC championship game against the defending Super Bowl champion Cowboys in Dallas.

Unlike the previous season's playoff loss to Dallas, when the Packers were out of the game by halftime, Favre was winning a shootout against Cowboys quarterback Troy Aikman, leading 27-24 after three quarters. But Dallas running back Emmitt Smith took over in the fourth quarter, scoring twice as the Cowboys rallied for a 38-27 victory.

During the next off-season, the Packers bolstered their defense for the 1996 season by signing tackle Santana Dotson and veteran safety Eugene Robinson, a perennial Pro Bowl player with the Seattle Seahawks.

Dotson joined run-stuffer Gilbert Brown in the interior. White and Sean Jones flanked them. Robinson lined up at strong safety next to free safety LeRoy Butler, whom Wolf called the leader of the defense. Newsome and Doug Evans were the corners. Simmons was at strongside linebacker. Brian Williams was on the other side and George Koonce was in the middle. When Koonce was injured, Ron Cox stepped in.

During their Super Bowl season of 1996, the Packers' defense limited opposing teams to 210 points; it had allowed 314 points a year earlier. The defense may have been the best in the NFL since that of the 1985 Bears.

White only had 8 $^1/_2$ sacks but constantly was double-teamed, which gave others opportunities to make plays. Butler had 6 $^1/_2$ sacks and five interceptions. The line limited opponents to an average of 88.5 yards rushing per game. The defense dominated at times.

Most people gave White credit for the way the team played.

"Reggie, you know everybody is always going to remember Reggie, but the other guys around him were good football players," said Brian Noble, a Packers linebacker from 1985-93 who was working as a broadcaster in Green Bay during that Super Bowl season. "I think they had the luxury and they had the ability to play a little bit better because of the level Reggie played at."

Veteran tight end Keith Jackson, who had been acquired late in 1995, returned for one last shot at the Super Bowl.

The Packers had all the pieces in place and were declared the team to beat before the season. They didn't disappoint. They went 7-1 in the Black and Blue, sweeping the Bears for the third straight year and losing only at Minnesota.

Injuries to wide receivers Robert Brooks and Antonio Freeman took weapons away from Favre. It showed during consecutive losses to Kansas City and Dallas that dropped Green Bay to 8-3 before Thanksgiving.

But Freeman came back from a broken wrist and the Packers picked up Andre Rison, who had been waived by Jacksonville.

The Packers finished 13-3, the best record in the NFC. After a first-round bye, they easily handled San Francisco 35-14 in the mud at Lambeau and moved into the NFC title game, this time against the Carolina Panthers, who in their second season went 12-4.

On January 12, 1997, the Packers appeared in a championship game at Lambeau Field for the first time since the famous Ice Bowl win over Dallas on December 31, 1967. That day, the temperature was minus-13 with a minus-46 wind chill. On this day, it was a relatively balmy three degrees with a minus-17 wind chill.

The Panthers played the Packers tough for almost a half, scoring ten points after a Favre fumble and interception. But Green Bay soon took control. Favre threw two touchdown passes and

Chris Jacke kicked three field goals for a 30-13 victory.

Despite the cold, fans stayed for a victory celebration as Packers players and executives stayed on the field and reveled in Green Bay's first championship win in 29 years. Many recall that moment more than the celebration after the victory in Super Bowl XXXI.

"That experience is something I'll never have again the rest of my life, that experience of being in Lambeau Field witnessing that game and the feeling of exuberance after that game," Wolf said. "I'd never experienced that anywhere, anytime, anyplace, nor will I ever again."

Two weeks later, a restless Harlan decided not to wait for the team bus and walked to the Louisiana Superdome.

The Packers took the lead early on a 54-yard pass from Favre to Rison, who duck-walked the final few yards into the end zone. Jacke kicked a field goal for a 10-0 lead.

New England battled back for a 14-10 lead at the end of the first quarter, but Favre was at his best in the second quarter.

He connected with Freeman on an 81-yard scoring pass, then a Super Bowl record, giving Green Bay the lead for good. After another Jacke field goal, Favre scored on a two-yard run near the end of the half to give the Packers a 27-14 lead.

"I remember at halftime we had a good lead," Harlan said. "I'm all by myself at halftime. I don't feel like eating. I go over and lean against a wall in the press box and I'm watching the band or whatever that was down on the field and I'm thinking, 'God, I wish this game was over.' We were so close."

The Patriots cut the Packers lead to 27-21 on an 18-yard touchdown run by Curtis Martin late in the third quarter.

But on the ensuing kickoff, the momentum swung back to the Packers. Desmond Howard took the kickoff, followed his blockers about 30 yards, then found a hole and sprinted the rest of the way for a 99-yard score that put the finishing touches on the Patriots.

Green Bay was Titletown again, thanks to Harlan, who signed Wolf, who brought Holmgren, Favre and White to Green Bay.

Each move was critical to the Packers' return to prominence, but Wolf took the biggest gamble on Favre, who just knew the kid was going to be a huge star in the NFL.

"To have an opportunity to get that player I thought was a no-brainer, and you know what, it turned out to be a no-brainer," Wolf said. "I was in it 41 years and that's the best player I'd ever

Defensive end Reggie White (left) and quarterback Brett Favre leave the field after helping the Packers beat the Bears 35-28 at Lambeau Field in 1995.

been associated with right there. I remember telling the executive committee what I thought of him as a player, and I'm sure they thought when I got done they'd hired some loony tunes from New York. He turned out to be pretty much everything I told them he would be.

"Let's face it. I hitched my career to that deal for Brett Favre. And you know what? I don't know about you, but I think I should be proud of it and I'm darned proud about what all he's done."

The Packers came back in 1997 with another 13-3 record, but they weren't as dominant. They made it back to the Super Bowl and were favored by 11 points against the Denver Broncos. Nobody gave Denver a chance. But the Broncos surprised the NFL by winning Super Bowl XXXII 31-24 in San Diego.

"We're a one-year wonder," Wolf said after the game. "Nothing but a fart in the wind."

The Packers were a little more than that.

From 1990 to 2005, they won six division titles to four for Minnesota, three for Chicago, two for Detroit and one for Tampa Bay, which moved to the new NFC South in 2001. From 1992 to 2004, the Packers went 13 years without a losing record.

They wouldn't have done it without Favre, who made others around him better. He also led by example, whether he played hurt or would do something like hurling his body at a 260-pound linebacker to clear a path for his running back. He was a throwback to the early days of the division.

"I think he could play anytime, that guy," former Lions linebacker and coach Joe Schmidt said. "He loves football, he loves to play. You know when he steps on the field he's the kind of guy who's going to give you 100 percent, bust his butt to get the job done, he'll play hurt, he'll do anything. That's what he brings to that football team, that's why they respect him so much and in turn they try to give their utmost to him. He has a lot of fire in him."

SPOTLIGHT: TWO WHO EPITOMIZE THE SPIRIT

Talk to Bud Grant about football and it doesn't take him long to use either "durable" or "durability" in a sentence.

The former coach of the Minnesota Vikings points to durability as one of the key components of the success his teams had during an 11-season run from 1968-78, when the Vikings won ten Black and Blue Division titles and played in the Super Bowl four times.

"When I first got into the league, Bud Grant preached all the time about durability," said former Vikings linebacker Scott Studwell, who played with Minnesota from 1977 through 1990 and later joined the team's front office. "It was one of the factors in his success, and his teams lined up and played every Sunday. It was such an important factor for him to be able to rely on players."

Check out the Vikings' all-time games played list, and the top is filled with guys who played for Grant.

Defensive end Carl Eller, a member of the Hall of Fame, missed just three games in 15 seasons for the Vikings and appeared in 209 during the regular season. Center Mick Tingelhoff, who wasn't even drafted, broke in with the Vikings in 1962, became the team's starter and never let go of the football, playing and starting in 240 consecutive regular season games.

While Tingelhoff's number is staggering, it's still a

distant second to the 270 put up by defensive end Jim Marshall, who played and started every game for Minnesota from 1961 through 1979. Throw in the 12 games he played for the Cleveland Browns the year before he arrived in Minnesota and Marshall played and started in 282 consecutive NFL games. Toss in the twenty playoff games he played and his streak is 302.

Marshall's streak was the longest in NFL history until 2005, when Jeff Feagles broke it. Respect Feagles for breaking the streak, but remember he is a punter, one who had played in 304 consecutive games through the 2006 season.

Marshall was special, considering that at the time he played, the average career of an NFL defensive lineman was maybe five years.

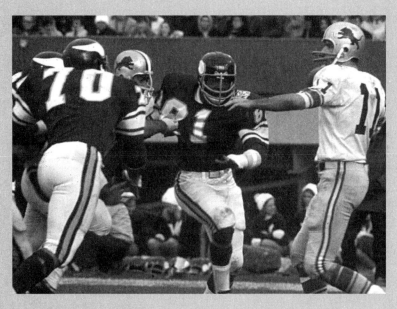

Vikings defensive ends Jim Marshall (70) and Carl Eller (81) converge on Lions quarterback Greg Landry during a game at the Met. During one stretch from 1968-74, the Vikings beat Detroit 13 straight times.

"Durability is the greatest ability you can have," Grant said while sitting in his office before the start of the 2005 season. "You can be the fastest guy in town, catch, run and throw. But if you're not durable, 8-8 (season record) is not going to win it for you. So durability, regardless of any ability you have, is the most important ability you can possess."

Marshall entered the NFL weighing 220 pounds and left in 1979 at 235, considerably lighter than the offensive linemen he battled every week. He'd get dinged, some weeks worse than others, but always came back.

"He was one of those people blessed with a great body," said Fred Zamberletti, who has been on the Vikings' training staff since 1961.

Grant will tell you that durability isn't happenstance.

"You say, 'Where do you get that?'" Grant asked. "Well, you have to have the right parents, that's the main thing. You have to have the right genes. Jim Marshall would get hit and he'd turn his ankle over and you could see it on films, his ankle would be turned right over.

"Well, he either broke his ankle or sprained his ankle so severely that some other guy would be out for the year. Jim Marshall would get a little swelling and in a week it would be gone or it would be gone enough so he could play. He had the mentality that if I'm hurt that means I have to play harder, I have to play better."

Former Packers center Ken Bowman, who played from 1964 through 1973, has great admiration for Marshall, who participated in two Pro Bowls and still holds the NFL record for most fumbles recovered by a defender with 29.

"It's very remarkable, especially playing the position he did, defensive end," Bowman said. "You're either trying to run the ball carrier down and you're coming from behind, and that's the easy part of the job. Or they're coming at you and you have to be the guy who tries to stand up the offensive lineman and make the tackle."

Entering the 2007 season, another Black and Blue player continues to amaze with his ability to play game after game after game. Brett Favre has been the starting quarterback for the Packers since the fourth game of the 1992 season. When the 2006 season ended, he had played in 207 consecutive games, starting in 205 consecutively. Include 20 post-season games and those numbers grow to 227 and 225.

One of the biggest compliments a player in today's era can receive is when a player from a different era says he could have played with him.

"I think Jim Marshall's streak is incredible, and I think Brett Favre's streak is incredible, too," said former Packers guard Jerry Kramer, who played many games against Marshall. "I'm a huge Brett fan and I think he could have played with our guys. He's one of those kids that just loves to play and it really doesn't matter how much he's making or what he's making, he just loves to play."

He must also have the durable genes Grant said Marshall possessed.

Favre has played with his shoulder separated, with badly sprained ankles, with hairline fractures in his thumb.

Some of his best games have come following injury. During his first season with the Packers he separated his left (non-throwing) shoulder early during a game against the Philadelphia Eagles. He came back to complete 23 of 33 passes for 275 yards in an upset victory. Defensive end Reggie White later called it a courageous performance.

He threw five touchdown passes on a bum ankle during a 1995 game against the Chicago Bears. Favre, a three-time NFL Most Valuable Player, is a shoo-in for the Hall of Fame after he retires.

THE MINNESOTA VIKINGS

Throughout the history of the Black and Blue Division, the most dominating of the four teams has been the Minnesota Vikings.

They've won the most division titles (16) and playoff appearances (24) and the fewest number of losing seasons (eight).

In comparison, the Packers have won eight division titles and made 13 trips to the playoffs; the Bears nine and 11; and the Lions three and seven. Tampa Bay, which played in the division from 1977 to 2000, won the other three division titles. There were no division champions in the NFL during the 1982 season when a strike wiped out seven games.

Vikings quarterback Fran Tarkenton signals a touchdown during a game against the Packers during the 1973 season at Lambeau Field. Tarkenton played with the Vikings from 1961-66, was traded to the Giants, then reacquired before the 1972 season. He guided the Vikings to the Super Bowl three times.

The Vikings have played in the NFC championship game eight times and in the Super Bowl four times. While the Packers and Bears are two of the most successful franchises in the NFL, with 21 championships between them, all but three of those came before the Black and Blue was officially formed.

The Packers won the first Super Bowl after the 1966 season and repeated the following year, after winning the Black and Blue title, or Central Division as it was officially known. Green Bay's other Super Bowl championship as a member of the division came in Super Bowl XXXI when quarterback Brett Favre guided the Pack to a 35-21 triumph over the New England Patriots.

The Bears and their famed 46 defense, the defense players of all eras call one of the best in the history of the game, won Super Bowl XX after breezing through the regular season with a 15-1 record.

The Vikings have had their signature teams. In 1969, led by the defensive line known as the Purple People Eaters, Minnesota allowed just 133 points, the second fewest ever in a 14-game season behind the 129 given up by the Falcons in 1977. Fast forward to 1998 when football was more offensive. The Vikings' high-octane offense that featured rookie receiver Randy Moss scored an NFL record 556 points.

Those are indeed impressive. But when there's talk of the truly great teams in the history of the NFL, the Vikings, fairly or not, are quickly dismissed for one reason: They've never won a championship.

"That doesn't diminish their talent," said Hall of Fame tight end Mike Ditka, who won an NFL championship as a player in 1963 and coached the 1985 Bears to victory over the New England Patriots in Super Bowl XX.

"I've always said that the worst thing that can happen in football is a team losing the Super Bowl. Everybody thinks they're not worthy of anything. You've got to understand what it takes to get to a Super Bowl. So the accomplishments of the Viking teams of the '70s are as great as anything I've seen.

"They just didn't come away with wins in the Super Bowl, but that doesn't diminish what a great run they had and what great teams they were and what great coaching they had. I think that's the biggest fallacy."

Maybe it's fitting to label the Vikings of that era as the best team not to win a championship. They certainly have enough players in the Hall of Fame to back that up.

The Vikings played at Metropolitan Stadium in the Twin Cities suburb of Bloomington. An old baseball park, the Met looked cold and forbidding, especially after November when snow banks formed a ring around the playing field. The setting was intimidating, not only for the teams that came in from the West Coast, but even for division rivals who had to play one game there year after year.

In the 1960s and '70s, the NFL's schedule generally had cold-weather teams in warmer climates near the end of the season. When the Vikings played at the Met after Thanksgiving, they were almost unbeatable during their best years, going 10-1 in regular-season games from 1969-77 and 8-3 in postseason games.

And the main reason why the Vikings rarely lost at home in those days was because of the men who stood on the front line. The Purple People Eaters consisted of Carl Eller and Jim Marshall at the ends and Alan Page and Gary Larsen in the middle. Eller and Page are in the Hall of Fame; Marshall, who never missed a game in 20 seasons, should be.

"I was a young player at the time," said Larry McCarren, a center for the Green Bay Packers from 1973-84. "I thought when you looked across the field and you saw Alan Page and you saw Carl Eller and Gary Larsen and Jim Marshall, that was the real NFL.

"When you're talking about the Black and Blue, you're talking about playing the Vikings at the old Met with steam coming off their helmets. To me that was a special experience. Every once in a while you'd see something and it would hit you. 'I'm playing in the real National Football League.' Being at the Met against those guys was one of those times."

For many years, the Vikings were unbeatable regardless of the month. Yes, they had talent, but the Vikings also had players who

Offensive tackle Ron Yary missed only two games during his career with the Minnesota Vikings. He played in seven Pro Bowls. Yary is in the Hall of Fame.

----

just wouldn't leave the field. It was a different era where pride mattered and there wasn't the constant substituting that fans see in today's game.

The heart of the team, offensive linemen Mick Tingelhoff and Ron Yary and defensive stalwarts Marshall, Page, Eller, Hilgenberg, Bobby Bryant and Paul Krause, rarely missed games. Broken bones didn't matter. If they could walk, they could play. And if those guys were playing, everyone else better be playing. The guy they didn't want to let down was Marshall, the team's leader.

"Jim Marshall happened to be our guy," said Bud Grant, the Vikings' coach from 1967-83, and again for one season in 1985. "He was our captain and he bought the program, played when he was hurt."

Marshall often gave away 20 to 30 pounds to linemen on the other side of the ball, yet he spent 20 seasons in the NFL, 19 in Minnesota, and never missed a start. He played in 282 consecutive games during the regular season, an NFL record that stood until 2001, when Jeff Feagles, a punter, broke it.

Grant gave out just one game ball as coach of the Vikings. It went to Marshall after he played his last home game in 1979.

Marshall set the tone. The others followed.

It's not a coincidence that of the 25 players who have participated in the most games in Vikings history, 15 played in at least two of the Vikings' four Super Bowl appearances.

During 11 seasons from 1968 to 1978, the Vikings won ten division titles, played in five NFL or NFC championship games and played in four Super Bowls. They were as dominating as any team in football over a sustained period. The only thing missing is a Super Bowl victory.

During that 11-year stretch, the first ten when the league played a 14-game schedule, the Vikings won ten or more games seven times. They also were almost unbeatable within their division.

From 1968 through 1978 the Vikings:

- Beat Detroit 19 of 22 times, winning 13 in a row from 1968-74.

- Beat the Bears 16 of 22 times, including one stretch of eight straight. Chicago was the only division team to beat Minnesota twice in a row during that period, winning both games in 1968. The Vikings won 12 of the next 14 games between the rivals.
- Whipped the Packers 18 times, losing three and tying once. The highlight for Green Bay during that eleven-year period was having the distinction of being the only other team to win an outright division title. That occurred in 1972, when the Packers clinched the Central with a 23-7 win at Minnesota in the second-to-last game of the season.

The Packers lost seven of those games to Minnesota by eight or fewer points.

"We always played them tough, but they just had better players," said Gale Gillingham, a guard for the Packers for ten seasons from 1966-74 and in '76. "It was always defensive. They just could score more points than us."

"They were confident, especially in Minnesota," said Charlie Sanders, who played tight end for the Lions from 1968-77. "Going to Minnesota, you just weren't going to beat them.

"They instilled that. Whether it was the weather or them coming out with no protection on their arms, they presented themselves as being superior. It was a mental thing. It affected you mentally in terms of handling the elements and playing with confidence. You always were on your heels because you knew they were there."

Grant used the weather to his advantage. He didn't allow heaters on his sidelines, which made the Vikings seem tougher than their opponents. Grant also let it be known that his players preferred playing in the mud and snow.

"We let (the media) perpetuate the myth and the players kind of bought into it," Grant said.

"That's a good designation, Black and Blue. The players bought into it. They liked that designation."

Carl Eller (81), Gary Larsen (center) and Jim Marshall receive some instruction during a game in the 1970s.

THE PURPLE PEOPLE EATERS

Led by the Purple People Eaters, those Vikings teams dominated and intimidated like few others in the history of the NFL. The Minnesota defense had a three-year stretch of dominance that seems mind-boggling. The Vikings limited opponents to 133 points in 1969, 143 in 1970 and 139 in 1971. All three of those totals were better than the 148 points the Packers allowed in 1962 when they compiled a 13-1 record with what some historians call one of the greatest defenses ever assembled. Scoring fewer than 14 points in those days against Minnesota usually meant a loss for opposing teams.

"Their dominance was because of their defensive team," said Joe Schmidt, a Hall of Fame linebacker for the Lions who became their coach in 1967, two years after he retired as a player. His teams beat Minnesota only once in 12 tries before he left coaching

The Purple People Eaters at Super Bowl VIII at Rice Stadium, Houston, Texas on January 13, 1974.

From left: Carl Eller (81), Gary Larsen (77), Alan Page (88) and Jim Marshall (70).

----

after the 1972 season.

"That front four was awesome," Schmidt said. "I mean they had great football players there. Of course, when they had (quarterback) Fran Tarkenton running around, he created a problem. But their whole deal was that defense. It was capable of making you turn the ball over, making you make mistakes. They lived off that defense."

During the 42 regular-season games during that three-year run from 1969-71, the Purple People Eaters and company allowed 415 points, or a remarkable 9.8 per game, posted seven shutouts and held teams to seven or fewer points nine other times. They forced opponents into 126 turnovers for an average of just over three per game.

The Purple People Eaters were at the heart of all that mayhem. If they weren't forcing fumbles, they were wreaking havoc on quarterbacks, who threw a total of 85 interceptions from 1969 through 1971.

Grant, the stoic genius, knew how to take advantage of the ever-changing conditions at the Met, especially in winter. He coached two seasons indoors at the Metrodome and said his game-day value was minimized significantly.

"The only decision I made was whether to call heads or tails," Grant said. "Everything changed when we went inside. I didn't like it."

Grant constantly checked the weather—two days before the game, an hour before kickoff, even at halftime. He knew which spots of the field were vulnerable to opposing players and he'd use that to the Vikings' advantage.

"We had this big scoreboard at the Met that blocked out the sun," Grant said. "I knew that in the fourth quarter when we were inside the 20-yard line that I could call a play where the defensive back would run backward and not have good footing."

Grant was a multisport star who grew up in Superior, Wisconsin, just across the harbor from Duluth, Minnesota. He attended the University of Minnesota, where he excelled in football, baseball and basketball. He was a first-round draft pick of the Philadelphia

Eagles in 1950 but opted to play with the NBA's Minneapolis Lakers for two seasons, helping the team win two titles.

Grant eventually played two seasons with the Eagles, leading them with 56 receptions in 1952, his second season. He then became the first player from the NFL to play out his option and sign with the Canadian Football League. He spent four seasons as a player with the Winnipeg Blue Bombers before he became the team's coach in 1957.

During his ten seasons with the Blue Bombers, Grant won 102 games and guided the team to four Grey Cup championships.

While Grant was becoming a coaching legend in Canada, the Vikings were going through growing pains during their first six years in the NFL.

From their inception in 1961 until 1966, the Vikings played in the NFL's Western Conference along with Chicago, Detroit, Green Bay, Baltimore, Los Angeles and San Francisco. The three older teams from the Midwest—the Bears, Lions and Packers—traditionally were by far the toughest physically. When the Vikings arrived, they played with the same fervor. They just didn't win many games.

Minnesota's first coach was Norm Van Brocklin, an old-school quarterback who a year earlier led the Eagles to the 1960 NFL championship in his final season as a player, beating the Packers 17-13.

Van Brocklin ran his training camp like a boot camp. Three practices a day were the norm. He berated and bullied his players.

Out of fear, the players responded, for a while. The Vikings won their first regular-season game, destroying the Bears 37-13 at the Met. In 1964, their fourth in the NFL, the Vikes compiled an 8-5-1 record, beating the Packers for the first time and the Baltimore Colts, who reached the NFL championship game that season.

"Van Brocklin was as ornery a sonofabitch as ever played the game," said Steve Sabol, president of NFL Films. "I remember when we used to do the highlight films for the Vikings in '64 and '65, Van Brocklin would have us put in a special section just on late hits and penalties because he felt that was the message he wanted to send to the other teams.

"When you play the Vikings, watch out, you better have it strapped on because we're going to come at you from every angle and maybe after the whistle once in a while. They were the only team where we would have a special section on just personal fouls and late hits. That was Van Brocklin saying they were a tough team and there wasn't anything wrong with one or two late hits or cheap shots."

Quarterback Fran Tarkenton was a third-round draft pick who made his debut in 1961, the same year the Vikings made a trade with Cleveland for Marshall. Defensive back Ed Sharockman, one of the Vikings' first real rough characters, was drafted in 1961 and began his career the following year.

Mick Tingelhoff, who never missed a start in 17 seasons, was signed as a free agent in 1962. The Vikings also drafted linebacker Roy Winston that year.

Wide receiver Paul Flatley and defensive end Carl Eller were among the draft choices in 1963 and 1964.

All of them eventually played for the Vikings in the Super Bowl.

Helping evaluate talent was Jim Finks, who joined the organization in 1964 and eventually became the team's general manager. With the Vikings, Finks built his reputation as an outstanding judge of talent. He later helped rebuild the Bears into Super Bowl contenders.

As the Vikings improved on the field, Van Brocklin's intimidation and verbal abuse was wearing on his players. Minnesota slipped to 7-7 in 1965 and to 4-9-1 in 1966. After that season, Van Brocklin resigned.

Grant, successful in anything he decided to do, was named the Vikings' second coach. He was tough and didn't lavish praise on his players, but he didn't criticize, either. The players considered him to be fair.

Tarkenton, dealt to the New York Giants in the offseason, was replaced by Joe Kapp. Of Hispanic descent, Kapp didn't possess Tarkenton's skills as a scrambler and passer but was a player who relished contact.

Grant's first Vikings team opened the 1967 season with four losses. But his first victory was memorable, beating the defending NFL champion Green Bay Packers 10-7 in Milwaukee. After starting 1-4, the Vikings went 2-4-3 and finished that first season under Grant with a 3-8-3 record.

The 1968 season brought three changes that would help give the Vikings a defense for the ages.

Gary Larsen, who had been a backup tackle for three years, replaced Paul Dickson in the interior. He joined Page and defensive ends Eller and Marshall to form a group that would come to be known as "The Purple People Eaters."

Paul Krause, who intercepted a league-high 12 passes for Washington as a rookie in 1964, was acquired in a trade with the Redskins.

Another acquisition was linebacker Wally Hilgenberg, signed by Finks for $100 off the waiver wire.

Hilgenberg was a former All-America player from Iowa who spent his first three seasons with the Lions. He missed the 1967 season because of a knee injury and was traded to the Pittsburgh Steelers, who eventually cut him. Late in the summer of 1968, Hilgenberg was contacted by Finks.

"He called me up after I got cut by Pittsburgh and said, 'We just picked you up from the waiver wire and you're a Minnesota Viking,'" Hilgenberg said.

"I packed my wife up, she was about seven months pregnant, and we drove from Detroit to Minneapolis. I came in, sat down with him for about 45 minutes and signed a contract, and he said, 'Get over to practice, we're getting ready,' and I went to my first practice."

Kapp, who had been a star in the CFL, was the quarterback. He was like Bobby Layne, who led the Lions to three NFL championships in the 1950s, a tough guy who threw an ugly pass but would do anything it took to win. Finks, who had been a general manager in the CFL, acquired Kapp in 1967, and he was the primary starter during Grant's first season.

The Black and Blue was up for grabs in 1968 because Lombardi no longer was the Packers' coach. The team's stars were aging and Lombardi hadn't done a good job of drafting players to be ready when rebuilding became necessary. After winning the first two Super Bowls, the Packers slipped to 6-7-1, opening the door for another team to win the division.

The Vikings' biggest rival that season was the Bears, another team starting life without a legendary coach. George Halas retired and was replaced by Jim Dooley.

The teams entered the final weekend both with 7-6 records. If they finished in a tie, the Bears would win the division and go to the playoffs by virtue of their two wins over the Vikings. Standing in the way of the playoffs were the Packers.

In Green Bay the thinking is this: If the Packers can't go to the playoffs, neither should the Bears. Playing at Wrigley Field, the Packers took satisfaction in knocking the Bears out of the playoffs with a 28-27 win.

The Vikings took care of business on the road, beating Philadelphia, 24-17, to earn a playoff berth in their eighth season of existence.

The following week, the Vikings traveled to Baltimore, which won the Coastal Division with a 13-1 record, the best in the NFL.

The Colts beat Minnesota, 24-14, in the Western Conference title game, then beat Cleveland a week later for the NFL title. Although they were 18-point favorites in the Super Bowl, the Colts committed five turnovers in a 16-7 loss to the New York Jets, whose quarterback, Joe Namath, had boldly predicted a victory for the AFL team three days before the game.

The Vikings' defense, brilliant at times in 1968, allowed 210 points. The offense also struggled with consistency. Kapp, not nearly as talented as Tarkenton, threw 17 interceptions and only ten touchdowns.

But Kapp was tough and Grant liked him. Grant also knew the defense was on the verge of greatness.

THE MINNESOTA VIKINGS

EIGHT SEASONS; FOUR SUPER BOWLS

Minnesota opened the 1969 season on the road with a 24-23 loss to the New York Giants but then won 12 straight games before resting their starters in the final week, a 10-3 loss to Atlanta. In between, the defense posted two shutouts and allowed seven or fewer points in four other games.

The Minnesota offense was workmanlike but could be explosive, scoring 50 or more points three times.

Kapp completed just over 50 percent of his passes but threw 19 touchdowns and only 13 interceptions. Gene Washington and John Henderson were the big-play ends, each averaging more than 16 yards per catch and catching 14 touchdown passes between them. Bill Brown and Dave Osborn were the unspectacular but tough running backs who both could move the chains and come out of the backfield to catch passes.

"I think that they probably were the first team to switch over to a more open offense," said Gillingham, who played in five Pro Bowls. "They could score points.

"They were running the West Coast offense before people heard about it. They threw to their backs a great deal. They threw a lot of short passes and always had receivers who could go deep."

In the opening round of the 1969 playoffs, the Vikings hosted the Los Angeles Rams at the frigid Met. Two years earlier, the Rams played the Packers in the opening round of the playoffs in Milwaukee. Some considered the Rams to have better talent, but the Packers handled the conditions better and breezed to a 28-7 win on a 20-degree day.

This time, the Rams seemed better prepared for the lousy weather. They built a 17-7 lead by halftime and led 20-14 going into the fourth quarter.

But Kapp scored the go-ahead touchdown on a run in which he hurdled Rams defensive back Jim Nettles at the two-yard line. Eller later sacked Rams quarterback Roman Gabriel in the end zone for a safety to put the finishing touches on a 23-20 comeback win.

"Everybody wants to win. Hell, wanting to win is nothing," Kapp said after the game. "Show me the people who are willing to do what it takes to win. You gotta be willing, not wanting."

The next weekend, the Vikings hosted the Cleveland Browns in the NFL championship game in eight-degree weather at the Met. Kapp scored the first touchdown after he collided with Brown on a botched handoff, then ran in for the score. Another highlight of the 27-7 win was a run by Kapp, who went right through linebacker Jim Houston.

"Knocked him out cold," Grant recalled.

Winning the 1969 NFL title meant a berth in the Super Bowl against the last AFL champions, the Kansas City Chiefs.

Three years earlier, the Chiefs played in the first Super Bowl and thought they had a chance of beating Lombardi's Packers. They played with Green Bay for a half, trailing 14-10 before 61,000 spectators at the 90,000-seat Los Angeles Coliseum. The Packers dominated the second half, scoring 21 unanswered points to win, 35-10, in the first championship game between the rival leagues.

The Chiefs swept through the AFL's final season in 1969 with an 11-3 record and won the league championship, 17-7, over Oakland.

The Vikings were favored by 13 points in the Super Bowl, a sign that oddsmakers considered the Jets' upset of the Colts, an 18-point favorite, a fluke.

In reality, the Chiefs probably were a better team than Minnesota. They had a better quarterback in Len Dawson, a better top running back in Mike Garrett and big-play receivers.

Kansas City scored the first 16 points and never looked back, beating the Vikings, 23-7, in New Orleans.

"I think the most exciting game for me in my entire career was probably when we beat Cleveland that year to earn the way to the Super Bowl," said Hilgenberg, who lives in suburban Minneapolis.

"We won the National Football League championship for the right to play for the world championship. I had a good game against Cleveland. I think that was probably one of the most exciting things that happened to me.

"Against Kansas City, we were a (heavy) favorite. We lost that game, and that was probably the most disappointing one. Going there the first time is probably the most exciting, but the most disappointing thing is to lose the first one, too."

While the Vikings players, coaches and management were most affected by the loss, old-guard NFL people were disappointed as well.

"When they lost that first time to Kansas City, I damn near cried," said former Packers linebacker Dave Robinson, who played on Green Bay's first two Super Bowl teams.

"I couldn't believe they lost to Kansas City. I always felt in my heart that the Jets' win against the Colts was a fluke and the Colts just weren't ready for the game. Talking to the Colts after the game, the way they approached the game, they weren't ready for it. The fact they didn't play Johnny Unitas until the end, I always thought it was a fluke. But when Kansas City came back and jumped on Minnesota, that's when I knew that the AFL versus the NFL was going to be some real battles."

The Vikings and Chiefs met again to open the 1970 season in Minnesota. At the Met, the Vikings didn't have any problems.

Gary Cuozzo was the quarterback, having replaced Kapp, who retired after a contract dispute. Minnesota dominated from the start and rolled to a 27-7 win.

The Vikings again finished 12-2 and easily won the Black and Blue, defeating the Bears and Lions twice each and splitting with the Packers in a couple of typically low-scoring games. The Packers won the first in Milwaukee, 13-10. The Vikings took the rematch at the Met, 10-3.

The Vikings were heavy favorites to return to the Super Bowl, but for one of the few times in the dead of winter, lost a home game, falling to the 49ers, 17-14 in an NFC divisional playoff game. The 49ers won the NFC West Division but weren't considered in the same class as the Vikings. The 49ers advanced to the NFC title game, losing to the Dallas Cowboys, who earlier in the season had been hammered 54-13 by the Vikings.

The Vikings went 11-3 in 1971 to win the Central, but again lost in the first round of the playoffs, this time to Dallas, 20-12, on Christmas Day at the Met.

In 1972, the Vikings fell to 7-7, finishing three games behind the Packers, who under second-year coach Dan Devine and behind the running of John Brockington and MacArthur Lane won their first division title since 1967.

Tarkenton was back with the Vikings that year, reacquired from the Giants in a multi-player trade. He put up good numbers, but the Minnesota running game had grown stale. Finks and Grant knew they needed somebody more explosive in the backfield.

Enter Chuck Foreman, a Black-and-Blue type of runner out of the University of Miami who was the twelfth overall pick in the 1973 NFL draft.

Foreman worked his way into the starting lineup in his rookie season, starting 11 games and rushing for 801 yards, the first Minnesota runner to rush for more than 700 yards since Bill Brown had 805 yards in 1968.

The beauty of the Vikings' early dominance of the Central Division was that they always had a good mix of veterans and younger players.

Defensive players who were with the Vikings for all four Super Bowl appearances were Bryant, Eller, Hilgenberg, Krause, Marshall and Page. Larsen and linebacker Roy Winston played in the first three. Defensive tackle Doug Sutherland, linebacker Jeff Siemon and cornerback Nate Wright were among the players who came in and filled holes.

On offense, linemen Tingelhoff and Yary were the only starters who played in all four Super Bowls. Guard Ed White started in the last three. So did tight end Stu Voigt, a punishing blocker who had a successful career after being a tenth-round draft choice out of the

University of Wisconsin. Tarkenton and Foreman also started in the last three Super Bowls.

Foreman and Oscar Reed started in the backfield in 1973, with Brown, Osborn and Ed Marinaro as the backups. The Vikings rushed for 2,210 yards, almost 500 more than the previous year.

Tarkenton, running less than during his first tenure with the Vikings, completed 61.7 percent of his passes and threw for 15 touchdowns. He still scrambled and presented the threat of the run, but more frequently waited for his receivers to get open, which was often.

"He was sort of the forerunner of some of the quarterbacks you see today," said Joe Schmidt, the former Lions linebacker and coach.

The Minnesota defense, which surrendered 252 points a year earlier, allowed just 168.

The Vikings finished a league-best 12-2 and defeated Washington at the Met, 27-20, in the first round of the NFC play-offs. Minnesota traveled to Dallas for the NFC championship game and humbled the Cowboys, 27-10, earning a Super Bowl berth for the second time.

This time, the Vikings weren't favored. The Miami Dolphins, who had won the previous Super Bowl after becoming the only team to go unbeaten and untied for an entire season, were back in the big game after losing just two games during the season.

Super Bowl VIII, played in Houston, was similar to the Vikings' loss in Super Bowl IV. They fell immediately into a hole as the Dolphins scored on their first two drives and limited Minnesota to seven plays in the first quarter. The Vikings never got untracked on offense and lost, 24-7.

"Everybody always asks me why we didn't win a Super Bowl and I always said we didn't score enough points," Hilgenberg said.

"I think the most we ever scored in a game was probably 14 points. In four Super Bowls."

The Vikings opened the 1974 season by winning their first five games. The fifth of those victories may have been a little payback for the Super Bowl defeats, at the expense of the AFC's Houston Oilers, who were humbled, 51-10.

Later in the season, the Vikings' 13-game winning streak over the Lions came to an end in uncharacteristic fashion. On October 20 at the Met, Detroit rallied from a 13-0 halftime deficit for a 20-16 win. The Lions were filled with so much emotion that they carried coach Rick Forzano off the field. Hours later, they were greeted by 200 fans when they reached the airport.

"I always tell Mike Lucci and my old buddies over there that they may have ended their streak against the Vikings, but they didn't end it against me because I was hurt that day and didn't play," said Hilgenberg, who never forgave the Lions for giving up on him after he blew out his knee in 1966.

"I took a lot of pleasure in those 13 wins, I'll tell you that."

The Vikings finished 10-4, good enough for another division title and home-field advantage in the playoffs. Minnesota beat the St. Louis Cardinals, 30-14, in the first round, then rallied for a 14-10 win over the Los Angeles Rams in the NFC championship game.

This time, the Vikings' Super Bowl opponent was an old NFL rival, the Pittsburgh Steelers, one of three teams moved to the AFC when the NFL and AFL merged in 1970.

Five years earlier, the Steelers had won just one game. But under the direction of coach Chuck Noll, Pittsburgh built a team around its defense, one that would have fit in nicely in the Black and Blue.

Super Bowl IX was played in New Orleans on a cold, sloppy day at Tulane Stadium. The only scoring in the opening thirty minutes came when Tarkenton was tackled in the end zone for a safety, giving the Steelers a 2-0 lead.

The game turned when Brown fumbled the opening kickoff of the second half. The Steelers recovered, went on to score a touchdown and won, 16-6.

Pittsburgh clinched the game with a seven-minute, 66-yard drive that produced a touchdown late in the fourth quarter after the Vikings had pulled within 9-6 by scoring when Terry Brown recovered a punt blocked by Matt Blair in the end zone.

"There's a reason why they call it the Super Bowl," Grant said. "Whoever coined that phrase, it's appropriate. It's one game, winner take all. The World Series is the best of seven. A team can get trounced in the first game and come back to win in five, six or seven games. That day against Kansas City, they were the better team. Now could we have beaten them four out of seven? Who knows?

"That game against Pittsburgh, it was another dreary day. Defense was good on both sides. We fumbled the kickoff and they went in to score and we had to play catch-up. On that particular day, they were better than we were."

Minnesota's last appearance in the Super Bowl was after the 1976 season. The Vikings were an NFC-best 11-2-1 and swept through Washington and Los Angeles in the playoffs, but were no match for the Oakland Raiders, putting up the 14 points Hilgenberg remembered as the most scored by his team in one Super Bowl.

Ken Stabler and the Raiders dominated Minnesota's once great but aging defense, scoring 32 points.

"Bud Grant was a hell of a coach, and to me, just getting there that often was a great achievement," Schmidt said.

"I respect that team today as much as any other team, but naturally, people want to judge you on winning the Super Bowl. They don't want to judge you on anything else."

Foreman was so upset after the game against the Raiders that he had trouble speaking to reporters following the loss, his third in the Super Bowl, the fourth for many of his teammates.

Several months later, Foreman expressed his frustration in an article in *Pro Quarterback Magazine.*

"That is what playing this game is really all about," Foreman said of his quest for a Super Bowl ring. "Sure, we like to be paid well and I've taken care of that aspect. But after the paychecks come in, what is there? You get some security, buy a nice home, good cars and the like, but then so do people who never play pro football.

"The one distinguishing mark for a pro football player to prove that he has been a champion is to be able to say, 'I played on the team that won the Super Bowl,' and then to flash that diamond ring. Then people know you've been the best and played with the best. When your career is over, short of being inducted into the Hall of Fame, nothing really matters more to a player.

"I admit I'm bitter over the fact that we failed three times while I've been with the Vikings. Each time I thought for certain that we would win. But we lost. Worse than losing was our inability to really play well, to the standards we expected of ourselves and which others expected of us.

"You're the champion when you play as well as you're supposed to, because that proves you're the best."

Foreman's anguish was probably felt by most of his teammates at the time. Through the years, though, at least some of the players are proud of the dominance they showed within their division and conference for a decade.

"We really had a good record, had a great team," Tingelhoff said almost thirty years after that last Super Bowl defeat. "The old guys are pretty proud of that. Not winning the Super Bowl will be on the record, too.

"But most of the guys I see every once in a while are pretty proud of the record we had, the team we had. When we get together for the annual golf tournament we still talk about this and that, different games from back then. I'm sure we all, myself included, would have liked to have won a Super Bowl. We were there, played in them, but it wasn't our day that day and we didn't win. Can't do nothing about it now."

Hilgenberg has similar feelings.

"When people are looking back and say the Vikings were there four times and lost four times do I regret it? Certainly," he said. "Would I have liked to have won one? Absolutely."

"On the other hand I'd like to think my perspective is I loved the game. I loved to play the game and it was a game. I remember walking out of the locker room after the Kansas City loss and my wife was crying. I asked, 'What are you crying about?' and she said, 'We lost the game,' and I said, 'Hey, if that's the worst thing that ever happens to us in life we'll be pretty grateful.'

"That's always been my perspective. I loved the game. I don't think anybody prepared any harder or played any harder than I did and I was very grateful for what I accomplished, for the talent I had. But as I look back on it, it was a great experience. My whole career was fun."

Grant retired after the 1983 season with 11 division titles and 12 playoff appearances. After Les Steckel led the Vikings to a 3-13 record in 1984, Grant returned and coached one more year in 1985, when the Vikings went 7-9.

Grant says not having won a Super Bowl doesn't eat at him.

"I don't spend a lot of time thinking about it," said Grant, whose office at Vikings headquarters is filled mostly with hunting artifacts.

"If we had won four, I wouldn't be any different. Chuck Noll won four and he wound up being fired. I wasn't."

AFTER THE DYNASTY

After the loss to the Raiders in Super Bowl XI, the Vikings won the Black and Blue the next two years, but needed tiebreakers to do so.

In 1977, Minnesota finished 9-5, failing to win at least ten games for the first time since 1972. The Bears, with Walter Payton rushing for 1,852 yards, also finished 9-5 and made the playoffs as a wild-card team. Though the teams split during the season, each winning at home, Minnesota was awarded the division title on a tiebreaker.

The Vikings beat the Rams 14-7 in Minnesota and advanced to the NFC title game for the third time in four years. They traveled to Dallas to play the Cowboys, who opened the season with a 16-10 win in overtime against the Vikings at the Met. This game wasn't as close. Dallas won easily, 23-6, then wrapped up a Super Bowl title with a 27-10 win over the Denver Broncos.

When the NFL went to a 16-game schedule in 1978, Minnesota went 5-2-1 against its Black and Blue rivals, which now included the Tampa Bay Buccaneers, and 3-5 in games outside the division. The Vikings and Packers both finished with 8-7-1 records. The playoff berth went to the Vikings, who went 1-0-1 in their two meetings with Green Bay.

Minnesota traveled to Los Angeles for the first playoff game and lost, 34-10, in the last game for Tarkenton, whose career started in 1961, and for Tingelhoff, who arrived in 1962.

"When I got here in '77, this was a team kind of in decline as far as the glory days," said former linebacker Scott Studwell, who played until 1990 and then joined the team's front office.

"This team had been together for so long and was coming off a Super Bowl season," Studwell said. "There were players who had been together fifteen, sixteen, seventeen years, had been together forever and were still playing well, although they were on the downside of their careers.

"They had been a team that could throw their hat on the field and win the game early in the '70s. By the middle '70s, they could still find a way to win, block a kick or pick up a fumble. They weren't blowing people away, but still found ways to win. Now we're going 8-8 and 9-7. We weren't able to step on the field and beat people. The other teams caught up to us."

During the team's golden era, at least five players made the NFC's Pro Bowl team each year. But from 1978-80, the only Vikings so honored were receiver Ahmad Rashad and linebacker Matt Blair. Those two went again in 1981, along with tight end Joe Senser. Over the next four seasons, the Vikings sent just three players to the Pro Bowl, a sign that the cupboard was bare of great talent.

Things started to improve for Minnesota during the late 1980s.

Jerry Burns, Grant's offensive coordinator, was named coach in 1986. By his second season, the Vikings were back in the NFC championship game, despite an 8-7 record (one game was canceled due to a players' strike).

The Vikings lost three of their last four games and limped into the playoffs, a team seemingly headed for a quick exit. Instead, they caught fire. Quarterback Wade Wilson led Minnesota to a 44-10 first-round playoff win at New Orleans, then passed for 298 yards in a 36-24 divisional playoff victory over Joe Montana and the 49ers in San Francisco.

Those wins catapulted the Vikings into the NFC championship game in Washington, but the Redskins prevailed, 17-10, in a defensive battle. Two weeks later in the Super Bowl, the Redskins scored 35 points in the second quarter on their way to a 42-17 victory over Denver.

In 1988, the Vikings had one of the more potent offenses in football. Minnesota scored 406 points and won the division with an 11-5 record. Wilson and Tommy Kramer combined to pass for more than 4,000 yards. Anthony Carter was their main target, with 72 receptions. Tight end Steve Jordan was a frequent target, with 57 catches.

In the playoffs, Minnesota beat the Rams 28-17 at the Metrodome to earn a berth in the NFC championship game for the second straight year. But the Vikings were no match for the 49ers, falling 34-9 in what turned out to be the best of Burns's six seasons as coach.

Dennis Green became coach in 1992 and guided the Vikings to the playoffs in four of his first five seasons but never won a postseason game. That changed in 1997 when the Vikings beat the New York Giants before losing in the second round to San Francisco.

In 1998, the Packers had been to two straight Super Bowls and had won three straight division titles. That dominance lasted until a Monday night game in the first week of October, when a rookie wide receiver helped change the balance of power in the Black and Blue Division.

The Packers had won 30 straight home games at Lambeau Field, including the playoffs, but the streak ended when Randy

Moss caught five passes for 190 yards and two touchdowns in a 37-24 drubbing of the Packers, who made the score close with two fourth-quarter touchdowns.

Moss stood six-foot-four, but he could run a 4.3-second forty-yard dash and changed the ways defenses played the Vikings. If you used an extra defensive back to try to contain Moss and Cris Carter, the Minnesota running game became more dangerous. If you dealt with those two receivers one-on-one, quarterback Randall Cunningham would find one or both of them open.

"That's when (Packers general manager) Ron Wolf decided he was going to get some taller corners to come in and play," said Paul Wiggin, the Vikings' senior consultant on pro personnel.

"We had chemistry. Everything about that team was great. Denny did a great job of coaching, and we stayed healthy."

The Vikings dominated the NFL in 1998, scoring a league-record 556 points. The only loss was a 27-24 setback to Tampa Bay that halted a seven-game winning streak. The Vikings just kept getting better throughout the season, ending with eight victories for a 15-1 record.

Minnesota's offense averaged 41.6 points over the final five weeks. It kept going in the playoffs with a 41-21 victory over the Arizona Cardinals.

The Vikings played the NFC championship game at home against the Atlanta Falcons, who were 11-point underdogs despite a 14-2 regular-season record.

Minnesota gave up an early touchdown and scored 20 unanswered points, appearing to be on its way to the Super Bowl for the first time since the 1970s. But the Falcons recovered a Cunningham fumble at the Minnesota 13 late in the first half, then scored a touchdown to cut the deficit to 20-14.

In the fourth quarter, the Vikings led 27-20 and were set to put the game away when Gary Anderson, who hadn't missed a field goal in 45 tries, lined up for a 38-yard attempt. He missed left by six inches.

The Falcons took over and drove for a tying touchdown before closing out a 30-27 upset victory on a field goal by Morten Anderson late in the first overtime.

It's a loss that still haunts Studwell.

"With that team, everything came together and they were playing on an emotional high so long and they were able to sustain it," he said. "Then it all came crashing down in the NFC championship game."

Minnesota went 11-5 and returned to the NFC championship game in 2000, losing badly on the road to the New York Giants, 41-0.

The Vikings have been to the playoffs just one time since.

SPOTLIGHT: THE BUCCANEERS

The **Tampa Bay Buccaneers** don't have a huge presence in this book.

Yes, they played in the Black and Blue Division, along with Chicago, Detroit, Green Bay and Minnesota, from 1977 until 2001.

They went through long periods of struggles at various times during those twenty-five years, but they did have some success, winning three division titles.

They also had some good tough players, most notably defensive end Lee Roy Selmon, defensive tackle Warren Sapp, linebacker Derrick Brooks, tight end Jimmy Giles and fullback Mike Alstott—guys who could play any time, with any team.

But even though they played in the Black and Blue Division for a quarter of a century, the Buccaneers were never considered a true Black and Blue team.

You can look at one major reason why: During their time in the Black and Blue, they were 0-21 when the temperature was forty degrees or colder. All but four of those defeats came against Black and Blue teams. And even when they played indoors in the Midwest after November, the Buccaneers won just one of seven games against either the Vikings or Lions.

"When you think of the Black and Blue Division, Tampa doesn't mentally get into your immediate thought," former Chicago Bears safety Gary Fencik said. "Part of the Black and Blue is about weather—cold weather, not hot weather.

"I remember playing outside before they built the new stadium in (Minneapolis), and going up there and pulling back the curtain and looking outside and seeing the wind blowing. It was cold, and back then both teams were on the same side of the field and I think there was some rule that if the home team decided not to use heaters then the other team couldn't use them.

"That's the Black and Blue, not playing in Tampa in December when it's 75 degrees and sunny."

Said Pat Yasinskas, who covered the Buccaneers for the *Tampa Tribune* from 1993-99: "Any time they went to Green Bay or Chicago in the winter, it was an automatic loss."

When the NFL realigned its divisions after the 2001 season, Tampa Bay was moved to the NFC South, along with Atlanta, Carolina and New Orleans, all southern teams.

"I thought they were a good team for a while, but obviously, they belonged in the South where they are now," former Packers guard Gale Gillingham said. "The Black and Blue was for the Midwest, old grudge matches. Now we're back to the old days again."

Former Packers general manager Ron Wolf didn't like having a division rival so far away.

"When we played a division game, the longest trip we had was when we took a bus to Milwaukee," Wolf said of the two-hour ride when the team was still playing two home games a year at County Stadium. "You'd have about 45 minutes by air to Detroit, Chicago and Minneapolis. That was the greatest thing about those three teams in the division. Then you had Tampa Bay. They didn't belong."

9

THE HALL OF FAMERS

Some of the greatest players, coaches and personnel men associated with the NFL spent most or part of their careers with Black and Blue teams since the early 1960s, when that phrase became synonymous with the franchises in Chicago, Detroit, Green Bay and Minnesota.

Since that time, 37 players, three coaches and one general manager involved with Black and Blue teams have been inducted into the Hall of Fame.

Twenty of the Hall of Famers were defensive players, guys like Ray Nitschke and Dick Butkus, names that sent shivers up the spines of the running backs and

----

The running back tandem of Paul Hornung (5) and Jim Taylor were on the roster during the Packers' first four NFL titles under Vince Lombardi in the 1960s.

quarterbacks who felt their wrath so many years ago.

The list of Black and Blue running backs includes bruising Jim Taylor, a man's man who played fullback during an era when those players were known more for grinding out the tough yards rather than being just a blocking back, and Walter Payton, whose nickname was Sweetness but whose demeanor on the football field was hardly that.

But nobody epitomizes what the Black and Blue is all about more so than the man who owned, coached and played for one team.

"When you think about the Black and Blue Division it all starts with one man, one name, one team and that's the Bears and George Halas," said Steve Sabol, president of NFL Films.

"Halas always believed that the game was built on the premise that a good player becomes less good when he's hit so hard that he doesn't want to be hit again," Sabol said. "And that's the mantra, that's the theme of that whole division. The Bears were the best team in that division, won the most championships, and everybody knew that to win that division you have to beat the Bears, and the way to beat the Bears is that you have to out-hit them."

Joe Schmidt, a linebacker for the Detroit Lions from 1953-65 and later the team's coach, remembers a winner-take-all game for the Western Conference title in 1956. It had been ten years since the Bears had played in an NFL championship game, and on this cold December day at Chicago's Wrigley Field, the Bears made their return with a crunching 38-21 win over the Lions. Bobby Layne, the Lions' tough-guy quarterback, had already led his team to two NFL titles in the 1950s and would do so again the following year. To beat the Lions, you needed to get Layne off the field.

Halas had taken a break from coaching during the 1956 and '57 seasons, but there's no doubt his influence still permeated among the players and their coach, Paddy Driscoll.

"They put the guy in, I forget the name, but they put the guy in for one play and he hits Layne across the head and knocks Layne out of the damn game," Schmidt recalled.

"Bobby never wore a mask, and this guy comes across and hits him with a forearm across the face, and Bobby went down and the Bears went on to win the game. Things like that happened. Plus, guys did things in a game that were not what I would call legal but it was part of football, you didn't think much of it."

The player was Ed Meadows.

"Bobby didn't have a chance," Lions coach Buddy Parker said in a *Chicago Tribune* story. "That Meadows was sent into the game for one purpose, to get Layne. It was a mission accomplished."

"Halas had that great expression whenever somebody on the opposing team was doing good, he would always say, 'Lay the bastard out,'" Sabol remembered. "Whenever I think of George Halas, I think of 'Lay the bastard out, lay the bastard out.'"

Halas founded the team in 1920. Known as the Decatur Staleys, they moved to Chicago in 1921 and won their first NFL title, still with the nickname of the Staleys. They became the Bears in 1922. Halas grew up in Chicago and was an outstanding athlete at the University of Illinois. After serving in World War I, he played right field for the New York Yankees before the team traded for Babe Ruth. A hip injury slowed his career and he turned to football.

He played end for the Bears during the 1920s before turning his attention solely to coaching and running the team. During the 1940s, the Bears were the class of the NFL. They won championships in 1940 and '41, winning the first of those games in a 73-0 rout of the Washington Redskins. That 1940 team was voted the greatest of the NFL by the National Academy of Sports Editors in 1963.

They repeated in 1941 after tying for the Western title with the Green Bay Packers with a 10-1 record. The Bears beat the Packers in a playoff game and capped another championship season with a 37-9 thumping of the New York Giants.

Halas's Bears went 11-0 during the 1942 season but were upset by the Redskins 14-6 in the championship game.

Halas took a leave from 1943 through 1945 to serve in World War II. The Bears won the 1943 championship, the only one during the Halas regime in which the Papa Bear wasn't on the sidelines.

The Bears dipped to a 3-7 record in 1945, but Halas returned to coaching after the war and brought the title back to the Windy City with a 24-14 win over the Giants in 1946.

Halas ruled the Bears with an iron fist and he was also heavily involved in all matters concerning the NFL. He's credited with helping steer the league toward sharing in television revenue, which allowed small-market teams like the Packers to survive.

Halas knew how to make a buck. When the Bears played at Wrigley Field the seating capacity was 38,000, but Halas could get that figure to the low 40,000s by selling every bit of space in the place. That included putting chairs up in the baseball scoreboard and fans on the benches of opposing players.

"I remember when I was a cameraman at a Vikings game and (Norm) Van Brocklin getting all upset because Fran Tarkenton was squatting on his helmet after he came off the field because there was no place on the bench for him to sit," Sabol recalled.

"And Van Brocklin saw five or six of these people in civilian overcoats and said, 'Who the fuck are you guys?' They had credentials on the visiting teams' bench.

"Van Brocklin complained to Pete Rozelle about it. That was the year that for the first time we started to use a camera that would just shoot close-ups. I was shooting the camera that day at Wrigley Field and actually shot some of these guys on the bench and figured they were probably team doctors or something."

Then-commissioner Pete Rozelle investigated Van Brocklin's complaint and asked Sabol if he could review the film of those people on Minnesota's bench. Once he saw the evidence, Halas was in trouble.

"Rozelle saw these guys on the bench and he called Halas, and said, 'George, what's going on? There's a lot of civilians on the bench,' and Halas goes, 'No, no I don't know anything about that.' Well, Pete said, 'You better take a look at this footage I got.'

"Well, he sent it to Halas and Halas was caught red-handed. He fined Halas $3,000 for conduct detrimental to the game. Halas found out that it was this NFL Films that had just been started by this father and son in Philadelphia. Halas wrote my dad a letter, and

I'll never forget the phrasing. He said, 'You and your pissant son have just cost me $3,000 and I don't ever want to see you ever again at a Bears game.' He tried to have us banned from the stadium, but Rozelle said obviously he couldn't do it. But it was dicey shooting in Wrigley Field the next two years because of what had happened.

"Who's to say? Maybe they were friends of Halas and would actually come back and tell Halas what was going on on that bench."

Halas's last title as a coach came in 1963, when he led the Bears to the Western Conference title with an 11-1-2 record. Along the way the Bears twice beat the two-time defending NFL champion Green Bay Packers, 10-3 and 26-7. The Bears set several team and NFL defensive records that season, including holding opponents to 144 points. That broke the 14-game record set the previous year by the Packers, who limited their foes to 148 points on the way to a 13-1 record.

In the 1963 championship game at Wrigley Field, the Bears beat the Giants, 14-10.

The following are Hall of Famers who spent at least one year with either Chicago, Detroit, Green Bay and Minnesota. Players who were with teams in the 1960s but left before the division was formed in 1967 are included because they helped create the Black and Blue style of play.

CHICAGO BEARS

DOUG ATKINS, defensive end, 1955-66: Atkins was huge during his era (six-foot-eight, 280 pounds) and also remarkably agile. Also had a reputation for being incredibly mean. Was elected to eight Pro Bowls with the Bears and made All-Pro three times. "Doug was the kind of guy you wouldn't want to piss off," former Packers guard Jerry Kramer said. "Ski (Packers tackle Bob Skoronski) would go, 'How's your day going, how's your family doing; how's your dog doing? I hear you have a pretty good huntin' dog,' He'd give him just general bullshit to keep Doug from getting angry. If you made him mad, he literally would throw you into your quarterback."

DICK BUTKUS, linebacker, 1965-73: Personified the Black and Blue Division. Ferocious player and considered by many to be the most intimidating in the history of the game. "I don't think there was anybody more intense than Dick," said former Packers offensive guard Gale Gillingham, who played against Butkus in college and the NFL. Known for his brutal hits, but people forget that when he had two good knees he may have been one of the more agile linebackers in the game. Recovered 25 fumbles, most in Bears history. Also picked off 22 passes. Voted to the Pro Bowl eight times, All-Pro seven times.

MIKE DITKA, tight end, 1961-66; coach, 1982-92: First tight end inducted into the Hall. Voted to the Pro Bowl five times. Set a rookie record with 56 receptions in 1961. Played a total of 12 seasons, two with Philadelphia and his final four with Dallas, where he earned a Super Bowl ring. His 427 career catches were most by a tight end until Kellen Winslow broke the record in 1980. As a coach guided the Bears to a 15-1 record in 1985 and to a 46-10 win over New England in Super Bowl XX. Won 112 games in eleven years as Bears coach. Later was head coach of the New Orleans Saints. "When I got to pro ball the first thing Willie Davis told me was, 'No matter what you do don't let Mike Ditka come down on me,' because Mike Ditka in the past could beat up on Willie Davis with a down block," former Packers linebacker Dave Robinson said. "So the only thing I was trying to do for Willie Davis when we played the Bears was to keep Mike Ditka off his legs."

BILL GEORGE, linebacker, 1952-65: Known for being the NFL's first middle linebacker by dropping off the front line in the 5-2 alignment in the 1954 season. Was All-Pro eight times and played in the Pro Bowl eight straight years from 1955-62. Was the defensive signal caller on Chicago's 1963 NFL championship team. Had 18 career interceptions.

GEORGE HALAS: The founder of the Bears, Halas won 318 games and six NFL titles as a coach. Halas coached some of the greatest players in the history of the game—Doug Atkins, Dick Butkus, Red Grange, Mike Ditka, Sid Luckman. He also had significant influence over everything concerning the NFL. "George carried so much weight that he practically could convince everybody what to do and how to do it," former Lions linebacker and coach Joe Schmidt said.

DAN HAMPTON, defensive end, 1979-90: Also played tackle during his career. Recorded 25 of his 82 sacks during his first three seasons. Teams couldn't beat him one-on-one but when he was doubled it opened the door for his teammates. Started 152 of the 157 games in which he played. One of nine members of the Super Bowl XX championship team to play in the Pro Bowl. "He was our inspirational leader," Ditka said.

STAN JONES, tackle-guard, 1954-65: Played offensive guard, tackle and defensive tackle in 1962 and '63 because of injuries. Was part of a defense that allowed a league-low 144 points in 1963. Played in the Pro Bowl eight times. Extremely durable, missing only two games during his first 11 seasons. Finished his career with the Washington Redskins in 1966.

WALTER PAYTON, running back, 1975-87: Rushed for at least 1,200 yards ten times and finished as the all-time leading rusher with 16,726 yards, a mark that stood until 2002, when Emmitt Smith passed him. Voted to the Pro Bowl nine times. Holds the NFL record for most 100 yards games with 77. Scored 125 career touchdowns. "I never played against a running back who had the timing that he had," said former Vikings linebacker Wally Hilgenberg. "When you come up as a linebacker to unload on one of these backs and you're going to stick him, Walter Payton, he would have a little pop where he would hit you. You didn't know whether you were the hitter or the hittee on any one of those tackles on him because he was just like a rock. It was just this incredible timing that he had and the ability to unload. You'd knock him down and he'd get up and hustle back to the huddle and the next play he's after you again. Great competitor, fun guy to play against.

GALE SAYERS, running back, 1965-71: Played just seven seasons because of knee injuries but still appeared in five Pro Bowls. Was Rookie of the Year over teammate Dick Butkus in '65 after scoring a then-NFL record 22 touchdowns, including a record-tying six in one game against San Francisco. Dangerous return man who had six touchdowns on kickoffs and two more on punt returns. Youngest player (age thirty-four) elected to the Hall of Fame. "I think the best two running backs I played against were Gale Sayers and Walter Payton," Hilgenberg said. "Gale, unfortunately his career got shortened because he had knee problems. But I remember him beating me on two consecutive plays in a row, one on a quick toss to the weak side one-on-one in the open field and him giving me that inside, outside move and he's gone down the field and I'm chasing him into the end zone."

MIKE SINGLETARY, linebacker, 1981-92: Two-time NFL Defensive Player of the Year who played in ten Pro Bowls, most by a Bear. Started 172 games, the most by a Bears defensive player. Was either first or second on the team in tackles in his final 11 seasons. Finished career with 1,488 tackles, 19 sacks and seven interceptions. "He was our coach on the field," Ditka said.

DETROIT LIONS

LEM BARNEY, cornerback, 1967-77: Burst into the NFL in a big way in 1967, making ten interceptions and returning three for touchdowns, including his first in a game against the Green Bay Packers. Selected to the Pro Bowl in seven of his eleven NFL seasons. Had 56 career interceptions for 1,077 yards (19.2 average) and seven touchdowns. Also was a dangerous return man for the Lions.

DICK (NIGHT TRAIN) LANE, cornerback, 1960-65: Regarded by many as one of the hardest-hitting cornerbacks ever. Played two seasons with the Rams and six with the Chicago Cardinals before finishing his career with the Lions. Had 68 career interceptions, including a record 14 when he was with the Rams in 1952, when the NFL played just 12 games. That record still stands. Also had 11 career fumble recoveries. Was known for a tackle in which he grabbed the opponent's neck or head, a technique that is now outlawed. The tackle was referred to as a "Night Train necktie." "I've never seen a defensive back hit the way he hit—I mean take them down, whether it be Jim Taylor or Jim Brown," Packers Hall of Fame cornerback Herb Adderley once said.

YALE LARY, defensive back/punter, 1952-53, 56-64: Played right safety on three championship teams with the Lions. Intercepted 50 passes throughout his career, returning two for touchdowns and averaging 15.7 yards on every return. Also a dangerous punt returner, bringing three back for touchdowns, and an extremely effective punter, averaging 44.3 yards per try. "He made our defense look good because we always had room to punt," said former linebacker Joe Schmidt, a teammate of Lary.

BARRY SANDERS, running back, 1989-98: Was heading toward the all-time NFL rushing record when he retired unexpectedly before the 1999 season after he already had run for 15,269 yards. Averaged 4.99 yards per carry, second only to Jim Brown (5.22) for backs with a minimum of 1,500 carries. Never rushed for less than 1,115 yards in a season. Career-best season was in 1997 when he rushed for 2,054 yards and averaged 6.1 yards per carry. "He may be the most elusive player ever to play the running back position," longtime Vikings personnel man Paul Wiggin said. "If you traced him, it's an interesting trace because he would go minus-one, minus-two, plus-two, 60, minus-one."

CHARLIE SANDERS, tight end, 1968-77: Caught 336 passes for 4,817 yards, high numbers for a tight end during the era in which he played. Was selected to the Pro Bowl seven times and to the NFL's All-Decade team of the 1970s. "Greg Landry told me once, 'You know, when I get into trouble I look for Charlie,'" said Jerry Green, who covered the Lions for the *Detroit News*.

JOE SCHMIDT, linebacker, 1953-65: Small for a linebacker but had great range. He was selected to the Pro Bowl ten times and helped the Lions to two of their three NFL championships in the 1950s. Coached the Lions to winning seasons in his last four years as coach and to a playoff berth in 1970. "He was the guy after practice running wind sprints on his own, hitting (tackling) dummies, doing this and that. He was one of the hardest working guys I'd ever seen," said former linebacker Wally Hilgenberg, who played two seasons with Schmidt in the 1960s.

GREEN BAY PACKERS

HERB ADDERLEY, cornerback, 1961-69: One of the most athletic players to ever wear a Packers uniform. Was named All-Pro five times. Played in the first two Super Bowls with the Packers and in two more with Dallas, where he played from 1970-72 before retiring. Made 48 career interceptions, including 39 with the Packers. Set a team record by returning three interceptions for touchdowns in 1965. Adderley was drafted as a running back and was moved to defense only in an emergency. Packers coach Vince Lombardi once admitted that he almost made a huge mistake with him. "I was too stubborn to switch him to defense until I had to," he said. "Now when I think of what Adderley means to our defense, it scares me to think of how I almost mishandled him." Adderley scored the final touchdown in Lombardi's final game as Packers coach, returning an interception 60 yards in a 33-14 victory over Oakland in Super Bowl II.

WILLIE DAVIS, defensive end, 1960-69: Played his first two seasons in Cleveland before coming to Green Bay in a trade. Davis holds the team record with 21 career fumble recoveries. Was named All-Pro five times and voted to the Pro Bowl five times. Part of a defense that held opposing teams without a touchdown fourteen times during the Packers five championship years ('61, '62, '65, '66, '67). Davis had three sacks in Super Bowl II, a 33-14 win over the Oakland Raiders. "The Black and Blue was an appropriate name for our division," Davis said. "I'm black, and on occasion, I was left blue after some games."

FORREST GREGG, right tackle, 1956, 1958-70: Vince Lombardi once referred to Gregg as the finest player he ever coached. That could be because one year Gregg was voted All-Pro at both tackle and left guard when he filled in for the injured Fuzzy Thurston. He held the Packers' record for durability by playing in 187 consecutive games, a record that stood until the 21st century, when Brett Favre broke it. Gregg was named to the NFL's 75th Anniversary team in 1994. Named All-Pro eight times and voted to the Pro Bowl nine times. Gregg ended his playing career with Dallas, then coached in Cleveland and Cincinnati, where he guided the Bengals to the Super Bowl in 1981. Coached the Packers from 1984-87.

TED HENDRICKS, linebacker, 1974: After playing out his option with Baltimore he played just one season in Green Bay. But it was memorable. Hendricks earned All-Pro honors after leading the Packers with five interceptions and setting a team record with seven blocked kicks. Earned a Super Bowl ring with Baltimore and another with Oakland. Showed Black and Blue toughness by playing in 215 straight regular season games. Finished his fifteen-year career with 26 picks, 16 fumble recoveries and four safeties.

PAUL HORNUNG, 1957-62, '64-'66: One of the most versatile players in NFL history. In 1960, when the NFL played a 12-game season Hornung set a league record with 176 points, a record that stood until LaDainian Tomlinson passed him during the 2006 season. Hornung scored 15 touchdowns and kicked 15 field goals and 41 extra points. Vince Lombardi famously said of Horning, "At midfield he's an ordinary player. Inside the 20, he smells the goal line." Hornung was suspended the entire 1963 season along with Lions defensive tackle Alex Karras for betting on football games. Came back in 1964 and wasn't the same player due to rust and injuries. He did have some flashes of brilliance in 1965 when he scored five touchdowns in a game against Baltimore and one month later in the NFL title game when he rushed for 105 yards and broke the game open with a 13-yard run for a touchdown to help the Packers to a 23-12 win over the Cleveland Browns. Was selected by the New Orleans Saints in the 1967 expansion draft but retired before he played a game due to a pinched nerve in his neck.

HENRY JORDAN, defensive tackle, 1960-69: Acquired in a trade after playing with the Cleveland Browns in 1957 and '58. Named All-Pro five straight times (1960-64). Was known for his colorful personality and his ability to stop the run. Once said of Vince Lombardi, "He treats us all the same, like dogs." One of his best postseason games was in the 1967 Western Conference playoffs when he had 3.5 sacks in a 28-7 win over the Los Angeles Rams. He died in 1977 at the age of 42.

JAMES LOFTON, wide receiver, 1978-86: Broke many of the team records held by the legendary Don Hutson. Caught 530 passes in a Packers uniform and remains the team's all-time leader with 9,656 receiving yards. Caught 50 or more passes in seven of his nine years with the Packers and was selected to eight Pro Bowls (seven while in Green Bay). Went on to play with four other teams. Was All-Pro four times, including two with Green Bay. "I had my battles with James," former Bears safety Gary Fencik said. "He was such a good receiver and one of the few receivers who really blocked. I can tell you that when a wide receiver puts as much effort into blocking, it puts additional effort on the defensive back in a way that guys who take plays off just don't execute."

VINCE LOMBARDI, coach, 1959-67: Green Bay was the worst team in the NFL before Lombardi arrived. By the time he left, Green Bay was known throughout the country after he guided the Packers to five NFL titles and the first two Super Bowl titles in a seven-year period. Sill the only team to win three consecutive NFL titles (1965-67). Packers won nine of ten playoff games under Lombardi, who compiled a 98-30-4 record. Retired after the second Super Bowl victory but came back as a coach in 1969, leading the Washington Redskins to a 7-5-2 record. He died of colon cancer in 1970.

RAY NITSCHKE, linebacker, 1958-72: Menacing style personified the image of the Black and Blue. Was named to the NFL's All-50- and 75-year Anniversary teams. Was a three-time All-Pro who was the heart of the Packers' defenses in the 1960s when the team won five titles. Played in 190 games and had 25 career interceptions. Was the MVP of the 1962 NFL title game, won by the Packers over the Giants, 16-7. Died in 1998. "Nitschke was a real great team player. He had a way about him, the ferocity of his commitment to the game I think intimidated even his teammates," said Steve Sabol, vice president of NFL Films. "When you think of great linebackers, you've got Butkus and Nitschke. Then there's Lawrence Taylor, who changed the game. Those three are at a unique level in my mind."

JIM RINGO, center, 1953-63: Durable and tough. Once held the NFL record for consecutive games played at 183, the first 126 coming when he was with the Packers. Was the anchor of the Packers' offensive line when they won their first two titles under Lombardi in 1961 and '62. Played in the Pro Bowl ten times, seven with the Packers. Ended his career by playing four seasons with the Eagles.

BART STARR, quarterback, 1956-71: The winningest quarterback of his era, leading the Packers to six conference titles, five NFL titles and the first two Super Bowl victories, earning MVP honors both times. Led the NFL in passing three times and named to the Pro Bowl four times. Coached the Packers from 1975-83, making the playoffs once. Scored the touchdown in the final seconds to win the Ice Bowl, keeping the ball on a quarterback sneak when he called for a fullback dive. That capped a 68-yard drive in the final 4:50, a drive which many of his teammates said was vintage Starr. "That drive, Unitas's drive leading to Ameche's touchdown in the 1958 championship, Elway's drive against Cleveland in the playoffs, those three to me are the great drives in football history, with the Packer drive being the first," Sabol said.

JIM TAYLOR, running back, 1958-66: A classic fullback whose bruising style punished opposing tacklers and kept the ball in the Packers' possession. Rushed for more than 1,000 yards in five straight seasons from 1960-64 and finished with 26 career 100-yard games and 8,207 yards for Green Bay. Played one season with the New Orleans Saints in 1967. "Jim Taylor was one of the toughest guys I ever played with," former Packers linebacker Dave Robinson said.

EMLEN TUNNELL, 1959-61: Became a star in the 1950s with the New York Giants, serving as one of their leaders on defense. Was the first African-American to play for the Giants and to be elected to the Pro Football Hall of Fame. Lombardi was the Giants' offensive coordinator when he was named Packers coach in 1959. Tunnell was going to retire but Lombardi talked him into going with him to Green Bay to help provide leadership. He played on Lombardi's first NFL championship team in 1961. When Tunnell retired, he held the NFL's all-time interception record with 79.

REGGIE WHITE, defensive end, 1993-98: White spent seven seasons in Philadelphia before signing a four-year free agent deal worth $17 million with the Packers. His arrival was key to the Packers because other talented African-American players soon followed White to Green Bay, including defensive line mates Sean Jones and Santana Dotson. White retired in 1998, then played one more season, with Carolina in 2000. He finished his career with 199.5 sacks, which was the all-time record until Bruce Smith passed him. Recorded three sacks for the Packers in Super Bowl XXXI against New England. "The thing about Reggie is that he played in an era when they liberalized the holding," Packers radio analyst and former center Larry McCarren said. "You could just latch on as long as your hands were inside. You could latch on but yet he was equally effective and equally outstanding against the run and the pass. Nobody could block the guy consistently one-on-one. He could take away a side of the field for the running game."

WILLIE WOOD, safety, 1960-71: Only one of six non-drafted free agents to make the Hall of Fame. Was a quarterback in college who went on to become one of the game's best free safeties. Had 48 career interceptions, including nine in 1962 when he led the NFL. Broke open a close game in the first Super Bowl with an interception and 50-yard return that led to the Packers' first of three touchdowns in the second half when they scored 21 points and went on to a 35-10 win over Kansas City. Played in eight Pro Bowls and was All-Pro six straight times from 1963-68. Was respected for his ability to play through injuries. His streak of playing in 166 straight games is third-highest in franchise history.

MINNESOTA VIKINGS

CARL ELLER, defensive end, 1964-78: Finished his career with one season in Seattle in 1979. Holds the Vikings sack record with 130. Played in six Pro Bowls and was named All-Pro five time. Was part of the famed Purple People Eaters defensive line that played in five NFC championship games and four Super Bowls. With Eller on one side and Jim Marshall at the other end, the Vikings' front four was one of the best ever in the NFL. "I have always told people that the two most blessed guys in the NFL during that era were Roy Winston and Wally Hilgenberg, because we got to play behind Carl Eller and Jim Marshall," Hilgenberg said. "When you have those guys at defensive end playing for you, and the way we ran our defense with the linebackers making all the calls, we were talking to those guys all the time, working stunts, working together, coordinating our efforts. We really knew what it was to play team defense."

JIM FINKS, general manager of Vikings, 1964-73, and of Bears, 1974-82: Excellent judge of personnel, built the Vikings and Bears into NFL powers. Hired Bud Grant as coach with the Vikings and Mike Ditka in Chicago. Vikings appeared in two Super Bowls when Finks was with the team and many of the players he drafted or traded for were part of all four Vikings' Super Bowl appearances.

BUD GRANT, head coach, 1967-83, '85: First person to be elected to both the Pro Football Hall of Fame and the Canadian Football League Hall of Fame. In twenty-eight seasons as a head coach won 290 games, including 168 with Minnesota. His Vikings teams won eleven divisional titles and played in the Super Bowl four times. "When you think of the Black and Blue, you think about Lombardi, Halas and Bud Grant," former Bears player and coach Mike Ditka said. Grant won four Grey Cups with the Winnipeg Blue Bombers.

JIM LANGER, center, 1980-81: Finished his career as a backup playing for his home-state Vikings after spending the '70s with the Dolphins, where he developed into one of the best centers in the history of the game. Participated in six straight Pro Bowls and played every snap on offense on Miami's 17-0 team.

PAUL KRAUSE, safety, 1968-79: Played first four seasons in Washington before being traded to Vikings, where he played for 11

Central Division championship teams and participated in four Super Bowls. The all-time NFL interception leader with 81. His ten interceptions in 1975 is a club record. Played in eight Pro Bowls and was All-NFL four times.

WARREN MOON, quarterback, 1994-96: Spent seventeen years in the NFL, mostly with the Houston Oilers. Threw 33 touchdown passes for the Vikings in 1995. His 49,325 passing yards are the fourth-most in NFL history. Also threw 291 touchdown passes and rushed for 1,736 yards. Was inducted into the Hall of Fame in 2006.

ALAN PAGE, defensive tackle, 1967-78 with Vikings, 1978-81 with Bears: Spent all of his sixteen years in the Black and Blue. Four-time NFC defensive player of the year and NFL MVP in 1971, when he led a defense that held opposing teams to 133 points. Quickness enabled him to record 148.5 sacks, recover 23 fumbles and block 28 kicks. "Just super quick and a very intelligent player," former Packers guard Gale Gillingham said. "He was one of those guys, if you didn't get him blocked he would make the play. He had the potential to disrupt."

JAN STENERUD, kicker, 1980-83 with Packers, 1984-85 with Vikings: Spent most of his Hall of fame career with Kansas City but played his final six ('80-'85) seasons in the Black and Blue. Led the Packers in scoring for three seasons, kicking 22 field goals in 1981, 13 in the strike-shortened season in 1982 and 21 in 1983. Made a total of 35 field goals during his two seasons with the Vikings.

FRAN TARKENTON, quarterback, 1961-66, '72-'78: Elusive quarterback whose scrambling could keep a play going for more than ten seconds. Showed star quality in his first game by coming off the bench to throw four touchdown passes in a 37-13 victory over the Bears in the Vikings' first game in the NFL. Was traded to the Giants after the '66 season but came back in 1972 and helped the Vikings reach three Super Bowls. "Francis was not a typical Black and Blue player, but that doesn't mean he wasn't tough," former Minnesota tight end Stu Voigt said. "He could take a hit." Passed for 47,003 yards, which set him apart from other Black and Blue quarterbacks of his era who played for teams that ran the ball more often. Tarkenton also ran for 3,686 during his career. Played in nine Pro Bowls and was the NFL's MVP in 1975.

RON YARY, offensive tackle, 1968-81: Finished his career by playing for the Rams in 1982. Was named All-Pro six straight seasons and played in seven Pro Bowls. Tough, durable player who missed only two games because of an injury, due to a broken ankle that sidelined him for two games in 1980. Started at right tackle in four Super Bowls.

The elusive Barry Sanders breaks free of Packers safety Mike Prior during a game in 1996.

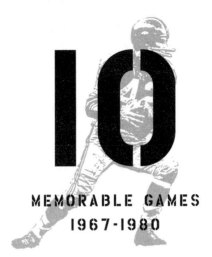

10

MEMORABLE GAMES
1967-1980

September 24, 1967
Lambeau Field
Packers 13, Bears 10

Bart Starr had perhaps his finest year in 1966 when he won the NFL's Most Valuable Player award after passing for 2,257 yards, 14 touchdowns, completing 62 percent of his passes and throwing just three interceptions, a number unheard-of for a starting quarterback.

He guided the Packers to a 12-2 regular season record and to a 34-27 win over the Dallas Cowboys in the championship game, throwing four touchdown passes.

Vikings quarterback Fran Tarkenton scrambles away from Packers tackle Dave Hanner during a game between the teams in Green Bay during the 1964 season.

That's why the start of the 1967 season was not typical for Starr, who before throwing the five picks against the Bears, had four passes intercepted the previous week, when the Packers and Lions played to a 17-17 tie.

In this game, the Packers took a 10-0 lead before halftime when second-year fullback Jim Grabowski scored on a two-yard run.

But the Bears forged a tie with a field goal by Mac Percival and a 13-yard run by Gale Sayers, whom the Packers otherwise held in check by limiting him to 63 yards.

The Packers finally won when they advanced to the Bears 39 in the final moments and Don Chandler booted a 46-yard field goal with just 63 ticks left on the clock.

The Packers weren't out of the woods, thanks to Sayers, who also was an outstanding kick returner. On some previous kicks, coach Vince Lombardi ordered Chandler to squib kick, to keep the ball away from Sayers.

On this last kickoff, Sayers sneaked up to the 30-yard line just before the kick, hoping to get his hands on the ball. But when it bounced, it hopped away from him.

October 15, 1967
Milwaukee County Stadium
Vikings 10, Packers 7

The Vikings entered this game without a win, losing their first four games under new coach Bud Grant by an average margin of 15.5 points a game.

But on this day, while playing at the second home of the Packers, Grant's team gave a snapshot of what they would be known for during the next decade: a dominating defensive team.

Minnesota held the defending NFL champions to 42 yards rushing and just one touchdown in beating the Packers, who had gone 17 games without a defeat going back to early in the 1966 season. In the first game of 1967 the Lions tied them, 17-17.

Zeke Bratkowski was at quarterback for the injured Starr and he and Carroll Dale combined on an 86-yard scoring pass in the first half that gave the Packers a 7-0 lead. The touchdown play was the longest of Dale's career. The Vikings were held scoreless until the fourth quarter, when quarterback Joe Kapp engineered two drives that produced ten points. The first resulted in a one-yard plunge by Bill Brown with 11:02 left. Fred Cox's extra point knotted the game at 7-7.

Late in the game, Earsell MackBee made a diving interception of a Bratkowski pass at the Packers' 43. Six plays moved Minnesota to the four and Cox came out and finished the upset with a 12-yard field goal with eight seconds remaining.

Fran Tarkenton, the Vikings' quarterback the previous six seasons, was traded during the off-season to the Giants. Kapp, who struggled as his replacement for much of the season, didn't complete any of the six passes he attempted in the first half against the Packers. He wound up with two completions in 11 attempts for 25 yards.

"Coach Grant has a lot more patience than I do," Kapp told reporters after the game. "He told me to forget about passing and just run the ball right at those Packers and sooner or later it would pay off. You gotta admit, he was right."

The Vikings' ground game totaled 158 yards against a defense that had five future Hall of Famers on the field that day.

November 3, 1968
Lambeau Field
Bears 13, Packers 10

Because of injuries, Sayers missed five of 14 games against the Packers during his career.

When Sayers did play, he hurt the Packers. His best performance in the rivalry came on an early November Sunday at Lambeau Field when Sayers rushed for a personal-best 205 yards on 24 carries.

Sayers later recalled he could have rushed for more than 300 yards had it not been for several runs being nullified because of penalties. Regardless, it was a terrific performance and it moved Lombardi, who had retired from coaching the year before but was still the Packers' general manager, to call it one of the greatest performances he had witnessed.

Still, the Bears had trouble getting in the end zone and the game was tied at 10-10 in the fourth quarter when they pulled something on the Packers that Lombardi had done to them four years earlier.

There's a little-used rule in the NFL that allows a team to attempt a field goal—without the opposing team rushing—following a fair catch of a punt. In 1964, near the end of the first half of a game between the teams at Lambeau, Lombardi took advantage of the rule and sent Paul Hornung out to kick a 52-yard field goal that helped the Packers to a 23-12 win.

After that game, Lombardi said, "The chance of your seeing it in your lifetime or me seeing it in mine are nil."

Four years later, he was proven wrong. The teams lined up for a punt by the Packers' Donny Anderson from the Green Bay 15. Sayers and Cecil Turner, who were back to field the kick, were told to signal for a fair catch. Anderson's short punt went to Turner, who signaled for a fair catch at the Green Bay 43 with 32 seconds left.

The Bears coaches yelled for their kicking team, which confused some of the players.

"I had never heard of a free kick," Bears kicker Mac Percival said years later.

When Percival figured out it was like lining up for a kickoff, it was a piece of cake. The NFL goalposts at the time were still on the goal line. Percival easily kicked a field goal and the Bears had their three-point victory in the only NFL game decided by a free kick.

Chuck Mercein, a running back who was born in Milwaukee and grew up in suburban Chicago, was in his second season with the Packers. After Packers kicker Errol Mann left the game with an injury after missing two field goals, Mercein, who was a running back and kicker in college at Yale, missed a 22-yard attempt in the fourth quarter. It was a memory he had blocked out of his mind until reminded of it thirty-nine years later.

"Kicking is all about timing," Mercein said. "At Yale I had the record for distance: 47, 48 yards something like that. I kicked a 45-yarder when I was with the Giants, so I had a pretty good leg.

"But if you didn't work on the timing with the snapper and the holder and the kicker, it's something that looks easy but it's not easy."

November 10, 1968
Metropolitan Stadium
Vikings 14, Packers 10

The Vikings completed their first season sweep of the Packers by knocking Packers quarterback Bart Starr senseless to the point where he couldn't remember anything.

Minnesota jumped out to a 14-0 lead but the Packers battled back and eventually cut the deficit to 14-10.

Vikings defensive end Carl Eller later unloaded on Starr while rushing him, hitting the quarterback so hard he was knocked out.

Starr left the game but later returned and moved the Packers into position for a field goal early in the fourth quarter. The Packers had a third and goal on the Minnesota 20 when Starr inexplicably called for the Packers sweep while the coaching staff stood on the sidelines in disbelief.

Donny Anderson gained just two yards and Mike Mercer trotted out for a field goal attempt that was blocked by Eller.

Starr never returned to the game.

"I'm having trouble remembering much about the second half," Starr confessed to reporters before they were shooed away by Lombardi, no longer the Packers' coach.

The loss for the three-time defending NFL champs dropped their record to 3-5-1.

December 15, 1968
Wrigley Field
Packers 28, Bears 27

The Packers entered the 100th meeting with their most hated rivals with no hope of winning a fourth consecutive NFL title. In fact, their 5-7-1 record entering the last game of the season ensured they would have a losing mark for the first year since 1958, the year before Lombardi arrived.

Lombardi no longer was on the sidelines, having retired from coaching after the win in Super Bowl II. He was still the team's general manager, and watched the games from the press box.

The Bears were also without their legendary coach, George Halas, who also retired from coaching the year before. The new coach, Jim Dooley, had guided his team to a 7-6 record, which in normal years wouldn't have been good enough for the postseason. But in the wild and unpredictable Black and Blue, the Bears controlled their destiny on this day.

Both the Bears and Vikings, who were playing Philadelphia, had 7-6 records. If the teams finished in a tie, the Bears would get the Central Division playoff berth based on their two wins over Minnesota during the season.

The Vikings beat the Eagles. But the Packers' ruined any thoughts the Bears had of returning to the playoffs for the first time since 1963 by beating them with a third-string quarterback.

Starr was injured and on the sidelines, unable to play. His replacement, Bratkowski, threw a touchdown pass but went down with an injury in the first quarter. Enter Don Horn, who came in and threw for 187 yards and a couple of touchdowns to help the Packers to a 28-10 lead after three quarters.

The Bears had injury problems of their own. Three offensive tackles went out in this game, forcing Dooley to use defensive tackle Dick Evey on a patchwork offensive line.

Regardless, Chicago came charging back with 17 points that left them trailing 28-27 following a 51-yard touchdown pass from

Jack Concannon to Dick Gordon with 3:58 to play, plenty of time to complete the comeback.

The Bears then forced the Packers to punt after three plays and got the ball back on their own 46 well before the two-minute warning.

After a couple of plays they had a first down on the Green Bay 44 and only needed about eight to 10 yards to get in field goal range for Percival. But Concannon was thrown for a four-yard loss on first down before firing two incompletions.

The Bears called timeout and started to send the field goal unit out for what would be a 55-yard attempt. Dooley changed his mind and sent the offense back out, but to no avail. Concannon had a pass picked off by Packers linebacker Ray Nitschke with 1:07 remaining that sealed the Bears' fate.

November 17, 1970
Tiger Stadium
Vikings 24, Lions 20

During a seven-year stretch, the Vikings beat the Lions 13 straight times, many times while being outplayed and many times when something unusual happened in the final moments.

This was one of those games.

Jim Lindsey, a third-string running back, was forced to play tight end for the Vikings. With just under two minutes to play and the Vikings 54 yards away from the end zone and trailing 20-17, Lindsey somehow slipped past defensive back Wayne Rasmussen and was wide open. Minnesota quarterback Gary Cuozzo threw a pass in his direction that appeared to be long. But Lindsey made a lunging catch at the 14 and staggered another ten yards to the four. A couple of plays later, Clint Jones scored his third touchdown of the game as the Vikings pulled off another improbable win against the Lions.

December 21, 1970
Tiger Stadium
Lions 20, Packers 0

The Lions were one of the NFL's dominant teams in the 1950s, playing in four championship games and winning three.

Since their last title in 1957, the Lions had some good teams that fell just short of reaching the playoffs. But that changed when the Lions, who needed a win to make the NFC playoffs, shut out the Packers for the second time during the 1970 season.

The Lions had a 3-0 lead at halftime and led just 6-0 going into the fourth quarter before Lem Barney, the Lions' cornerback and return specialist, personally delivered a playoff berth to his teammates.

Early in the fourth quarter, Barney's 65-yard punt return set up a 13-yard scoring pass from Greg Landry to tight end Charlie Sanders. Later in the quarter, he scored Detroit's second touchdown by picking off a Starr pass and returning it 49 yards for a score.

Barney capped a day in which he had 223 return yards (on punts, kickoffs and interceptions), or 99 more yards than the Packers mustered on offense.

"On the interception I noticed that Bart Starr had been throwing outside patterns all day, so I played harder to the outside and managed to pick that one off," Barney told reporters after the game. "I had Forrest Gregg and one other big guy to beat and I just barely got around 'em and into the end zone."

The Lions finished with a 10-4 record, good for second place in the division behind the Vikings, who won it with a 12-2 record.

The victory was satisfying to Lions coach Joe Schmidt, a former linebacker who was a part of two championship teams as a player.

"The most satisfaction I get is when I walk from that dugout into the dressing room after a win," he said.

The game featured a mild skirmish in the fourth quarter between Donny Anderson and Lions defensive tackle Alex Karras.

"We were fighting," Anderson said after the game. "If he

doesn't like contact, he shouldn't be in the game. I've been getting hit for five years. I don't know why he doesn't expect to get hit every once in a while."

Anderson, who had his best year in the NFL, entered the game with 836 rushing yards, but was held to 17 yards on 13 attempts.

The game turned out to be the last for coach Phil Bengtson, Vince Lombardi's successor after the 1967 season. The Packers finished 1970 with a 6-8 record, giving Bengtson a three-year mark of 20-21-1.

The Lions' offense faltered the following week in the playoffs, failing to score in a 5-0 loss to the Dallas Cowboys.

Years later, middle linebacker Mike Lucci said, "I really thought we had a good enough team to go to the Super Bowl."

September 20, 1971
Tiger Stadium
Vikings 16, Lions 13

ABC began its second season of *Monday Night Football* in Detroit with a game between two teams from the Black and Blue Division that had qualified for the playoffs the previous year.

The Vikings were two seasons removed from playing in the Super Bowl. The Lions finished second in the NFC Central the previous year with a 10-4 record and lost in the playoffs to the Cowboys.

Five days before the game, the Lions released Karras, who was thirty-six and hadn't been as productive as he was earlier in his career when he was one of the most feared linemen in the game. His departure was a storyline for the game, as was the Vikings' recent dominance of the Lions, who had lost the previous six meetings between the teams.

On the morning of the game, ABC broadcaster Howard Cosell and his wife were taking a walk in downtown Detroit when a thief broke into their hotel suite and stole a watch and $40. Hours later, the Vikings stole a game from the Lions.

Detroit jumped out to a 13-0 lead, but the Vikings came roaring back and eventually took a 16-13 advantage on Fred Cox's third field goal of the game in the fourth quarter. On the other side, Errol Mann was having a horrid night. Near the end of the game, the Lions drove inside the Minnesota 30, but Mann shanked a 33-yard attempt that would have tied the score.

"You're going to have days like this," Mann said after the game. "But you hope you can schedule them on Tuesday and Wednesday, Thursday or Friday and not on game day. I misjudged this week."

The victory was the seventh straight for Minnesota over Detroit. That streak would reach 13 before the Lions finally ended it in 1974.

"It was like, shit happens," Lucci said years later of the Vikings' streak. "I mean they were a helluva football team and they deserved to win most of them, but there were two or three instances where any other team would have won the game."

Said Stu Voigt, who was a tight end in several of those games with the Vikings: "We always felt the Lions had a good team. They had players like Mike Lucci and Larry Hand. But we'd always find a way to win."

November 14, 1971
Metropolitan Stadium
Vikings 3, Packers 0

The Vikings were well on the way to their fourth consecutive Black and Blue title; the Packers were headed toward a second consecutive losing season under first-year coach Dan Devine.

But on a chilly day at the Met, the Packers thoroughly dominated the Vikings. They rushed for 245 yards against the Purple People Eaters, who hardly looked like the fearsome front line that had dominated the Central for three years. They held the Vikings to 87 yards total offense with a defensive effort Packers coaches said was one of the best they had been associated with.

These statistics made the final outcome all the more frustrating: Vikings 3, Packers 0.

"The Packers played as sound a football game as anybody has played against us the last three years," Grant said following the game.

Indeed. So what happened?

The Packers had a second and eight on the Vikings ten with eight minutes remaining. Scott Hunter elected to go for a touchdown rather than keep the ball in the middle of the field for a field goal. He threw a pass intended for tight end Rich McGeorge, whom Hunter later said was open by several steps. The ball wasn't thrown well and was intercepted by Vikings safety Charlie West, who returned the ball to midfield.

The Vikings then moved into field goal range for Fred Cox, who kicked a 25-yard field goal for the only points of the game.

But that wasn't the Packers' only scoring chance. Three times they were stopped inside the ten.

They were frustrated the most in the second quarter when they faced third and goal from the one and twice gave the ball to Anderson, who was stopped both times. There was another time when the Packers had a second and eight on the Minnesota ten and Anderson fumbled after being hit and the ball was snapped out of the air by Vikings safety Paul Krause. Another time, Scott Hunter intended a pass for Anderson, but it was intercepted on the three.

Why Anderson was getting the ball all the time was a mystery because rookie John Brockington was having a huge day. He eventually finished with 149 rushing yards.

Almost thirty-five years later, former Packers linebacker Dave Robinson became agitated when asked about the defeat.

"I don't know how to say this tactfully except Dan Devine was the most stubborn-assed coach I ever had," Robinson said.

"We're down inside the five-yard line, the score was 0-0 and he refused to kick the field goal. Check the records on this: John Brockington had 190 yards rushing, something like that, a huge day rushing. Every time we got down inside the ten-yard line, Dan Devine would not let John Brockington carry the ball.

"You know what he said? 'They're looking for Brock so we won't run him.' The man had 100-some yards all day. Let them look for him. Brockington was running all over them. And why doesn't he kick the field goal down there? We're down there three times and he doesn't kick it once?

"That game will haunt me as long as I live. Our defense was killing them that day. Man, was I mad. As a defensive guy when you hold a team like Minnesota in Minnesota scoreless for three quarters in a slugfest, I can't believe he wouldn't kick a field goal."

October 20, 1974
Metropolitan Stadium
Lions 20, Vikings 16

The Lions, who had found all kinds of ways to lose to the Vikings for six seasons, finally found a way to win, and in Minnesota of all places.

The Vikings, always difficult to beat at the Met, fell this day to the Lions, 20-16, when Altie Taylor scored on an eight-yard run with 11 minutes left in the game.

In previous years, the Vikings would find a way to come back and extend the streak, and they almost did this time. But Barney intercepted a Tarkenton pass in the end zone with six seconds remaining. The Lions were so ecstatic that they carried first-year coach Rick Forzano off the field.

A month earlier, the Vikings' streak reached 13 with a 7-6 victory in Tiger Stadium in a defensive battle. Chuck Foreman scored the only touchdown on an 11-yard run.

"I'm glad I can go out a winner," said Detroit center Ed Flanagan, who was going to play in the World Football League after the season. "The Minnesota game has been close some other times with a minute to go but they always won it. This time we did it."

When the Lions arrived back in Detroit that night, a crowd of 100 greeted them at the airport. The headline in Monday's *Detroit Free Press* read, "Worm Turns... Lions Finally Beat Vikes, 20-16."

September 26, 1976
Pontiac Silverdome
Vikings 10, Lions 9

Vikings coach Bud Grant never liked wasting time. When on the road, the team typically arrived at the stadium about 60 minutes prior to kickoff. Most teams would arrive maybe two hours before kickoff.

On this day, though, the Vikings got into a traffic jam on the way to the Lions' indoor stadium in suburban Pontiac, and a trip that should have taken five minutes took much longer and resulted in the game starting 22 minutes after the scheduled 1 p.m. kickoff.

"Bud likes to arrive at the stadium one hour before game time," a Vikings spokesman said in newspaper accounts of the game. "We always check with as many people as possible and with the bus company as to when we should leave the hotel. We've been doing this for ten years and this has never happened before."

The NFL fined the Vikings, who arrived at the stadium around 12:50. Once they got settled, they were given a short time to warm up and the game started.

Despite being outgained 183-68 in the second half and 251-173 for the game, they kept the Lions out of the end zone. One time they stopped quarterback Greg Landry on fourth and goal from the one.

With two minutes left, Mann lined up for a short field goal but Joe Reed bobbled the snap. He got the ball down and Mann hurried a kick that was blocked by Nate Allen.

The Lions got the ball back but failed to get out of bounds on two plays. They did get close enough for Mann to try a 57-yard field goal attempt that fell short as the clock expired.

October 31, 1976
Pontiac Silverdome
Bears 14, Vikings 13

Three weeks before meeting them in Chicago, the Vikings took a hard-fought, 20-19 decision over the Bears, sending Walter Payton to the sidelines with a hit that knocked him senseless, then holding him on a fourth-and-short play in the fourth quarter when the Bears were trying to move into range for a winning field goal attempt.

It was their eighth straight win over the Monsters of the Midway and many of the final outcomes had been close.

But in the rematch, Chicago finally got some payback on a chilly, windy afternoon that was supposed to be Fran Tarkenton's day.

The Vikings quarterback came into the game needing only 91 yards to pass Johnny Unitas as the NFL's all-time passing leader. Tarkenton achieved that when he connected on a 24-yard play with Chuck Foreman in the second quarter to surpass Unitas' mark of 40,239 passing yards. Tarkenton went on to throw for 272 yards, but it was in a losing effort.

"My goal is to give a quality performance each week," he said in a story that appeared in the *Chicago Tribune*. "Really, what concerns me in any game is our team performance. Obviously we didn't perform very well today."

The Vikings outgained the Bears by 200 yards, had more first downs, 23-7, and ran more plays, 87-48. But the Bears never trailed, scoring first on a 39-yard run by Payton following a 15-yard punt into the wind by the Vikings' Neil Clabo.

The Bears' clinching touchdown early in the fourth quarter came after a 15-yard punt by Clabo. Johnny Musso scored on a 3-yard run, but not before he fumbled the ball into the end zone and frantically recovered it to put Chicago up by two scores.

"My heart stopped. The Lord is taking care of me," Musso said. "I know that if I didn't get in, this Italian boy would be in trouble."

While the Vikings' punting game suffered, Bears punter Bob

Parsons managed to average 35.4 yards per kick. He also kept one drive alive by completing a pass while in punt formation.

The loss was the first of the year for the Vikings, who would go on to their fourth Super Bowl appearance in eight years. The Bears, who would finish 7-7, were showing signs of improvement under second-year coach Jack Pardee.

November 20, 1971
Soldier Field
Bears 10, Vikings 7

On a cold, gray day when the wind gusted up to 23 miles per hour, Payton ran into the NFL record books.

Earlier in the season, Payton tied the Bears' single-game rushing record with 205 yards against the Green Bay Packers. On this Sunday, he established an NFL record with a 275-yard performance in a big division game against the Vikings.

Payton broke the NFL record of 273 yards established a year earlier by the Buffalo Bills' O.J. Simpson in a Thanksgiving Day game against the Detroit Lions.

Payton carried the ball 40 times, a number that surprised him.

"Forty?" he said in a story that appeared the next day in the *Chicago Tribune*. "It felt like about 20. I didn't know it was that many. I did have to suck it up a little at times."

While Payton was surprised by how many times he carried the ball, his quarterback and coach were just as stunned.

"An NFL record?" asked quarterback Bob Avellini, who attempted just seven passes, completing four.

"Did Walter set a record?" Pardee asked. "I had no idea."

The *Tribune* reported that Payton ran over the Vikings' left side 25 times, including 16 sweeps that produced 157 yards.

Payton scored the game's only offensive touchdown on a sweep in the first half to help the Bears take a 10-0 lead. Vikings linebacker Matt Blair provided the only touchdown for his side with a blocked punt that was recovered for a touchdown.

That may have led to a decision by Pardee to go for a touch-down on fourth down from the Vikings' six late in the game rather than kick a field goal. Payton got the ball and gained four yards to pass Simpson but came up two yards short of a touchdown.

"I felt that was the only way we could lose, for them to block a kick and return it 90 yards for a touchdown like they did against Los Angeles last year," Pardee said.

The victory evened the Bears' record at 5-5. They went on to win their final four games and earn a playoff spot for the first time since 1963. The Vikings also finished 9-5 and made the playoffs for the ninth time in ten years.

In the Vikings' locker room, Foreman, who gained just 40 yards on 14 carries, seemed envious of the offensive line Payton had playing in front of him.

"The way we played, if I had carried 40 times I probably would have gotten 80 yards," Foreman said in the *Tribune* story. "I think the Bears have the best offensive line in football. It's unbelievable the way they have pride in Walter Payton and pride in themselves."

November 27, 1977
Lambeau Field
Vikings 13, Packers 6

When you think of the early days of the Black and Blue, a couple of things generally come to mind: low scores and nasty weather.

Sometimes the weather was worse than nasty, as it was on this day at Lambeau Field when six inches of snow fell, covering the field in a blanket of white.

This was OK for the Vikings, whose motto always seemed to be: "The worse the weather, the better it is for us."

Along with the snow, the temperature was twenty-six degrees, which seemed like a Jamaican vacation to the Vikings.

"Naw, it wasn't real cold today," said Mick Tingelhoff, then a

37-year-old center for the Vikings. "Heck, sometimes snow is kind of fun."

Grant didn't mind the weather, saying it took away some of the Packers' home-field advantage.

Green Bay took a 6-0 lead in the first quarter on a three-yard run by quarterback David Whitehurst but was shut out the rest of the way, finishing with just 169 total yards.

The Vikings, who totaled only 218 yards, did all of their scoring in the second period. Fran Tarkenton threw a 40-yard touchdown pass to Sammy White and Fred Cox then kicked the extra point for a 7-6 lead. He added two field goals later in the quarter.

Several thousand people didn't use their tickets, the largest number of no-shows at Lambeau Field since 9,163 stayed home for Green Bay's 28-7 win over the Bears on November 30, 1975. The Packers were suffering their fifth consecutive losing season and eighth in the ten years following the team's last championship.

"Those who chose not to come missed something," Packers coach Bart Starr said after the game. "That's not a jab at them. It was a thrill to be coaching and a thrill to be playing. It was a great game from a standpoint of enthusiasm."

November 26, 1978
Lambeau Field
Packers 10, Vikings 10 (overtime)

Both teams entered the game tied for first with 7-5 records. The Packers, trying to win the division for the first time since 1972, started the season 6-1, but were mired in a three-game losing streak. The Vikings were still the power in the division but nowhere near the team that went to the Super Bowl four times from 1970-77.

In this game, the Packers intercepted Tarkenton four times and outgained the Vikings, 318-293. But with two minutes left and holding a 10-3 lead, they couldn't stop Tarkenton, who drove his team 57 yards in 11 plays. The touchdown came with ten seconds left when the quarterback tossed a five-yard scoring pass to Ahmad Rashad to send the game into overtime. Rashad was covered well by Mike McCoy, but made a nice catch before stepping out of bounds.

"I thought I had good position on him. I just couldn't get both hands on the ball," McCoy said after the game. "I looked at him and his eyes got bigger and I knew the ball was coming. I jumped up and he got both hands on the ball and I got one. I thought he was out of bounds but I wasn't really sure. So I couldn't start ranting and raving."

In the extra session, both teams had a chance to win. The Vikings' Rich Danmier was wide right on a 21-yard field goal with four minutes remaining in overtime. Late in the period, the Packers' Mike McCoy intercepted Tarkenton, then fumbled with teammate Dave Roller recovering on the Minnesota 43 with 1:06 to play. Quarterback David Whitehurst moved the Packers to the 23, but Chester Marcol was wide left on a 40-yard field goal try with 17 seconds remaining.

After the game, Grant thought the fans got their money's worth despite a typical low-scoring divisional game.

"I think you saw a very exciting football game," Grant said. "Nobody likes a no-hitter, I suppose, but there were fumbles, interceptions and fine offensive plays. If you want to be a critic, and I suspect that some of you do, you could say there were a lot of mistakes. But it was interesting from a fan's standpoint."

While the tie left both teams tied for the Black and Blue lead, there was a level of frustration in the Packers' locker room after the game because they knew they had wasted a huge opportunity to beat the Vikings. They also knew that if the teams ended the season tied, the tiebreaker would go to Minnesota based on its 21-7 win in the first meeting between the teams.

That's exactly what happened. Both teams ended with 8-7-1 records and the Vikings went to the playoffs.

September 2, 1979
Soldier Field
Bears 6, Packers 3

In the season opener for both teams, the Bears and Packers failed to produce a touchdown and the teams combined to produce the fewest points in a Packers-Bears game since a 1959 game won by the Packers, 9-6. That, by the way, was Vince Lombardi's first victory as a head coach in the NFL.

In this game the Bears did all of their scoring in the first half on a pair of field goals by Bob Thomas. The second, a 19-yarder, came just before halftime after the Packers stopped Payton twice near the goal line. The Packers' only points came after they drove to the Bears 11 but were forced to settle for a 28-yard field goal by Marcol in the third quarter.

The Bears held the Packers to 149 yards and sacked Whitehurst six times.

Payton, who won the NFL rushing title in 1977 and 1978, gained 125 yards against the Packers, but needed 36 carries and averaged just 3.5 yards per carry. After the game he paid the Packers' defense a high compliment.

"They are just about the toughest I've had to face," Payton said in a *Chicago Tribune* story. "At the very least I would rate them in the top five I've had to face.

"They made it tough everywhere we went. They came off the ball and forced things away from the flow."

Later that season the Bears beat the Packers at Lambeau, 15-14, giving the Bears an 11-9 edge in victories during the 1970s. In those 20 games, three were decided by one point, three by a field goal and two by six points.

September 7, 1980
Lambeau Field
Packers 12, Bears 6 (overtime)

Funny how a game that was boring for more than 60 minutes turned into one of those that rank among the most memorable of the rivalry. Chester Marcol, who would be released a few weeks later, had a short field goal attempt in overtime blocked by future Hall of Famer Alan Page. But instead of the ball being recovered or even returned for a gain by the Bears, it bounced right back to Marcol, who scooped it up and scampered around left end for the only touchdown of his career.

"Lindsay Nelson, who was doing the telecast for CBS, couldn't get out what happened," Packers historian Lee Remmel recalled. "He kept saying, 'Chester Marcol, Chester Marcol, Chester Marcol.' That's all he could say."

The game was nondescript before then. Four field goals—two each by Marcol and Bears kicker Bob Thomas—accounted for the only points in regulation. The overtime was the first ever between the teams in their long and storied rivalry.

The Packers moved into field-goal position with a 32-yard pass from Lynn Dickey to James Lofton that helped set up Marcol's 34-yard attempt with nine minutes left in the extra period.

Page, one of the game's all-time great kick blockers, told his teammates he was going to get a hand on Marcol's kick.

"The next morning I read in the paper that Alan Page had told everyone in the huddle, 'You guys on the outside just be ready because I'm going to block this field goal and then get the ricochet back and just run it for a touchdown and we'll win the game,'" recalled Dickey. "He blocked it and of course it came like a rifle right back to Chester. When things like that happen you just look up in the air and go, 'It's nothing I did, it was just meant to be.'"

Bears safety Gary Fencik cringed at the memory.

The game was a monumental win for the Packers, who scored just 17 points during five preseason games in which they went 0-4-1. In the final one, a 38-0 loss to the Broncos in Denver, Packers defense end Ezra Johnson was seen eating a hot dog on the bench. Starr first suspended Johnson for the season opener, then changed his mind. Fred vonAppen, the Packers' defensive line coach, was so appalled by Starr's decision that he resigned four days before the game. Starr, also the team's general manager, was entering his sixth season as coach and had just one winning season. The strain of vonAppen's resignation showed when he addressed members of the Packers organization.

"Bart called us all together and you could tell the pressure was really weighing on him," Remmel said. "The team had not played well during the preseason and then this happened. He felt it was a huge calamity. He was so emotional a couple of times while addressing us that he turned his back trying to compose himself.

"I felt we didn't have a prayer of winning this game. Oddly enough, it was another typical tight-fisted dogfight. We went into overtime and you know what happened."

The game was memorable to Packers center Larry McCarren, and not just because of the outcome. During training camp he had undergone hernia surgery. He was listed as questionable and didn't think he'd be able to play. McCarren was entering the season with 63 straight starts and Starr wanted to see McCarren keep the streak alive, so he asked McCarren about the possibility of playing a few snaps.

"Bart said that the night before: 'We're going to play you to keep your streak alive, play you a couple plays and get you out,'" McCarren said. He wound up playing the entire game.

"When I heard the double thud, and that's what a blocked kick sounds like, you hear the kick and then the double thud is it got blocked, and when I heard that, I thought, 'Oh, my God, this thing is going on forever,'" McCarren recalled.

"Then out of the confusion, you see some activity and I saw us going in and the official giving the touchdown sign. I was thrilled, but I had personal reasons for that for more than the victory because I was ready for that thing to end."

December 7, 1980
Soldier Field
Bears 61, Packers 7

Exactly three months after kicker Marcol picked up a blocked field goal and scored a touchdown to beat Chicago, the Bears gained some payback with their biggest margin of victory in the history of the rivalry.

Walter Payton ran for 130 yards for the Bears, who totaled a whopping 594 yards.

"It seemed like every other minute I heard, 'And that's a new Chicago Bear record,'" McCarren said. "And they were just blasting it. I don't blame them. This was a classic case of when things are being played out and a team has it working and the other one doesn't. That's professional sports."

The weekend started ominously for the Packers, who had to bus to Chicago the day before the game because an unseasonably mild weather front stalled in the Green Bay area and covered the city in fog. When the Packers got to Chicago the temperature was still very un-December like.

"If I remember, it was 62 or 63 degrees," Packers quarterback Lynn Dickey said. "When we finally got to Chicago, Jan Stenerud and I went out to grab something to eat and it was very balmy that evening walking down the streets of Chicago. I woke up the next morning and it was still really warm. It was so warm that it caused a lot of condensation on the Astroturf.

"I remember Jan opening up the game going up to kick off and his feet just went right over the top of his head. The kick did like a line drive, never got two feet off the ground and he went right down on his side. I want to say we scored first; I think I hit Lofton with a little slant and he runs it for a touchdown and so we're ahead, 7-0. And they scored 61 straight. Nothing went right for us and everything went right for them."

Indeed. Vince Evans passed for 318 yards and three touchdowns, the first Bears quarterback to throw for more than 300 yards in ten years.

"I just think it was a great game," Fencik recalled. "Those are games that defenses pray for. I know offensively you want to score a lot of points, but when it gets that bad you're paying no attention to the run and all you're doing is getting sacks and hopefully interceptions and fumbles.

"It was a great day and we beat the crap out of them. There are days that you remember during the course of a season and particularly the second game in a division rivalry, it's not that far away from the previous game. If you've got any sense of IOUs, you're looking out for certain people."

Bears defensive end Dan Hampton had this to say about the game: "We wanted to score 100 points. It couldn't have happened to a nicer bunch of pricks."

Starr was upset that Payton was put back into the game and that the Bears were still blitzing when the score was 48-7. Bears backup quarterback Mike Phipps was also throwing passes late in the game. When the game ended, Starr raced across the field and confronted Bears coach Neill Armstrong. He was more upset that defensive coordinator Buddy Ryan was blitzing Whitehurst, who was playing for the first time that season.

"I felt there was an excessive effort on the part of Ryan to take advantage of an inexperienced quarterback and continue to literally rub it in," Starr said in *Mudbaths and Bloodbaths*, a book on the Bears-Packers rivalry. "I harbor no feelings about it now, but at the time, I was really ticked off."

Recalled McCarren, "The whole thing was out of the ordinary from start to finish, and certainly the finish of the game was out of the ordinary."

MEMORABLE GAMES
1981-1990

November 22, 1982
Soldier Field
Bears 20, Lions 17

Mike Ditka's first victory as a head coach came almost three months after the season opener. The Bears lost their first two games, and then Ditka had to endure a two-month players' strike before the season resumed.

When it did, the coach, his players and Bears fans got a glimpse of what life was going to be like with Jim McMahon at quarterback.

He put the Bears in a hole with two

Packers quarterback Don Majkowski (7) celebrates the instant-replay call confirming his game-winning touchdown pass to Sterling Sharpe with 32 seconds remaining against the Chicago Bears on Nov. 5, 1989. The Packers won 14-13.

early interceptions that helped the Lions take a 14-3 lead. But McMahon never lost his confidence and Ditka never thought of taking him out of the game.

Good thing. The Bears got back into it when McMahon threw a 28-yard touchdown pass to Emery Moorehead.

With two minutes left in the game and the scored tied at 17-17, the Lions were threatening with a first down on the Bears 48 when Chicago's defense gave a preview of how good it was going to be three years later. First, safety Gary Fencik tackled Billy Sims for a four-yard loss. On the next two plays, Mike Singletary and Steve McMichael each sacked quarterback Eric Hipple for a total of 21 yards in losses.

The Lions punted and the Bears took over on their 42 with 49 seconds to play. The big play was a 44-yard pass from McMahon to Moorehead to the Lions' one-yard line that set up John Roveto's 18-yard field goal that rewarded Ditka with his first win.

The player everyone was talking about after the game was the cocksure McMahon.

"He's running around the field, pointing at guys to go down-field and I'm saying, 'Look at this guy, he's only a rookie,'" line-backer Al Harris said in the *Chicago Tribune*'s account of the game.

"One time, he was trying to call an audible and the clock was running down and he just said, 'Oh, shoot,'" Bears safety Jeff Fisher said. "That was an audible we hadn't heard before. Oh shoot."

What impressed McMahon's teammates were his poise and his refusal to panic after making two early mistakes.

"You've got to be pleased with his poise," running back Brian Baschnagel said. "Those kind of quarterbacks don't come around too often."

December 18, 1983
Soldier Field
Bears 23, Packers 21

The Packers held a 21-20 lead and needed to hold off Chicago to clinch a playoff berth for the second straight year. But the Bears had other ideas; the Packers lost and Bart Starr was out of a coaching job the next day.

Jim McMahon drove his team from the Bears' 36 to inside the Green Bay 10, where Bob Thomas eventually kicked a 22-yard field goal with ten seconds remaining that left both teams with 8-8 season-ending records.

In the fourth quarter, the Packers noticed on the scoreboard that the Los Angeles Rams had defeated the New Orleans Saints. All they needed was to win to be playing a post-season game the following week.

But the Green Bay defense, which had allowed more than 27.4 points per game, failed one more time and Starr, the quarterback of five NFL championship teams for the Packers during the 1960s, was let go after compiling a 52-76-3 record in nine seasons as coach. His coaching staff was also fired.

"The decision was difficult, not only because of what it means to Bart Starr, because Bart is almost synonymous with the Green Bay Packers, but also of what it means to the coaching staff," Judge Robert Parins, the team's president, read from a statement.

"The decision, while difficult, is not made out of emotion or frustration, but on an overall evaluation on the needs of the franchise. We feel the position of head coach needs a fresh look."

Gale Gillingham, a Packers guard from 1966-74 and '76, played with Starr and for him.

"When they let him go finally, he was actually doing a good job," Gillingham recalled years later. "Why they pulled the plug on him when they did, I never did figure that out."

In that fateful last game, Starr was criticized by the media for letting the clock run down as the Bears drove down the field.

When asked after the game about not using his timeouts, he snapped, "That's our business."

Years later, Starr admitted he erred by not stopping the clock in *Mudbaths and Bloodbaths*, a book on the Bears-Packers rivalry.

"I blame myself totally for that loss," he said. "I should have taken the timeouts. I should have done that, rather than just let a no-decision continue, thinking we could block any kick. We were so good at blocking kicks; that was the decision. But I knew better, and if we had taken a timeout sooner, we might have had a chance to get back down the field and kick one ourselves."

September 19, 1985
Minneapolis Metrodome
Bears 33, Vikings 24

Both the Bears and Vikings had 2-0 records heading into this nationally televised Thursday night game. Bears quarterback Jim McMahon didn't start because of injuries, but it was later learned it really had more to do with coach Mike Ditka being upset about McMahon's refusal to stop head-butting his teammates after touchdowns.

His replacement, Steve Fuller, moved the Bears but couldn't get into the end zone and midway through the third quarter the Vikings held a 17-9 lead.

McMahon spent much of the game following Ditka up and down the sideline, pleading with his coach to put him into the game. Ditka finally agreed. What followed was one of those things that made the 1985 Bears so special and showed the world what a competitor McMahon was.

On his first pass, he threw a 70-yard touchdown pass to Willie Gault to pull the Bears within a point.

Chicago got the ball back on a turnover and McMahon immediately connected on a 25-yard scoring pass with Dennis McKinnon for a 23-17 lead.

Later and still in the third quarter, the Bears got the ball back and McMahon struck again, this time completing a 68-yard drive with a 43-yard touchdown pass to McKinnon that gave Chicago a 30-17 advantage.

In just six minutes, 40 seconds, McMahon completed 5-of-7 passes with three going for touchdowns.

McMahon finished with eight completions in 15 attempts for 236 yards.

"I haven't played on national television for so long, I wanted to show my friends I could still play," McMahon told the *Chicago Tribune* after the game.

"I was praying he was coming in," McKinnon said. "He is known to have miracles happen."

The Vikings cut the gap to 30-24 in the fourth quarter, but Kevin Butler's fourth field goal of the game iced the win for Chicago, which improved to 3-0.

Bud Grant, who was back coaching the Vikings after spending a year in retirement, said of the Bears: "They're an up-and-coming team. One or two plays could have made a difference in this game. Next time, it might be different."

It wasn't. In the rematch at Soldier Field, the Bears, on their way to a 15-1 record and a Super Bowl victory, won going away, 27-9.

October 21, 1985
Soldier Field
Bears 23, Packers 7

William Perry, a rookie defensive tackle who already had been making a name for himself because of his size and gap-toothed grin, became a household name during a nationally televised Monday night game at Soldier Field.

Perry, listed at 310 pounds but rumored to be as much as 380, lined up as a fullback five times that night for the Bears, who came in with a 6-0 record and were already showing the football world they were on the way to a very special season.

On Perry's first play the Bears had the ball at the Packers' two. McMahon handed the ball to Walter Payton, who had an easy path into the end zone running behind Perry. The mammoth rookie obliterated linebacker George Cumby—giving away at least 100 pounds to the fake fullback—almost five yards deep into the end zone.

"I only have one obligation, and that's to block the linebacker," Perry told the *Chicago Tribune* after the game. "Whoever else got in the way, I took him out, too. Cumby didn't say anything. I think I rung his bell."

Perry wasn't finished. He came in the next time the Bears had the ball. On the Green Bay one, Perry took a handoff from McMahon and rumbled into the end zone, which sent a jolt of electricity through the Soldier Field crowd. He came back again later in the quarter and led Payton into the end zone one more time, again knocking down the determined, but undersized, Cumby, listed at a generous 225 pounds.

Perry had lined up as a fullback the week before against San Francisco. But the fact he became a national celebrity against the Packers was something that pleased the Bears, who were developing a hatred for second-year Packers coach Forrest Gregg.

As a player, Gregg, a Hall of Fame offensive tackle, was a part of five championship teams with the Packers during the 1960s when the Packers dominated the rivalry with the Bears. Now it was the Bears turn, and coach Mike Ditka took extra pleasure when he could beat his old rival. It probably wasn't an accident that he waited until playing the Packers to put Perry in a situation that would result in a Chicago touchdown.

"A great moment. God, he hit George Cumby, didn't he?" Bears safety Gary Fencik said more than twenty years later. "God, he just crushed him. Yeah it was really enjoyable because of Forrest Gregg. The tough thing about a rivalry is that you have to have enough wins on both sides in order for the intensity to really heat up. And even though the Packers weren't winning a lot, they had a character you didn't like, Forrest Gregg. He'd be talking to you on the sidelines. You'd make a tackle and be getting up and he was jawing at everybody.

"It just personified all your hatred about the Packers was in their coach instead of an individual player. The players themselves couldn't match their coach."

For Perry, enough endorsements came his way to set him up for life. An above average tackle, he's probably known more for what he did during a few games on offense. In the rematch with the Packers that season he caught a touchdown pass.

Brian Noble, then a rookie linebacker for the Packers, remembers feeling bad for Cumby on that night at Soldier Field.

"I had taken George's job that year. George wasn't even playing in the game but he played on goal line, 'cause I moved to outside linebacker down on the line," Noble said. "So here you're asking a 220-pound George Cumby to take on a 380-pound guy, you know, and stop him dead in his tracks.

"When you get down on the goal line, realize this: that the offensive and defensive linemen, all they do is make a pile. And then it's the linebackers that usually are doing all the running into each other making the play. Basically, they isolated George by himself on the weak side and handed Fridge the ball. And, you know, obviously, George wasn't the only one that they did that to, but it was kind of a slap in the face. Needless to say we had to live with that the entire rest of the season, with all his commercials. We, for the most part, made him famous just on that because, although he was a decent football player, I mean, that made him who he is."

Later in the game, the Bears ticked off the Packers again by passing five times late in the fourth quarter while holding a 16-point lead.

"They blitzed on every down," a blunt Ditka said after the game. "You're going to burn out your players by running them into a brick wall. We tried to throw the ball. Maybe if we'd hit one we'd have gotten them out of it."

The Packers were also upset because they felt that quarterback Lynn Dickey was physically abused by Bears defensive linemen Richard Dent and Dan Hampton after throwing an interception in the first quarter. Of course, they blamed Ditka.

"I don't know Ditka very well but from what I understand I'm not very surprised," Packers cornerback Tim Lewis told the *Green Bay Press-Gazette* after the game. "It's a very heated game when you see every six plays guys pushing each other around."

October 19, 1986
Minneapolis Metrodome
Vikings 23, Bears 7

From 1985 through 1987, the Bears lost just one game against a division rival. It came on this Sunday when Tommy Kramer threw two touchdown passes during his first eight plays to give the Vikings a 13-0 lead.

The crowd of 62,851, the largest to see a Vikings game in Minnesota, roared its approval as the Vikings snapped the Bears' 12-game winning streak (including three playoff games). Fuller was at quarterback, subbing for the injured McMahon. But once he was put in the 13-point hole, he didn't have a chance.

"We beat Chicago," Minnesota defensive tackle Tim Newton said in a *Chicago Tribune* story. "Everyone's going to say, 'Well, McMahon wasn't playing.' I don't think that would've made any difference today. McMahon isn't the offensive line or the defensive line."

The victory improved the Vikings' record to 5-2. They'd finish at 9-7 and miss the playoffs. The Bears won the division with a 14-2 record.

"They beat us the way you're supposed to win football games," Ditka said. "Took it to us and shoved it down our throat."

November 23, 1986
Soldier Field
Bears 12, Packers 10

The Bears had a 9-2 record and the Packers were 2-9 when they met in late November. One team was the defending Super Bowl champion and heading back to the playoffs. The other was on the way to a 4-12 record.

But as they say, the records don't matter when the Bears and Packers get together. And the rivalry, which had turned nasty in the mid-'80s, got downright ugly in this game.

Midway through the second quarter, McMahon had just thrown a pass that was intercepted by the Packers' Mark Lee. Packers defensive end Charles Martin hesitated for a moment, then went up to McMahon, picked him up and body-slammed him to the ground. He was immediately ejected by referee Jerry Markbreit.

Some of the Packers didn't see the play because they were celebrating the interception. But when they saw the replays, many of the veterans were furious at Martin.

Brian Noble, was a second-year linebacker for the Packers. He remembered watching Martin depart the field.

"He walks through that tunnel at Solder Field and just got pelted," Noble recalled. "I mean I've seen cars go through car washes that didn't get as wet as Charlie did going through that tunnel. It was unbelievable."

The Bears were riled up on the sidelines. Later, William Perry viciously hit Packers quarterback Randy Wright just after he released a ball that ended in a touchdown pass. He wasn't penalized, although the Packers felt he should have been.

In the end, Green Bay had a chance to win. Holding a 10-9 lead, the Packers appeared to be driving to another score with just under seven minutes left in the game. On first and ten at the Bears 30, halfback Gary Ellerson was hit by linebacker Mike Singletary, who forced a fumble that was recovered by the Bears.

The Bears then took over and moved into position for a 32-yard field goal by Kevin Butler that gave the Bears a 12-10 lead with 2:37 to play.

After the game, Noble went into the Bears' locker room and apologized to Ditka for the actions of some of his teammates, notably Martin.

"I wanted him to understand that I had no part of that," Noble said years later. "I kind of conducted myself in a specific manner and wanted (him) to know that's not the way I play the game and that's not the way I want my teammates to play."

December 6, 1987
Minneapolis Metrodome
Bears 30, Vikings 24

Mike Ditka knew how to stoke a rivalry, and to have fun.

He didn't like the Metrodome, the Vikings' indoor stadium that looked like it had a big bubble over it. He called it the Rollerdome.

Vikings general manager Mike Lynn sent Ditka a pair of roller skates and the Bears' coach promptly put them on and skated around Halas Hall three days before the game.

Ditka's intent, really, was to create diversion before a key Black and Blue game, one that would result in Chicago's fourth straight division title with a victory.

Ditka got his win, but not without a fight.

After his team twice wasted 13-point leads, Ditka watched as backup quarterback Mike Tomczak threw a 38-yard touchdown pass to Dennis Gentry with forty seconds remaining to rally the Bears from a 24-23 deficit.

"Unbelievable," said Ditka, wearing a Viking helmet with horns as he met the media. "They proved they had the guts to do it. I said all week Dennis Gentry was going to be MVP. Don't ask me why."

The Metrodome was ready for Ditka after his weeklong insults. The scoreboard read: "Welcome to the Rollerdome."

The Bears' winning score came after the defense stopped the

Vikings on four straight running plays near the goal line following a lost fumble by Tomczak.

"The goal-line stand was incredible," Ditka said. "I've been excited, but I've never felt this way. Every cliché you teach your kids about never giving up, they proved."

Years later, Ditka said he was just trying to inject a little life into the game with his roller-blading antics.

"I was just having fun," he said. "Nobody would ever do that today because the league is so stuffy. I'll say it, it's stuffy.

"They want every coach to be so proper. I listen to these guys talk in press conferences, I can't tell if they won, they lost, whether the dog died, I don't know what the hell is going on. Have a little fun. It's only football; it's not brain surgery. If you win, you're gonna have a job, if you don't win, chances are you're not going to have a job. I had a lot of fun with it and I refuse to look at it any other way."

October 15, 1989
Minneapolis Metrodome
Vikings 26, Packers 14

A week earlier, the Packers faced Herschel Walker when he was wearing a Cowboys uniform.

Two days after that game, he was traded to the Vikings. Five days later, Walker rushed for 148 yards on 18 carries, or 104 more than he had the previous week against Green Bay.

Vikings coach Jerry Burns, whose team was in desperate need of a solid running back, was thankful he played Walker as much as he did. He originally said Walker would see limited action.

"When I saw him run, I changed my mind," Burns said. "I'm not the smartest guy in the world, but I'm not a complete idiot, either."

Walker, the former Heisman Trophy winner from Georgia, was unhappy with how he was being used in Dallas.

"When I step on the field, that's where I feel at home," Walker said. "I think today I ran the ball the way I've been saying Herschel has got to run."

The Vikings sacked Packers quarterback Don Majkowski seven times. Defensive tackle Keith Millard had four of those sacks, giving him 12 for the season. He finished with 18, which wasn't even best on his team. Linebacker Chris Doleman had 21 to lead the NFL.

The Vikings were 3-2 before trading for Walker. They finished 10-6, tied for the division title with the Packers and won the play-off berth on a tiebreaker. They lost in their first-round playoff game to San Francisco.

The game was Walker's best of the season. He finished the season with 669 rushing yards in nine games.

In his last game before becoming a Viking, Walker carried only 12 times for 44 yards against Green Bay. He arrived in Minnesota Friday after the Cowboys traded him and was only supposed to see limited action.

The trade decimated the Vikings, who had been considered a Super Bowl-caliber team. They traded five roster players and six draft picks over the next three years, including three in the first round.

November 5, 1989
Lambeau Field
Packers 14, Bears 13

There were about four minutes left in the game when Majkowski, his team trailing by six points and trying to break an eight-game losing streak against the Bears, threw an interception at a point in the game when the Packers couldn't afford a mistake.

Understandably, Majkowski was downtrodden as he trotted off the field, hearing some scattered boos from Packers fans believing that the losing streak against Chicago was going to continue. But Packers coach Lindy Infante came up to his quarterback and expressed nothing but optimism.

"Lindy grabbed me by the facemask and he said, 'Look at me.'

He said, 'Look at me, Donny,'" Majkowski recalled more than sixteen years later.

"He goes, 'We need you to keep your head in this game because you're still going to be the hero today in this game. We've gotta have you. Keep your head up. You're still going to win this game. You're going to be the hero.'"

Infante was right, but Majkowski's heroics became overshadowed in what has become known in the Bears-Packers rivalry as "The Instant Replay Game."

The Packers got the ball back and Majkowski engineered a 14-play drive that culminated with the quarterback throwing a 14-yard touchdown pass on fourth and goal that tied the game at 13-13 with just 32 seconds remaining.

The play broke down early and Majkowski was forced to improvise. Running to his right and being pursued by the Bears' Trace Armstrong, he spotted Sharpe, planted his foot and tossed a well-thrown pass to his favorite receiver.

Touchdown, thought the crowd, but then a flag was thrown from the other side of the field by line judge Jim Quirk, who was positioned on the line of scrimmage and indicated Majkowski crossed the scrimmage line before throwing the pass.

The Bears began to celebrate and the Packers protested. Up in the press box sat replay official Bill Parkinson. This was the first year that the NFL was using instant replay to review close plays and rather than the referee reviewing from the field, it was done by another official away from the action.

For five minutes, the players and the Lambeau Field crowd waited for what seemed like an eternity as Parkinson watched the play over and over. Bears players were convinced Majkowski's foot was over the line of scrimmage, which would negate the score. Majkowski's teammates kept asking him and he tried reassuring them that the play was legal.

Finally, Parkinson made his call, overruling Quirk. Chris Jacke kicked the extra point and moments later the game ended, as did Chicago's eight-game winning streak against Green Bay.

"I'm not saying this because it was me that did the play, but my foot was on the 15-yard line when I threw that ball. I was a yard behind the line of scrimmage," Majkowski said. "I mean, you can listen to the commentators. Dan Fouts was doing the game and he even said, 'He's a yard behind the line of scrimmage. This is going to be a touchdown. It's not even close.'

"And it wasn't. When they reviewed it, they got it right and I made a nice throw across the field and Sterling did a great job of finding an open seam and I put it in there. You know the rest is history. It was a great, great play on the last play of the game, crunch time. So that was my defining moment as a Green Bay Packer."

Just before Quirk's call was reversed, Bears linebacker Mike Singletary tried getting into Majkowski's head.

"Singletary came over to me during the review period and he said something kind of sarcastic like, 'That was a great game, kid. Too bad you guys still aren't going to beat us,'" Majkowski recalled. "And I said something like, 'Hey, it's not over yet, Mike. Hold on to your horse.'

"And when they reviewed it and it came down, the referee said, all you could basically hear was, "After further review we have a reversal," and that's basically all you could hear. The crowd went nuts and Singletary kind of looked over at me shaking his head and I just winked at him.

"It was kind of a cocky, cool moment, like man, how sweet was that? It was a great moment. The fans went nuts. It was the most emotional moment in my career. I never cried ever during my career, except for after that when we kicked the extra point and we won the game. Aw, gee. So much emotion overcame me at that point. It was like I had tears of joy, like crying after that game which never, ever happened to me throughout my whole career.

Some Bears players said after the game that the call shouldn't have been reversed. Among the loudest was linebacker Ron Rivera.

"I don't think that's right. They could go back every play and pick out all the infractions, and the game would never be completed. I think they've got to do something about it," he said in a story that appeared the next day in the *Milwaukee Sentinel*.

"Sometimes I feel they ought to just put twenty-two robots in uniform and let them play, or get a couple of computer operators and let them play it on a video game."

Bears president Michael McCaskey was so disgusted with the reversal that for years he had the Bears' public relations staff put an asterisk next to the game in the section with the Bears all-time results. At the bottom was a notation: "Instant Replay Game."

November 25, 1990
Minneapolis Metrodome
Vikings 41, Bears 13

Following a 6-10 season in 1989, the Bears were back to being the Bears in 1990, winning ten of their first eleven games in assuming control of the division.

The Vikings were on a three-game winning streak but still under .500 (4-6) because of an earlier five-game losing streak.

But on the last Sunday of November, the Minnesota defense had its way with quarterback Jim Harbaugh, sacking him seven times and forcing him into two fumbles that the Vikings used for scores that gave them early control.

The Bears, who came into the game as the least penalized team in the NFL with a little more than four per game, were whistled for eight.

On this day the Vikings were simply better.

"I don't feel as bad as probably a lot of people think I should," Bears coach Mike Ditka said. "Once the truck hit me, I didn't bother getting up. I just lay there and watched."

"There is not a whole lot Mike Ditka could have done today," Harbaugh said following his first start in a domed stadium. "I mean, it is not like he had a uniform. We just didn't play very well, didn't execute very well in every phase of the game. There is not a lot for him to get frustrated about. It wasn't his fault."

12

MEMORABLE GAMES
1991-2006

September 1, 1991
Soldier Field
Bears 10, Vikings 6

Games between division foes had been higher-scoring affairs the previous two seasons, but on opening day in 1991 the Bears won what appeared to be a throwback game.

The Bears had not won a game by scoring as few as 10 points since beating the 49ers 10-9 three years earlier. In ten years, the Vikings had lost only one game giving up ten points, a 10-9 setback to the Eagles in 1989.

The Vikings' Chris Dishman drops a potential interception during a Monday night game against the Packers on Nov. 6, 2000. Antonio Freeman caught the ball before it hit the ground, got up and ran in for a touchdown that gave Green Bay a 26-20 victory in overtime.

This was the first game the Bears played since 1978 without Dan Hampton, their defensive leader who retired following the 1990 season. The Chicago defense repeatedly came up with big plays to keep the Vikings from scoring.

A pair of interceptions by strong safety Markus Paul ended two drives, and another by cornerback Donnell Woolford after Richard Dent pressured the quarterback set up an insurance field goal in the fourth quarter by Kevin Butler.

Later, with a 10-6 lead, the Bears defense was called on to stop a Vikings drive that had advanced to the Bears' 13 with 1:13 left. On third down and one, Vikings quarterback Wade Wilson had a pass tipped that was intended for tight end Steve Jordan. Paul was there to make his second pick.

"Markus Paul played an excellent football game," coach Mike Ditka said after the game. "He made two great interceptions. Steve McMichael made the play. I mean, he tipped the ball. But Markus made a great play on the first interception."

Without Hampton, McMichael and William Perry were forced to play more snaps without rotating.

"I am proud of the way the defense bowed their neck up at the goal line," McMichael said in a *Chicago Tribune* story the following day. "We turned them back three times. That's something special."

October 6, 1991
Soldier Field
Lions 24, Vikings 20

The Lions had opened the season with a 45-0 loss to the Redskins in Washington. Remarkably, they bounced back from that defeat and won their next four games, beating division rival Green Bay to begin the streak.

But the streak appeared to be coming to an end against the Vikings, who held a 20-3 lead early in the fourth quarter.

Then, lightning struck. Rodney Peete started the comeback by throwing a 68-yard touchdown pass to Robert Clark with 8:10 remaining. Looking for a quick hit, Detroit successfully executed an onside kick, which Derek Tennell recovered.

Almost four minutes later, the Lions pulled to 20-17 following a 16-yard touchdown pass from Peete to Willie Green.

The Lions kicked away this time and held the Vikings on downs, forcing a punt. Taking over on its 28, Detroit marched 72 yards, scoring the winning touchdown with 36 seconds remaining on a 15-yard run by Barry Sanders.

"I coached in a lot of games, I played in a lot of games, but that fourth quarter by this total team is the best football I've been associated with in my life," an ebullient Wayne Fontes said after the game. "When they ask me someday about the things I remember, I'll remember this comeback."

Going into the game, the Vikings had won eight of the previous nine games with the Lions. But the comeback win on this day started a modest three-game winning streak for Detroit versus Minnesota.

Pontiac Silverdome
November 28, 1991
Lions 16, Bears 6

Thanksgiving was indeed a special day for these two Black and Blue teams playing a game with first place at stake.

The Bears came into the game with a 9-3 record; the Lions were a game behind at 8-4 and looking to atone for a 20-10 loss at Soldier Field earlier in the season.

The Bears figured if they stopped Barry Sanders, they'd win. Sanders was held to 62 yards on 19 carries, but Chicago turned the ball over six times, four on interceptions by quarterback Jim Harbaugh.

Harbaugh also threw an incomplete pass intended for running back Neal Anderson on fourth and goal from the one with the

Bears down, 13-6. Had Anderson caught it, the score would have been nullified because Anderson had been out of bounds, then came back onto the field.

The Lions also struggled on offense but did enough to squeeze out a win and move into a tie for first place with three games remaining. They'd eventually win the division with a 12-4 record, one game in front of the Bears.

The highlight of this game was a confrontation on the sidelines between Ditka and defensive end Richard Dent, who had been challenging the officials on a call. Ditka didn't care for that and got in his player's face.

Bears middle linebacker Mike Singletary tried being peacemaker after the game.

"It's not anybody's fault. But whenever a player talks, he's wrong," Singletary told the *Chicago Tribune* after the game. "I know that and Richard knows that. I know he's frustrated when he sees calls that should be going the other way. It's frustrating for everybody. But we have to be quiet. There are only so many coaches, and there is definitely only one head coach. We have 47 players, and that's the way it's supposed to be.

"I mean, a coach shouldn't have to argue with any player. He shouldn't have to go through all of that. It breaks up the continuity of what we're trying to do. But I understand why Richard was upset. At the same time, we just can't do that.

"The ref really was getting upset. And I think that if Richard had said one more thing, he would have thrown a flag, because he had told him to keep quiet and that wasn't happening."

December 19, 1993
Milwaukee County Stadium
Vikings 21, Packers 17

Different team, same result.

Jim McMahon, who beat the Packers for so many years

when he was with the Bears, did it again, this time with the Vikings. McMahon improved his record as a starter to 10-1 over the Packers by throwing three touchdown passes to keep Green Bay from locking up a playoff berth and the Vikings in the playoff picture.

"We could win this thing yet," McMahon told a reporter from the *Chicago Tribune* after the game. "Wouldn't that tick them off? It's nice beating the Packers twice, and the Bears."

Both teams eventually made the playoffs, along with the Lions.

"This is the kind of game we envisioned when we brought Jim in here," Minnesota coach Dennis Green said after the game.

The victory gave Green a 4-0 record against Packers coach Mike Holmgren. The two were assistants together on Bill Walsh's staff in San Francisco.

"Right now they have our number; it's very painful," Green Bay running back Edgar Bennett said.

The Packers had a chance with just over a minute left, getting the ball back on the Minnesota 47. But Brett Favre's first pass was intercepted, ensuring another loss to Minnesota.

"That jinx stuff and all of that is a bunch of bull," said Favre, who couldn't explain it. "Frustrating."

September 4, 1994
Lambeau Field
Packers 16, Vikings 10

Holmgren finally beat the Vikings and Green, ending a four-game losing streak against his former coaching mate with the San Francisco 49ers.

But Holmgren had more on his mind than beating the Vikings the day before when Packers All-Pro receiver Sterling Sharpe didn't show up to practice because of a contract dispute. Later on Saturday, the Packers announced that Sharpe could miss the season. The sides worked out an agreement before the game and Sharpe caught a touchdown to help the Packers open the NFL's 75th season with a win.

"Say what you want; those types of things are distractions," Holmgren said after the game. "You try to battle through or ignore or deal with it the best way you can. We're all human. I applaud the players. They played hard. They didn't let it bother them too much. I was probably the one it bothered."

When Sharpe didn't show up to practice, Favre criticized him. But the two were on the same page on Sunday and Favre even helped on a reverse when he delivered a block that enabled Sharpe to gain eight yards.

"He played his butt off, and I have no grudges against him because I threw the ball to him," Favre said.

Favre was fortunate to have Sharpe and not Minnesota's receivers, who combined to drop six balls, one fewer than Sharpe caught. That ruined the debut of Warren Moon as the Vikings' quarterback. He threw three interceptions and failed to get his team into the end zone. The Vikings' only touchdown was scored by defensive end James Harris, who scored after picking up a fumble by Favre.

October 20, 1994
Minneapolis Metrodome
Vikings 13, Packers 10 (overtime)

This was a throwback Black and Blue game, dominated by the defenses and won by the team whose only touchdown came on a defensive play.

This was also the first time Favre didn't finish a game because of injury. He suffered a hip pointer in the first half and was replaced by Mark Brunell, who guided the Packers to a touchdown in which he scored on a five-yard run that gave his team a 10-7 lead just before halftime.

Brunell and the Packers were 17 seconds from a victory before

Minnesota's Fuad Reveiz kicked a 29-yard field goal to send the game into overtime.

The Vikings won the toss and got the ball first in the extra session. Moon completed passes of eight and nine yards to put Reveiz in position to win the game with a 27-yard field goal.

Minnesota's only touchdown came in the first quarter when cornerback Anthony Parker picked up a fumble by teammate James Harris, who lost the ball after intercepting a Favre pass. It was Minnesota's fourth defensive touchdown of the season.

"We didn't make many plays on offense. We made a lot on defense," Vikings coach Dennis Green said. "They didn't make many offensive plays, either, Sterling Sharpe included. But they made a lot on defense."

"Classic Black and Blue Division game," Vikings linebacker Jack Del Rio told reporters after the game.

There was one play in which Packers defensive end Reggie White threw receiver Cris Carter into Warren Moon and eventually chased the Vikings quarterback down for a 15-yard sack.

This was also one of those border battles where it seemed at times that were more Packers fans in the Metrodome than Minnesota fans.

"Some new guys on our bench were asking, 'Is this our stadium?'" Parker said.

December 1, 1994
Minneapolis Metrodome
Vikings 33, Bears 27 (overtime)

The Vikings ended a three-game losing streak in spectacular fashion.

In overtime, following a missed 40-yard field goal by Chicago's usually reliable Kevin Butler, Moon and Cris Carter hooked up on a 65-yard touchdown play to put a sudden end to an entertaining Thursday night matchup of teams battling for a division title.

Moon and Carter had discussed the play near the end of regulation. When they finally got the ball, Carter ran a "shoot" route, running to the flat and then turned up field when he saw an opening.

"We felt he would be wide open," Moon said.

"I knew the game was over," Carter said.

Carter outran Bears safety Shaun Gayle into the end zone. It was his ninth catch of the game and 102nd of the season.

"It's just one of those things," Gayle told reporters after the game. "The guys played really hard. You just have to give credit to the Vikings. They scored when they had to."

The Vikings were trailing 24-19 when Del Rio came up with a fumble by Lewis Tillman at the Bears' 15-yard line with just over six minutes remaining in regulation.

On fourth and goal from the one, Moon threw a touchdown pass to Carter, and the Vikings then successfully completed a two-point conversion for a 27-24 lead.

Butler kicked a field goal that sent the game into overtime.

The outcome left both teams tied for first with 8-5 records. All four Black and Blue teams would make the playoffs that season.

November 5, 1995
Minneapolis Metrodome
Vikings 27, Packers 24

In Green Bay, it's known as the T.J. Rubley game.

The Metrodome had turned into a House of Horrors for Holmgren, who lost his fourth straight game in the facility, and his third straight in the final moments.

In this one, Favre suffered a badly sprained ankle and had to leave a game due to injury for just the second time since becoming a starter. The first time had been the previous year in the same facility.

Ty Detmer, his backup, went down, which forced Holmgren to bring in Rubley, a third-stringer who hadn't played a game in two years.

After this one, he would never play another for the Packers.

The score was knotted at 24-24 with just over a minute to play. The Packers faced a third down at the Vikings 38, needing a foot for a first down. Kicker Chris Jacke already had kicked three field goals, including one from 50 yards. All he needed was a couple more yards.

The play Holmgren sent in to Rubley was a quarterback sneak. But when Rubley noticed a safety moved up, he called an audible.

He rolled right but within seconds, several Vikings defenders were bearing down on him. Looking in the direction of Mark Ingram and Antonio Freeman, Rubley erroneously threw across his body into traffic. There was only one guy who possibly could make that throw and he was on the bench, with a sprained ankle.

The pass was intercepted by linebacker Jeff Brady, a former Packer.

"I called a quarterback sneak," Holmgren said. "He changed the play. He thought he had the choice."

With 50 seconds left from his own 28, Moon, the Vikings' quarterback, completed passes of 23 and 22 yards to Jake Reed and eventually got his team to the Green Bay 22. Fuad Reveiz then came out and booted a 47-yard field goal to give the Vikings another win over the Packers.

"I made a mistake and compounded it," Rubley told reporters after the game. "It probably ended up costing us."

It cost Rubley his job. He was released the following day.

November 12, 1995
Lambeau Field
Packers 35, Bears 28

During his four seasons as Packers quarterback, Favre had displayed enough flashes of brilliance to justify general manager Ron Wolf using a first-round draft pick to trade for him in 1992.

But on this day, with first place on the line against the Bears, Favre not only turned in one of the very finest performances of his career but one of his most courageous.

The previous week he had severely sprained his left ankle on the Astroturf against the Vikings. For much of the week there was doubt about Favre's status for the game. Even after he saw Favre take a handful of snaps in practice the Friday before the game, Holmgren, Green Bay's fourth-year coach, wasn't sure his quarterback would be able to play.

On the day of the game, Favre's ankle was wrapped as tight as it could be. Lacking his usual mobility, Favre completed 25 of 33 passes for 336 yards and five touchdowns. The five touchdown passes tied a franchise record.

The Packers needed every one of those to beat the Bears and take control of the Black and Blue.

"The things that I do well, improvise, make things happen, I've never really had to play a game where I just had to sit in there and play a control game," Favre told reporters after the game. "Before the game, me and several players were saying that this was as nervous as we had been in years, probably dating back to college.

"It was such a big game, against the Bears, with first place up for grabs and I'd been hurt all week and didn't know if I was going to come back and play. It was kind of a buildup process."

His touchdown passes ranged from one to 44 yards. Running back Edgar Bennett and wide receiver Robert Brooks caught two each and running back Dorsey Levens caught the other.

"Nothing he does surprises me, good or bad," Holmgren said after the game about Favre.

In the visiting dressing room, the Bears had doubts about how bad Favre's ankle was, and they weren't lavish in their praise.

"You guys can talk about Favre all you want," Bears linebacker Vinson Smith said to reporters.

"He's a good player, OK? Is that what you want to hear? He's not Troy Aikman."

September 22, 1996
Minneapolis Metrodome
Vikings 30, Packers 21

The Packers were lucky they only played one game a year at the Metrodome. Had they played more, maybe they never would have won the Super Bowl.

For the fifth straight year under Holmgren, the Packers continued to struggle under the bubble in Minneapolis.

It didn't matter that the Packers came into the game with a 3-0 record and an average winning margin of 29.7 points per game. For one week, they were not the king of the Black and Blue, Minnesota was.

The Vikings, also 3-0 and not expected to do much in 1996, overcame a 21-17 deficit in the third quarter and took the lead for good on a 37-yard touchdown run by running back Robert Smith. Dennis Green, who improved his personal record over Holmgren to 7-2, used the no-respect ploy with his team the week of the game.

"I said, 'People are saying Green Bay is number one. They're not saying it's Dallas or San Francisco. They're saying we're about number ten. That's a good matchup,' Green told his troops. "I'm not sure who's number one now."

Led by defensive tackle John Randle, who had two sacks and forced Brett Favre into two of his three fumbles, the Vikings finished with seven sacks. On offense, they controlled the ball and ran 27 more plays (76 to 49) than the Packers. By the end of the game, the Green Bay defense couldn't catch its breath.

"They weren't prepared to play that kind of game," Smith said. "They had easy going in the second half (of earlier games) and didn't have to play a full 60 minutes."

The Vikings lost the following week to the Giants, and after a win against Carolina, fell out of the division race with four straight losses. The Packers, who won the Black and Blue with a 13-3 record, gained payback in the final week of the season with a 38-10 whipping of the Vikings at Lambeau.

October 12, 1997
Soldier Field
Packers 24, Bears 23

Bears coach Dave Wannstedt rolled the dice at the end of the game, and although his gamble failed, his call was respected in both locker rooms.

The Bears scored a potentially tying touchdown with 1:54 remaining on a 22-yard pass from Erik Kramer to Chris Penn.

During the drive, the Bears' coaching staff decided to go for a two-point conversion if they scored the touchdown.

The Packers were 4-2, the Bears 0-6. It's not like the season hung in the balance.

So when Penn's touchdown pulled the Bears within 24-23, the decision was made to try to take the lead.

The Bears went with a swing pass to running back Raymont Harris, a somewhat risky play. But Kramer overthrew his teammate and the Packers held on for the win.

"It would have been surprising if their situation was different, if they weren't 0-6," Packers center Frank Winters told reporters after the game. "It was a gutsy call by Dave (Wannstedt). He needed a win bad."

Bears players supported their coach.

"It is a tough call," Kramer said. "I'm glad I didn't have to make it, but I like the aggressive nature of going for it. If you (get it), it looks great."

"What did we have to lose?" asked receiver Curtis Conway. "We had to go for it. That was the best call all game."

Earlier in the quarter, the Bears gambled on a fourth and goal from the one when Kramer tried scoring a touchdown to tie the game with a quarterback sneak. He was stopped, although at first it appeared he scored.

"I can definitely say I was across," Kramer said. "The problem was I was lying on top of a couple linemen and I got pushed back."

After the game, Wannstedt was not second-guessing himself on the two-point call.

"Would I do it again? Definitely," he said.

October 6, 1998
Lambeau Field
Viking 37, Packers 24

Several days before the Packers and Vikings would match unbeaten records in a Monday night game at Lambeau Field, Holmgren had this to say about Vikings receiver Randy Moss, a rookie who was off to an incredible start to his NFL career.

"I just hope he doesn't kill us," Holmgren said during a press conference.

The Packers, who had played in the two previous Super Bowls and had won three consecutive Black and Blue Division titles going into the 1998 season, accomplished a lot of that because of how they took care of business on their home turf.

Green Bay hadn't lost at Lambeau since the first game of the 1995 season and entered the matchup against its division rival with a 25-game home winning streak, just two short of the league record established by the Miami Dolphins from 1971-74. The Vikings had been a thorn in the Packers' side during the 1990s, the only division team with any considerable success against them during the Brett Favre era.

While Favre had lost his share of games to Minnesota away from Lambeau, he hadn't lost to them at Lambeau since taking over the starting quarterback job.

That changed on a rainy, muddy night in front of a national television audience, and it was because Moss helped drive a stake through the Packers' heart.

Moss caught five passes for 190 yards, including two for touchdowns of 52 and 44 yards as the Vikings decisively beat Green Bay, sending a message that there was a new sheriff in the Black and Blue. And this was a thumping. The Vikes had a 37-10 lead before giving up a couple of fourth-quarter touchdowns.

"The guy's for real, and they find ways to get him the ball," Packers cornerback Tyrone Williams said of Moss after the game.

The Vikings beat the Packers in all facets of the game. Doug Pederson, Green Bay's backup quarterback suffered a broken jaw and Packers safety LeRoy Butler badly sprained an ankle.

The Packers' defense had allowed 230 yards per game through the first quarter of the season. In this game the Vikings had 330 by halftime before finishing with 545 yards. Randall Cunningham, the veteran of 13 NFL seasons, completed 20 of 31 passes for 442 yards and four touchdowns.

"It's unbelievable," Boomer Esiason said during the Monday night telecast, probably echoing the thoughts of viewers around the country. "He just throws it up there for these guys. This is like a circus out here."

"It was the greatest night of my career," Cunningham said.

The other Minnesota receivers also contributed. Cris Carter caught eight balls for 119 yards and Jake Reed had four receptions for 89 yards and one touchdown.

"We knew the only way to beat Green Bay was to keep putting it up," said Brian Billick, then Minnesota's offensive coordinator. "We took advantage of our receivers. You could see their dilemma: They couldn't get that extra help to Randy. I mean, how do you leave Carter and Reed to do that?"

The Vikings went on to win the division with a 15-1 record. The Packers wouldn't win another Black and Blue title until 2002.

Moss's domination had a significant impact on Packers general manager Ron Wolf. The following spring he used his first three draft picks on cornerbacks in an attempt to shut down Minnesota's passing attack.

November 7, 1999
Lambeau Field
Bears 14, Packers 13

The Bears entered the 159th meeting versus their bitter rival with a ten-game losing streak against the Packers. They also were carrying heavy hearts because six days earlier, Walter Payton, the running back who had given his heart and soul to the Bears and the city of Chicago during a 13-year career in which he became the NFL's all-time leading rusher, died following a battle with liver cancer.

The week had been difficult for the Bears and anyone who knew Payton, one of the game's most fierce competitors and genuinely decent people.

Before leaving for Green Bay the day before the game, the team attended a memorial service for Payton at Soldier Field. At the end of the service, thousands of fans who had gathered in tribute to Payton shouted in unison, "Beat Green Bay. Beat Green Bay."

The next day, the Bears did, and some probably believed Payton was there to help.

The Packers missed an extra point after one of their two touchdowns. At the end of the game, Packers kicker Ryan Longwell lined up for a 28-yard field goal attempt after Brett Favre had driven the Packers into position to win the game.

As Longwell booted the ball, Chicago's Bryan Robinson leaped like never before and blocked the kick to snap the losing streak to the Packers and give the Bears their first win at Lambeau since 1992.

"I think Walter Payton actually picked me up, because I know I can't jump that high," Robinson said.

Added coach Dick Jauron, "We've got to believe (Walter Payton) had a hand in the final play."

The Bears rushed for a season-high 162 yards, with four players sharing the load. They did it by grinding it out the way Payton did as a player. The Bears wore a patch with Payton's number 34 as a tribute to the fallen hero.

"We've got the patch on our chests and everybody's saying to themselves, 'There's no way we're going to lose this game,'" running back James Allen said. "We showed today through all the ups and downs that we stuck together, and through the tragedy, we found some happiness. And that's bringing us together, bringing the city of Chicago together, bringing ex-Bears and current Bears together. That's the impact Walter had on everybody."

The victory was unlikely because the Bears entered the game without starting quarterback Shane Matthews and then lost backup Cade McNown early in the game to a knee injury. Jim Miller came in and finished the game.

"We don't want to use Walter Payton's death in a cheap fashion," Miller said. "This game was not won for Walter Payton, but I will say this. If everybody on our team plays with the effort that 34 played with, I'll guarantee we would never lose a game."

November 6, 2000
Lambeau Field
Packers 26, Vikings 20 (overtime)

Playing in a light rain and on a muddy track at Lambeau Field, Packers receiver Antonio Freeman scored one of the most remarkable touchdowns in team history.

The Packers faced a third and four at the Vikings 43 on their first possession of the extra period. Favre decided to go deep with Freeman as the intended target. What happened in the next few seconds will be talked about time and again by all who saw it.

Freeman slipped and fell, apparently out of the play. The ball went into the hands of Minnesota cornerback Chris Dishman, who had possession for a second before dropping it. Lying on the ground, the ball dropped to Freeman, bouncing off his left arm before he gained control by pulling the pigskin to his chest.

Freeman got up, and since he had not been touched by a Vikings player, ran into the end zone to give the Packers a victory on *Monday Night Football.*

"As I rolled back, I got an early Christmas gift, I guess," Freeman said. "Hey, who said football was all skill? Tonight, we got our lucky bounce."

The Packers had been struggling during Mike Sherman's first year as coach and entered the game with a 3-5 record against the Vikings, who were leading the division with a 7-1 mark.

After the game, Sherman was asked if the Packers had benefited from a miraculous play.

"No, I wouldn't call it a miracle," Sherman said. "I'd call it a happy moment. It was an even game and we made a play, a very special play, at the end. It's a great win."

One which the Packers were fortunate to get. They were outgained in total yardage, 407-298, but the Vikings committed five turnovers, which kept the game close.

November 22, 2001
Pontiac Silverdome
Packers 29, Lions 27

The Lions sent many of the 77,000 who attended the final Thanksgiving Day game at the Silverdome home early after falling behind 29-13.

Those who stayed witnessed a valiant comeback led by a rookie quarterback who came up just short against the Packers, who held on to hand Detroit its tenth straight loss of the season.

Mike McMahon was playing quarterback in place of Lions' starter Charlie Batch, whose injured groin and ineffective play sent him to the bench. With six minutes to play, McMahon was sacked on third down, but a defensive holding penalty on cornerback Mike McKenzie gave the Lions new life.

On fourth and four, McMahon hit Johnnie Morton for nine yards. Later, McMahon was sacked on fourth down but the Lions kept the ball because Green Bay's Vonnie Holliday was called for a facemask penalty. On fourth and ten, he found Anderson for 14 yards. On fourth and seven, McMahon was sacked, but a facemask penalty on the Packers allowed the Lions to keep the ball. That set up Lamont Warren's one-yard touchdown run with 1:17 to play.

McMahon then scrambled in for the two-point conversion that cut Green Bay's lead to 29-21.

"When McMahon was in, our inability to tackle him was the turning point in the game," Packers coach Mike Sherman said.

When Jason Hanson's onside kick was recovered by the Lions at the Packers' 31, those who remained at the Silverdome were glad they did.

McMahon faced another fourth down but threw a touchdown pass to rookie Scotty Anderson that pulled the Lions within 29-27 with ten seconds left. But the miracle comeback ended with McMahon throwing up a pass on the two-point try for a tie that didn't get near a teammate. He had scrambled to the right trying to run, before turning around and running the other direction.

"I thought I could get to the corner," McMahon said, "but guys are too fast in this league."

The Lions, who had been playing in Pontiac since 1975, moved to Ford Field in downtown Detroit in 2002.

November 2, 2003
Minneapolis Metrodome
Packers 30, Vikings 27

One of the things that makes Brett Favre special is his ability to play with pain and do absolutely anything to help his team win.

He did both in a Sunday night matchup in a place where he usually struggled. Favre entered the game with a 2-9 record (won in '97 and '00) at the Metrodome. He left with a rare win after throwing three touchdown passes despite playing with a hairline fracture on his thumb.

"Pain was there on every pass," Favre said. "If you're going to play, you suck it up. I wanted this game. . . . Considering everybody except my teammates was expecting me to play differently, I wanted to come in and prove everybody wrong."

He also proved his ability to dish out punishment. With the score tied at 20-20, he helped spring Ahman Green for a 17-yard gain with a punishing block on Vikings cornerback Denard Green. After the block, Favre bounced to his feet and pumped his fist in the air.

"That's what type of guy he is," Ahman Green said of Favre. "We're out there giving our bodies for 60 minutes. Whatever we have to do to help our teammates, Brett is going to do."

The Packers went on to score the go-ahead touchdown later in the drive.

The game served as payback for a 30-25 loss at Lambeau against Minnesota in the season opener. After that game, Vikings defensive tackle Chris Hovan referred to the Packers as a "finesse" team and not as physical as the Vikings.

"I guess they forgot we played a second game," Packers guard Marco Rivera said. "We hung it on the blackboard."

September 19, 2004
Lambeau Field
Bears 21, Packers 10

During the Brett Favre era going back to 1992, the Packers had won 20 of 24 games against the Bears, many of them blowouts. That made some question whether or not this rivalry was still worth getting excited about.

When Lovie Smith was introduced as Bears coach eight months before this game, he said he wanted to end Favre's dominance of the Packers. He said he also knew how to beat Green Bay, having been a part of four victories as an assistant coach with Tampa Bay and St. Louis.

Smith was true to his word. In his second game as Chicago's head coach, he watched his team dominate the Packers, jumping out to a 21-3 lead by the third quarter that silenced the Packer faithful at Lambeau Field.

"I bet it's more of a rivalry now than it was on Saturday," Bears quarterback Rex Grossman said.

Thomas Jones rushed for 152 yards, leading a Chicago rushing attack that gained 182 yards. Favre threw for 252 yards and a score but he was intercepted twice. The Bears scored one of their touchdowns when linebacker Brian Urlacher stripped Ahman Green of the ball and safety Mike Brown scooped it up and ran 95 yards for a touchdown that gave the Bears a 14-3 lead just before halftime.

"I made statements about the rivalry, and my team backed me up quite a bit with their effort," Smith said after the game.

"We tried using everything," Smith said of his motivational tactics. "We talked about the streak and all the national media calling us cupcakes. But really, deep down inside, it came down to we came up here and thought we could win the football game."

There were some in the Packers' locker room who felt Urlacher might be getting preferential treatment for being a star. On Brown's fumble return, he pushed Favre at the 20 but a flag wasn't thrown. Later, it appeared he slipped while covering tight end Bubba Franks, who caught a touchdown pass that was called back because he was called for pushing off on Urlacher.

"We can't say too much about calls because the league comes down on us," fullback William Henderson said. "They'll give us that courtesy phone call or letter about the bad calls. But what can you do?"

December 25, 2005
Lambeau Field
Bears 24, Packers 17

In the long history of these two franchises, neither had played on Christmas. It wound up being a more memorable day for the Bears, who jumped out to a 24-3 lead and clinched their first division title after some preseason publications had predicted a last-place finish.

Chicago started the season 1-3, but then turned things around with a defense that was being compared to the one on the Super Bowl XX champion team.

This victory gave the Bears an 11-4 record. They eventually finished 11-5 and, after a first-round bye, lost in the NFC semifinals to the Carolina Panthers.

"It says a lot about people who make predictions," defensive end Adewale Ogunleye said in a Chicago Tribune story.

"It's everybody's guess. It was an insult to me (calling the Bears) the 32nd team in the country. You had San Francisco, who hadn't done anything, and you put them in front of us."

The Packers also had been put in front of the Bears. This would be a long season for Brett Favre and company. After a 4-12 record, coach Mike Sherman, who had led the team to three straight division championships (2002-04), was fired.

Favre threw four interceptions, including one by Lance Briggs, who returned it ten yards for a touchdown that gave Chicago a 17-point lead late in the third quarter.

Making his first start in 15 months, quarterback Rex Grossman completed 11 of 23 passes for 166 yards and one touchdown with one interception. Running back Thomas Jones rushed for 105 yards on 25 attempts.

13

PLAYOFF GAMES

All four teams went into the final weekend with a scenario in which they could win the division title. In the end, the Vikings did with a 10-6 record, followed by the Packers, Lions and Bears, who all finished 9-7.

In the playoffs, the Packers hosted and beat the Lions while the Vikings hosted and lost to the Bears. Both the Packers and Bears lost the following week.

Only two other times have Black and Blue teams played each other in the postseason.

Green Bay's Michael Hawthorne sacks Minnesota quarterback Daunte Culpepper during a playoff game in Green Bay in January, 2005.

January 8, 1994
Pontiac Silverdome
Packers 28, Lions 24

This was the first playoff game between Black and Blue teams. This also was Brett Favre's first post-season experience and the Packers' first time back in the playoffs in 11 seasons, while the Lions were returning for the first time since advancing to the NFC title game following the 1991 campaign.

The Lions jumped out to a 17-7 lead on a 15-yard interception return by Robert Jenkins, who picked off a pass by Favre in the third quarter. But Favre came back and threw his second touchdown pass to Sterling Sharpe to cut the Lions' lead to 17-14. Then, near the end of the quarter, Packers rookie safety George Teague had the biggest play of his career by returning an interception thrown by Erik Kramer 101 yards for a touchdown. Instead of the Lions going in for a touchdown and a ten-point lead, the Packers bolted to a 21-17 lead.

Teague ran down the left sideline escorted by several teammates.

"I don't know if you saw me running down the sidelines with him," Packers coach Mike Holmgren joked after the game. "A big, big play. Maybe the play of the game."

It turned out to be the play of the third quarter. The Lions came back and took a 24-21 lead on a five-yard run by Derrick Moore in his only carry of the game. Barry Sanders, who did everything but score, rushed 27 times for 189 yards.

Then Favre provided the Packers with what Holmgren later called their "Play of the Year."

On second down at the Lions' 40, Favre dropped back, scrambled to his left and suddenly saw Sterling Sharpe open in the end zone, but on the right side. Didn't matter. Favre threw across his body to Sharpe, who gathered in his third touchdown of the day as the Packers came back for an important playoff victory.

They lost the next week to Dallas. But two years later they were in the NFC title game and the year after that won the Super

Bowl. Maybe things wouldn't have happened that way had Favre not made his play.

"Again, it's one of those things when you think you're out of it and suddenly you're in it," former Packers General Manager Ron Wolf recalled years later. "Suddenly you're playing another week. It was just a great, great feeling."

Years later, former Lions linebacker Chris Spielman, who was on the field when Favre threw the pass, marveled at the quarterback's athleticism.

"He's running left and he throws across his body across the field," Spielman said. "Those were the kind of plays we came to expect from him."

December 31, 1994
Lambeau Field
Packers 16, Lions 12

The year before, the teams met in the playoffs in the sterile Pontiac Silverdome.

This time it was at Lambeau Field on New Year's Eve. Rain and snow that fell before the game turned Lambeau into a mud pit, the perfect setting for a playoff battle between two old rivals.

The previous year's victory, delivered on Favre's remarkable pass to Sharpe, came despite a 169-yard rushing effort by Sanders, who had turned into the NFL's most dangerous back.

This time, the Packers built a game plan to stop Sanders. Boy, did they ever.

The Packers played eight men near the line of scrimmage for the entire game, watching Sanders's every move. Fritz Shurmur, finishing his first year as Packers' defensive coordinator, put defensive end Reggie White at tackle, which confused the Lions in their blocking schemes. Sanders carried 13 times and was held to a career-low minus-one yard. Sanders was the type of runner who could be stopped for little or no gain several times, but then break a team's back with a 60- or 70-yard burst. But the Packers' game plan made sure he was shadowed every step he took. In the muck and snow at Lambeau, footing was treacherous and he was never able to get that burst he was known for.

Other Lions backs didn't do any better. Detroit finished with minus-four yards on the ground, a playoff record for fewest rushing yards. Shurmur, who was from Wyandotte, Michigan, just downriver from Detroit, played ball at Albion (Michigan) College. He replaced Ray Rhodes, a respected coordinator popular among the players who took a head-coaching job with the Eagles. Shurmur butted heads with some of his players during his first year, but there was no doubt he earned a lot of respect for designing a game plan that stopped Sanders.

"Fritz Shurmur coached against Barry Sanders many times," recalled Bob McGinn, the Packers' beat reporter for the *Milwaukee Journal Sentinel*. "Often, he was red-faced after games when Sanders would have a huge day. The one thing that Fritz always preached to his players was to take a shot at him. In other words, don't wait. If Sanders was coming your way, run up and go for the tackle. If you miss, you miss. But at least you took a chance and at least made Sanders make an evasive move that might make him easier for the next guy to tackle.

"Shurmur moved Reggie White from his normal left end position to tackle for almost the entire game. It messed up the Lions' blocking combinations. That, combined with a slow field, led to a minus-one total for Sanders, the lowest of his six-year career to that point. If anyone questioned how well Shurmur would fare as the first-year replacement for Ray Rhodes, this game answered that."

"That, I think is one of the most under-appreciated performances by a defense," Spielman said. "What did they hold Barry to, minus how many yards? It was an incredible performance by their defense."

Despite that defensive dominance, the Packers held a tenuous 16-10 lead when the Lions drove to the Packers' 11 in the final moments. But the defense rose to the challenge one more time and got the ball back four plays later, holding the Lions on downs. Green Bay took a safety rather than punt in the final seconds and won, 16-12.

Players were covered in mud and the defenses dominated, giving the fans a game that was pure throwback Black and Blue. Twenty-nine years earlier in the 1965 NFL championship game, the Packers held the great Jim Brown to 50 yards in similar conditions in a 23-12 win. Holding a runner of Sanders's ilk to negative yardage might be one of the great defensive efforts ever by any team.

"It has to be," Wolf said years later. "If somebody were to tell you that you were going to be able to do that you'd have the person committed.

"As running backs go, certainly in our time we didn't play a better running back anywhere, anytime, and that includes the guy in Dallas," Wolf said of former Cowboys back Emmitt Smith, the NFL's all-time leading rusher. "But to be able to do that just speaks volumes for the job Fritz Shurmur did as a coach. There's a guy who will never get his due, but he did that game."

January 1, 1995
Minneapolis Metrodome
Bears 35, Vikings 18

Twice during the regular season the Vikings defeated the Bears, the first time by 28 points and the second time in overtime when the Bears could have won in regulation had Kevin Butler not missed a chip-shot field goal.

The Vikings won the Black and Blue with a 10-6 record behind a strong defensive line that had allowed a league-low 68 yards rushing per game. The Bears had quarterback issues all season.

But on the first day of a new year, Steve Walsh survived a shaky start and led the Bears to an upset win before a shocked crowd at the Metrodome.

Walsh, originally signed as a backup to Erik Kramer, was 8-3 as a starter during the regular season. But he struggled near the end of the season and had been ineffective the year before in a 13-3 loss to New England. A win in that game would have meant a home playoff game for the Bears.

Walsh completed 15 of 23 passes for 221 yards and two touchdowns and directed touchdown drives of 80, 75, 71 and 60 yards.

Rookie running back Raymont Harris, not intimidated by a Minnesota defensive front that included All-Pro John Randle, broke the game open with a 29-yard touchdown that gave the Bears a 21-9 lead.

"I knew I hadn't been playing as well the last three weeks, but it wasn't all me," Walsh said in a *Chicago Tribune* story that appeared a day after the game. "The whole offense hadn't been playing as well. Certainly it's a confidence-builder to go out against a defense like that and put (so many) points on the board. It doesn't matter where you win, but it is a double dip to get it here against the Vikings."

January 9, 2005
Lambeau Field
Vikings 31, Packers 17

The rivals were meeting for the first time in the playoffs and a wild game was expected because the Packers had won both regular-season meetings by identical 34-31 scores.

In fact, two weeks earlier the Packers clinched the Black and Blue title and home-field advantage for the playoff game when Favre drove the Packers into position for Ryan Longwell to kick a winning field goal as time expired at the Metrodome.

The Vikings backed into the playoffs, losing seven of their final nine games to finish with an 8-8 record. Plus, they had lost 20 of their previous 22 games in outdoor stadiums. Coming into Lambeau, where the Packers always seemed to dominate, seemed like a daunting challenge.

It wasn't. Minnesota sprinted out to a 17-0 lead behind the play of Daunte Culpepper and Randy Moss. When the Packers pulled within 24-17, Moss caught a touchdown pass from Culpepper in the fourth quarter, then celebrated by pretending to moon the Packers' crowd, rubbing his backside against the goalpost for added affect.

"Just trying to have a little fun," Moss said.

Vikings center Matt Birk said the Vikings were motivated by the two previous three-point losses to the Packers and from a perceived lack of respect for their 8-8 record.

"Where else would you rather play, to come here with no pressure as the sixth seed?" Birk said. "It was a great situation for us."

Packers quarterback Brett Favre, who threw for seven touchdown passes and a total of 601 yards in the two regular-season wins over the Vikes, was intercepted four times, helping put the Packers into a hole from which they couldn't fully escape. His play and the Packers' inability to tackle the Vikings, made for a miserable one-and-done playoff scenario.

"I can handle losing, but losing the way we lost, not playing smart, was disappointing," Packers coach Mike Sherman said.

14

ALL-TIME
BLACK & BLUE TEAM

S ince 1967, thousands of players have worn the uniforms of the Chicago Bears, Detroit Lions, Green Bay Packers and Minnesota Vikings.

Coming up with an all-time Black and Blue Division team was extremely difficult. Do you choose the dirtiest players at every position? The players who rarely missed games or practice? Those who earned the most post-season honors?

Perhaps a combination of all three. The author selected his 40-man team (that was the NFL roster size in 1967) based on his research and comments made by those interviewed for the book. Call it the Black

----

Bears running back Walter Payton struts back to the huddle after a play during a Monday night game against the Packers early in the 1986 season.

and Blue Fantasy team.

Only players who were with a team when the division was officially formed in 1967 were considered.

OFFENSE

JAMES LOFTON, WR, Packers, 1978-86: A gifted receiver who broke many of Don Hutson's receiving records in Green Bay. Possessed world-class speed but also wasn't afraid to dish out punishment. "James and I had our battles," former Bears safety Gary Fencik said. "He was such a good receiver and one of the few receivers who really blocked. I came in when you could hit wide receivers anytime, anywhere. The five-yard bump rule came into play three or four years later. James and I both made a Pro Bowl and we had a discussion. He thought I was a cheap-shot artist and I thought he was a cheap-shot artist. It didn't change the way we played but I think it changed the way we thought of each other." Is in the Hall of Fame.

SAMMY WHITE, WR, Vikings, 1976-86: Averaged more yards per catch for his career (16.3) than Randy Moss, Cris Carter, Anthony Carter and Ahmad Rashad, and was more physical. "He was tougher than boot leather," former Vikings coach Bud Grant told the *Milwaukee Journal Sentinel*. "He practiced every week, played every game. He got beat up a little bit, but he was tough."

HERMAN MOORE, WR, Lions, 1991-2001: During a three-year stretch from 1995-97 caught 333 passes, including a then league-record 123 in 1995. "Herman Moore often was overshadowed by the magic of Barry Sanders," said Pat Yasinskas, pro football writer for the *Charlotte Observer*. "But the guy still put up huge numbers with Scott Mitchell and a cast of characters at quarterback."

CHARLIE SANDERS, TE, Lions, 1968-77: Brought finesse to the position, but also could battle the best of the linebackers. "I remember him, first of all, as a spectacular tight end, very acrobatic," former *Detroit News* writer Jerry Green said. "He could block." Is in the Hall of Fame.

STU VOIGT, TE, Vikings 1970-80: Epitome of a Black and Blue player. Weighed just 225 pounds and didn't back down from anyone. His nickname was Hacksaw. "Just a tough, tough guy," former Packers linebacker Dave Robinson said.

RON YARY, T, Vikings, 1968-81: Athletic, intelligent and nasty—three perfect traits for a Hall of Fame lineman. "The man had a mean streak on the field," former Vikings offensive line coach John Michels said in *Tales from the Vikings Locker Room.* "He literally wanted to destroy his opponent. He took it so personally and wanted to dismantle his opponent." Is in the Hall of Fame.

LOMAS BROWN, T, Lions, 1985-95: Played the first 11 years of an 18-year career with the Lions. Made the Pro Bowl six times in Detroit and seven overall. "He wasn't a mauler in the run game, but he was a consummate pass blocker at left tackle," retired *Milwaukee Journal Sentinel* football writer Cliff Christl recalled. "And he played 18 years in all. Any team worth anything needs a mainstay at left tackle. Brown fits the bill.

TIM IRWIN, T, Vikings 1981-93: "The guy nobody ever, ever messed with was Tim Irwin," Grant told the *Milwaukee Journal Sentinel.* "He was our cop. We had a defensive end named Doug Martin and they got in a little scrap. Martin took a swing at him and Tim grabbed him by the throat, threw him on the ground and said, 'If you ever do that again, I'll kill you.' That's the kind of guy he was."

GALE GILLINGHAM, G, Packers, 1966-74, 76: A big guard who was ahead of his time in terms of size and speed. "Maybe the best offensive lineman of the Lombardi Era, although he wasn't drafted until 1966," said Christl. "Probably belongs in the Hall of Fame, but played mostly on losing teams after Lombardi departed and endured knee problems after Dan Devine briefly switched him to defense in 1972. All in all, Gillingham was the epitome of an NFC Central guard: Dominant, mean and a rare talent."

RANDALL McDANIEL, G, Vikings, 1988-99: One of the best linemen in Vikings' history, played in 12 Pro Bowls. "If you went after Randall on the field, he'd come right at you and was ready to fight until one of you was dead," John Michels said in *Tales from the Vikings Locker Room.*

GEORGE SEALS, G, Bears, 1967-71: Switched to defensive tackle in 1969. Was tough on both sides of the ball, a real bruiser who never backed down from anyone. "There was one game when I had an interception and I was running up the field and George came and just clubbed me, knocked me to my knees," former Packer Dave Robinson said. "Four plays later, George pulled on a long trap and I got a good shot on him, put him on his back. People suddenly said we had a rivalry, really slugged it out when we played each other. People thought we had a big feud going, but George and I were friends. We'd just laugh about it."

ED FLANAGAN, C, Lions, 1968-74: Had a heated rivalry with Dick Butkus and was one of the few centers not intimidated by him. "Flanagan used to cut him," said former Lions linebacker Mike Lucci. "Flanagan was a hell of a center but not overly physically imposing, so he would go out there and cut Butkus, grab him a little bit and would block him pretty good.

JAY HILGENBERG, C, Bears, 1981-91: Undrafted out of college, but proved all the scouts wrong by making the Pro Bowl seven times. Always played with a chip on his shoulder and never forgot that he was skipped over in the draft. "I wanted to play against first-round draft choices because they get out there on that field and that first-round draft choice can't bring his press clippings, or his PR department, or his coach out there on the field with him," Hilgenberg said. " And I can go out there and make my name off him."

BRETT FAVRE, QB, Packers, 1992-present: Heading into the 2007 season, he hadn't missed a start since becoming the Packers' starting quarterback in 1992. Plays hurt, will throw a block, just a tough guy who is respected by players who played long before him. "The best football player I've ever seen, period," Larry McCarren said. "I haven't seen them all, but he's the best."

JOE KAPP, QB, Vikings, 1967-69: Led the Vikings to their first two division titles. Would rather run through people than around them. Knocked out Cleveland's Ken Houston while scoring a touchdown in the 1969 NFL championship game. "Fran Tarkenton was a scrambler but Joe Kapp was different," Robinson said. "The best word for Joe Kapp is competitor. He was a great competitor. I enjoyed playing against him."

JIM MCMAHON, QB, Bears, 1982-88; Vikings, 1993; Packers, 1995-96: Teammates loved him because he was highly competitive and would play hurt. Once after scoring a touchdown he gave the finger to Packers coach Forrest Gregg. What more needs to be said?

WALTER PAYTON, RB, Bears, 1975-87: Finished his career as the NFL's all-time rushing leader, but known as a guy who could stay on his feet while being hit over and over. "Sometimes you didn't appreciate what Walter did until you watched the highlight film at the end of the year," Fencik said. "You'd see the hits that he would take, or maybe more appropriately that he would deliver. Plus the fact that he never ran out of bounds, the pride he took in blocking and picking up blitzes, really being a complete football player." Is in the Hall of Fame.

BILL BROWN, FB, Vikings, 1967-74: Earned the nickname "Boom-Boom" for his running style. Dished out as much punishment as he took. Was a fullback at the University of Illinois, which also produced such tough guys as Ray Nitschke and Dick Butkus. Reportedly suffered four concussions, all by ramming into the goalpost on plunge plays. "He was a throwback type of player," former Vikings coach Bud Grant said.

MACARTHUR LANE, RB, Packers, 1972-74: Was a halfback but played with the mentality of a fullback. "Mac Lane would go out there against full-grown linebackers and knock them a—over tea kettle," Larry McCarren told the *Milwaukee Journal Sentinel.* "Mac Lane marched to his own drummer and nobody messed with the tune. He was one of those guys who had an aura that you just knew, 'You don't mess with this dude.'"

BARRY SANDERS, RB, Lions, 1989-98: Every team needs a breakaway threat and Sanders was one of the best. Left the game in good health after ten seasons and 15,269 yards rushing. "He may be the most elusive player ever to play the running back position," said longtime Vikings personnel man Paul Wiggin. "If you traced him it's an interesting trace because he would go minus 1, minus 2, plus 2, 60, minus 1." Is in the Hall of Fame.

DEFENSE

REGGIE WHITE, E, Packers, 1993-98: One of the more dominating defensive players in the history of the NFL. Played in 13 straight Pro Bowls. Clearly, he was blessed with special talent, but you don't dominate the way he did without being a highly competitive player,"

Cliff Christl said. "Maybe he picked his spots more with Green Bay than he ever did with Philadelphia, but he could still throw an offensive tackle around like a rag doll. His signature club move was a perfect fit for the Black and Blue Division." Is in the Hall of Fame.

ED O'BRADOVICH, E, Bears, 1967-71: Looked like a guy you wouldn't want to mess with, on the field and off. During one game against the Vikings, five guys blocked him on one play. "When the fifth one finally got me, [Dick] Butkus came up to make the tackle and got all the credit," O'Bradovich told the *Chicago Sun-Times* in 2003.

JIM MARSHALL, E, Vikings, 1961-79: Never missed a game in 20 seasons, starting in all 282 games he played. That alone gets him on the team. "Jim Marshall was the emotional leader on our ball club and Jim Marshall was a great leader," said former Vikings linebacker Wally Hilgenberg, who played 11 seasons with Marshall. "Everybody looked up to him and saw how he played with the intensity and tenacity. He had the desire to be an overachiever rather than an achiever. That was Jim Marshall. He was Mr. Viking."

ALAN PAGE, T, Bears and Vikings, 1968-81: Never missed a game during his fifteen-year career. Was the first defensive player to win the NFL's Most Valuable Player award (1971). Had incredible quickness but also strength to handle bigger offensive linemen. "Page was one of those special, special players," said Larry McCarren, the former Packers' center. "He was one of those guys, if you didn't get him blocked he would make the play." Is in the Hall of Fame.

DAN HAMPTON, T-E, Bears, 1979-90: One of the leaders of the Super Bowl XX champion team. Tireless worker. "He was an Arkansas farm boy," Cliff Christl recalled. "Woo pig sooey! What better background to prepare someone for playing in the slop and mud of Lambeau; and the Packers seemed to bring out the best in Hampton. When the Bears crushed the Packers, 61-7, in 1980, Hampton lamented that they hadn't scored 100. Anybody who could endure 10 knee operations—five on each knee—and make the Hall of Fame had to be as tough as they come."

JOHN RANDLE, T/E, Vikings, 1990-2000: Known for his eccentric behavior (he'd paint his face for games) and for trash-talking. But he backed it up by making the Pro Bowl seven times and recording ten or more sacks in eight seasons. Had a rivalry with Packers quarterback Brett Favre, but the two respected each other. Randle made a commercial in which he chased a chicken wearing a Brett Favre jersey. At the end of the commercial, he ate the chicken.

CHRIS SPIELMAN, MLB, Lions, 1988-95: Physically tough player who refused to leave the field. Once played a game after having a large mass drained from his right shoulder. His coaches asked him to sit out a week but he refused. "I approached the game that somebody was trying to take my job," he said.

DICK BUTKUS, MLB, Bears, 1965-73, and RAY NITSCHKE, Packers, 1958-72: The two go hand in hand. The toughest of the tough. Co-captains of the team. "I think of those Green Bay and Chicago teams, you've got Nitschke and Butkus, two pretty strong metaphors for what that division really represented," Fencik said. "Just tough, tough football teams that really, in most cases, relied upon a strong defense and a strong running game." Both are in the Hall of Fame.

DAVE ROBINSON, LB, Packers, 1963-72: One of the NFL's best outside linebackers during the late 1960s, earning All-Pro recognition three straight years. Tough guy who could cover. "Dave Robinson was a man, a real man" said Willie Davis, a Hall of Fame defensive end for the Packers. "He'd have tight ends begging by the end of the game."

DOUG BUFFONE, LB, Bears, 1967-79: An outside linebacker who didn't receive the recognition that Butkus did but was considered just as tough. "With Butkus and Buffone it almost was like winning didn't matter as much as them trying to be the toughest team," recalled Stu Voigt, the former Vikings' tight end. "I got to know those guys, Butkus and Buffone. They were funny guys but they had that mentality they had to be the toughest on the field."

OTIS WILSON, LB, Bears, 1980-87: Was overshadowed by Mike Singletary, although Wilson may have been the better athlete. "Wilson was the original 'Woofer,'" said Don Pierson of the *Chicago Tribune*. "Singletary told stories of having to calm him down because Otis would start telling (opposing players) what he planned to do to them and Singletary was afraid it wasn't hyperbole."

BOBBY BRYANT, CB, Vikings, 1968-80: Played at around 170 pounds but could dish out punishment and take it. "I can tell you on two different occasions after he made a tackle he came over to me and said, 'Wally, my shoulder's out, put it back in,'" Wally Hilgenberg recalled. "And his shoulder was literally dislocated. I would jerk on it and pull it down and it would pop back into place. He would never leave the field."

VIRGIL LIVERS, CB, Bears, 1975-79: Stood just 5-feet-8 and weighed 175 pounds. Had the mentality football coaches love. "Tough little guy, so tough that after one game in which he got hit in the balls, he was standing at his locker with a towel wrapped around his waist and I asked him how he was," Don Pierson recalled. "He casually pulled up the towel and exposed a ruptured testicle that was about the size of an orange. I just about fainted."

ED SHAROCKMAN, DB, Vikings, 1967-72: The Vikings always had strong players in the secondary during the early years of the division. Sharockman was regarded as one of their toughest. "He had to play tough because he wasn't a great cover guy," Vikings scout Jerry Reichow told the *Milwaukee Journal Sentinel.* "So he tried to light you up when he had a chance."

LEROY BUTLER, S, Packers, 1990-2001: Tough, aggressive defender who made 38 interceptions and also recorded 20 sacks. Played in the Pro Bowl four times. "LeRoy Butler was the real leader of our defense when we went to the Super Bowl," said former Packers general manager Ron Wolf.

GARY FENCIK, S, Bears, 1976-87: Wasn't drafted when he finished his career at Yale. Was signed by Jim Finks and helped the Bears to Super Bowl XX. John Madden once referred to him as clean dirt, because of his toughness and Yale pedigree. "Coming out of an Ivy League school and to earn the respect of the fans (of teams) that you're playing (against) is a compliment and the epitome of how people expect players in the Black and Blue Division to play," Fencik said. "It's hard-nosed, tough, take-no-prisoners type of football. I take that as a great compliment."

DOUG PLANK, S, Bears, 1975-82: There were more talented players, but Plank's mentality was to get in the biggest hit. "It started when I was eight," Plank told the *Pittsburgh Tribune-Review* in 2006. "My mother took us out and signed us up for pee-wee football. I couldn't believe you could knock people down and get a pat on the back."

SPECIALISTS

FRED COX, K, Vikings, 1967-77: Played fullback at the University of Pittsburgh and would play that position on the Vikings' scout team during practices. Played one game with three beer cans filled with ice strapped to his lower back to alleviate pain.

BOBBY JOE GREEN, P, Bears, 1967-73: Averaged 42.6 yards during a fourteen-year career. Fit the Bears' tough-guy mentality. "Bobby Joe would hit you," Doug Buffone told the *Milwaukee Journal Sentinel*. "They made our punters go through tackling drills and everything."

APPENDIX

AWARDS, STANDINGS AND SCORES

LEAGUE MVPS

ALAN PAGE, Vikings, 1971 (Associated Press)

FRAN TARKENTON, Vikings, 1975 (Associated Press, Pro Football Writers of America)

WALTER PAYTON, Bears, 1977 (Associated Press, Pro Football Writers of America, Newspaper Enterprise Association)

WALTER PAYTON, Bears, 1985 (Newspaper Enterprise Association, Maxwell Club of Philadelphia)

BARRY SANDERS, Lions, 1991 (Maxwell Club of Philadelphia)

BRETT FAVRE, Packers, 1995 (Associated Press, Pro Football Writers of America, Sporting News, Maxwell Club of Philadelphia)

BRETT FAVRE, Packers, 1996 (Associated Press, Pro Football Writers of America, Sporting News, Maxwell Club of Philadelphia)

BRETT FAVRE, Packers, 1997 (Associated Press (tie))

BARRY SANDERS, Lions, 1997 (Associated Press (tie), Pro Football Writers of America, Sporting News, Maxwell Club of Philadelphia)

RANDALL CUNNINGHAM, Vikings, 1998 (Maxwell Club of Philadelphia)

POSTSEASON BY THE NUMBERS

SUPER BOWL APPEARANCES (9): The Vikings have the most with four. They played in Super Bowls IV, VII, VIII and X. The Packers have three: II, XXXI and XXXII. The Bears played in Super Bowls XX and XLI.

SUPER BOWL WINS (3): Super Bowl II—Packers 33, Oakland 14. Super Bowl XX—Bears 46, New England 10. Super Bowl XXXI—Packers 35, New England 31.

NFC CHAMPIONSHIP GAME APPEARANCES (17)

Vikings (8): 1969; 1973; 1974; 1976; 1977; 1987; 1998; 2000.
Bears (4): 1984; 1985; 1988; 2006.
Packers (4): 1967; 1995; 1996; 1997.
Lions (1): 1991.

OVERALL RECORD IN DIVISION GAMES

	W	L	T	Pct.
Vikings	143	91	3	.612
Packers	120	112	5	.517
Bears	108	127	2	.459
Lions	96	137	6	.412

VIKINGS

vs. Packers	41-37-1
vs. Bears	45-33-1
vs. Lions	57-21-1

PACKERS

vs. Vikings	37-41-1
vs. Bears	43-35
vs. Lions	40-36-4

BEARS

vs. Vikings	33-45-1
vs. Packers	35-43
vs. Lions	40-39-1

LIONS

vs. Vikings	21-57-1
vs. Bears	39-40-1
vs. Packers	36-40-4

DIVISION CHAMPIONSHIPS

VIKINGS (16): 1968; 1969; 1970; 1971; 1973; 1974; 1975; 1976; 1977; 1978; 1980; 1989; 1992; 1994; 1998; 2000
BEARS (9): 1984, 1985; 1986; 1987; 1988; 1990; 2001; 2005; 2006
PACKERS (8): 1967; 1972; 1995; 1996; 1997; 2002; 2003; 2004
LIONS (3): 1983; 1991; 1993
Note: There was no division champion in 1982 because of the strike; Tampa Bay won division titles in 1979, 1981 and 1999.

YEARLY STANDINGS

1967

	W	L	T	Pct.	Pts.	Opp.
Packers	9	4	1	692	352	209
Bears	7	6	1	538	229	219
Lions	5	7	2	417	260	259
Vikings	3	8	3	273	233	294

Division scores

Bears 17, Vikings 7	Vikings 10, Lions 10 (tie)
Bears 10, Vikings 10 (tie)	Lions 14, Vikings 3
Vikings 10, Packers 7	Packers 13, Bears 10
Packers 30, Vikings 27	Packers 17, Bears 13
Bears 14, Lions 3	Packers 17, Lions 17 (tie)
Bears 27, Lions 17	Packers 27, Lions 17

1968

	W	L	T	Pct.	Pts.	Opp.
Vikings	8	6	0	.571	282	242
Bears	7	7	0	.500	250	333
Packers	6	7	1	.462	281	227
Lions	4	8	2	.333	207	241

Division scores

Bears 13, Packers 10	Bears 27, Vikings 17
Packers 28, Bears 27	Bears 26, Vikings 24
Lions 23, Packers 17	Lions 42, Bears 0
Packers 14, Lions 14 (tie)	Lions 28, Bears 10
Vikings 26, Packers 13	Vikings 24, Lions 10
Vikings 14, Packers 10	Vikings 13, Lions 6

1969

	W	L	T	Pct.	Pts.	Opp.
Vikings	12	2	0	.857	379	133
Lions	9	4	1	.692	259	188
Packers	8	6	0	.571	269	221
Bears	1	13	0	.071	210	339

Division scores

Vikings 24, Lions 10	Vikings 31, Bears 0
Vikings 27, Lions 0	Vikings 31, Bears 14
Lions 13, Bears 7	Packers 17, Bears 0
Lions 20, Bears 3	Packers 21, Bears 3
Vikings 19, Packers 7	Packers 28, Lions 17
Vikings 9, Packers 7	Lions 16, Packers 10

1970

	W	L	T	Pct.	Pts.	Opp.
Vikings	12	2	0	.857	335	143
Lions	10	4	0	.714	347	202
Packers	6	8	0	.429	196	293
Bears	6	8	0	.429	256	261

Division scores

Packers 20, Bears 19	Vikings 24, Bears 0
Bears 35, Packers 17	Vikings 16, Bears 13

Lions 40, Packers 0   Lions 28, Bears 14
Lions 20, Packers 0   Lions 16, Bears 10
Packers 13, Vikings 10   Vikings 30, Lions 17
Vikings 10, Packers 3   Vikings 24, Lions 20

1971

	W	L	T	Pct.	Pts.	Opp.
Vikings	11	3	0	.786	245	139
Lions	7	6	1	.538	341	286
Bears	6	8	0	.429	185	276
Packers	4	8	2	.333	274	298

Division scores

Vikings 24, Packers 13   Vikings 16, Lions 13
Vikings 3, Packers 0   Vikings 29, Lions 10
Bears 20, Vikings 17   Packers 17, Bears 14
Vikings 27, Bears 10   Packers 31, Bears 10
Bears 28, Lions 23   Lions 31, Packers 28
Lions 28, Bears 3   Lions 14, Packers 14 (tie)

1972

	W	L	T	Pct.	Pts.	Opp.
Packers	10	4	0	.714	304	226
Lions	8	5	1	.607	339	290
Vikings	7	7	0	.500	301	252
Bears	4	9	1	.321	225	275

Division scores

Packers 20, Bears 17   Bears 13, Vikings 10
Packers 23, Bears 17   Vikings 23, Bears 10
Packers 24, Lions 23   Lions 14, Bears 0
Packers 33, Lions 7   Lions 38, Bears 24
Vikings 27, Packers 13   Vikings 34, Lions 10
Packers 23, Vikings 7   Vikings 16, Lions 14

1973

	W	L	T	Pct.	Pts.	Opp.
Vikings	12	2	0	.857	296	168
Lions	6	7	1	.464	271	247
Packers	5	7	2	.429	202	259
Bears	3	11	0	.214	195	334

Division scores

Lions 30, Bears 7   Vikings 22, Bears 13
Lions 40, Bears 7   Vikings 31, Bears 13
Vikings 23, Lions 9   Bears 31, Packers 13
Vikings 28, Lions 7   Packers 21, Bears 0
Vikings 11, Packers 3   Lions 13, Packers 13 (tie)
Vikings 31, Packers 7   Lions 34, Packers 0

1974

	W	L	T	Pct.	Pts.	Opp.
Vikings	10	4	0	.714	310	195
Lions	7	7	0	.500	256	270
Packers	6	8	0	.429	210	206
Bears	4	10	0	.286	152	279

Division scores

Bears 10, Packers 9   Vikings 11, Bears 7
Packers 20, Bears 3   Vikings 17, Bears 0
Packers 21, Lions 19   Vikings 7, Lions 6
Lions 19, Packers 17   Lions 20, Vikings 16
Vikings 32, Packers 17   Bears 17, Lions 9
Packers 19, Vikings 7   Lions 34, Bears 17

1975

	W	L	T	Pct.	Pts.	Opp.
Vikings	12	2	0	.857	377	180
Lions	7	7	0	.500	245	262
Bears	4	10	0	.286	191	379
Packers	4	10	0	.286	226	285

Division scores

Lions 27, Bears 7	Vikings 28, Bears 3
Bears 25, Lions 21	Vikings 13, Bears 9
Vikings 25, Lions 17	Bears 27, Packers 14
Lions 17, Vikings 10	Packers 28, Bears 7
Vikings 28, Packers 17	Lions 30, Packers 16
Vikings 24, Packers 3	Lions 13, Packers 10

1976

	W	L	T	Pct.	Pts.	Opp.
Vikings	11	2	1	.821	305	176
Bears	7	7	0	.500	253	216
Lions	6	8	0	.429	262	220
Packers	5	9	0	.357	218	299

Division scores

Bears 24, Packers 13	Vikings 20, Bears 19
Bears 16, Packers 10	Bears 14, Vikings 13
Packers 24, Lions 14	Vikings 10, Lions 9
Lions 27, Packers 6	Vikings 31, Lions 21
Vikings 17, Packers 10	Lions 10, Bears 3
Vikings 20, Packers 9	Bears 14, Lions 10

1977

	W	L	T	Pct.	Pts.	Opp.
Vikings	9	5	0	.643	231	227
Bears	9	5	0	.643	255	253
Lions	6	8	0	.429	183	252
Packers	4	10	0	.286	134	219
Bucs	2	12	0	.143	103	223

Division scores

Bears 30, Lions 20

Bears 31, Lions 14

Vikings 30, Lions 21

Vikings 14, Lions 7

Vikings 22, Bears 16

Bears 10, Vikings 7

Vikings 19, Packers 7

Vikings 13, Packers 6

Bears 26, Packers 0

Bears 21, Packers 10

Lions 10, Packers 6

Packers 10, Lions 9

Packers 13, Bucs 0

Vikings 9, Bucs 5

Lions 16, Bucs 3

Bears 10, Bucs 0

1978

	W	L	T	Pct.	Pts.	Opp.
Vikings	8	7	1	.531	294	306
Packers	8	7	1	.531	249	269
Lions	7	9	0	.439	290	300
Bears	7	9	0	.439	253	274
Bucs	5	11	0	.313	241	259

Division scores

Packers 24, Bears 14

Bears 14, Packers 0

Packers 13, Lions 7

Packers 35, Lions 14

Vikings 21, Packers 7

Vikings 10, Packers 10 (OT, tie)

Bears 19, Lions 0

Lions 21, Bears 17

Bucs 16, Vikings 0

Vikings 24, Bucs 7

Packers 9, Bucs 7

Packers 17, Bucs 7

Vikings 24, Bears 20   Lions 15, Bucs 7
Vikings 17, Bears 14   Lions 34, Bucs 23
Vikings 17, Lions 14   Bucs 33, Bears 19
Lions 45, Vikings 14   Bears 14, Bucs 3

1979

	W	L	T	Pct.	Pts.	Opp.
Bucs	10	6	0	.625	273	237
Bears	10	6	0	.625	306	249
Vikings	7	9	0	.438	259	337
Packers	5	11	0	.313	246	316
Lions	2	14	0	.125	219	365

Division scores

Bears 6, Packers 3   Bears 35, Lions 7
Bears 15, Packers 14   Lions 20, Bears 0
Packers 24, Lions 16   Bucs 31, Lions 16
Lions 18, Packers 13   Bucs 16, Lions 14
Vikings 27, Packers 21 (OT)   Bucs 21, Packers 10
Packers 19, Vikings 7   Bucs 21, Packers 3
Bears 26, Vikings 7   Bucs 17, Bears 13
Vikings 30, Bears 27   Bears 14, Bucs 0
Vikings 13, Lions 10
Vikings 14, Lions 7

1980

	W	L	T	Pct.	Pts.	Opp.
Vikings	9	7	0	.563	317	308
Lions	9	7	0	.563	334	272
Bears	7	9	0	.438	304	264
Bucs	5	10	1	.344	271	341
Packers	5	10	1	.344	231	371

Division scores

Bears 24, Lions 7

Bears 23, Lions 17

Lions 27, Vikings 7

Vikings 34, Lions 0

Vikings 34, Bears 14

Vikings 13, Bears 7

Packers 16, Vikings 3

Packers 25, Vikings 13

Packers 12, Bears 6 (OT)

Bears 61, Packers 7

Lions 29, Packers 7

Lions 24, Packers 3

Bears 23, Bucs 0

Bears 14, Bucs 13

Lions 24, Bucs 10

Lions 27, Bucs 14

Packers 14, Bucs 14 (OT, tie)

Bucs 20, Packers 17

Vikings 38, Bucs 30

Vikings 21, Bucs 10

1981

	W	L	T	Pct.	Pts.	Opp.
Bucs	9	7	0	.563	315	268
Lions	8	8	0	.500	397	322
Packers	8	8	0	.500	304	264
Vikings	7	9	0	.438	325	369
Bears	6	10	0	.375	253	324

Division scores

Packers 16, Bears 9

Packers 21, Bears 17

Lions 31, Packers 27

Packers 31, Lions 17

Vikings 30, Packers 13

Packers 35, Vikings 23

Vikings 24, Bears 21

Vikings 10, Bears 9

Vikings 26, Lions 24

Lions 45, Vikings 7

Bucs 21, Vikings 13

Vikings 25, Bucs 10

Bucs 21, Packers 10

Bucs 37, Packers 3

Bears 28, Bucs 10

Bucs 20, Bears 10

Bucs 28, Lions 10

Bucs 20, Lions 17

1982

	W	L	T	Pct.	Pts.	Opp.
Packers	5	3	1	.611	226	169
Vikings	5	4	0	.556	187	198
Bucs	5	4	0	.556	158	178
Lions	4	5	0	.444	181	176
Bears	3	6	0	.333	141	174

Division scores

Vikings 34, Lions 31
Lions 17, Bears 10
Bears 20, Lions 17
Packers 26, Vikings 7
Vikings 35, Bears 7

Lions 30, Packers 10
Lions 27, Packers 24
Vikings 17, Bucs 10
Bucs 23, Lions 21
Bucs 23, Lions 21

1983

	W	L	T	Pct.	Pts.	Opp.
Lions	9	7	0	.563	347	286
Packers	8	8	0	.500	429	439
Bears	8	8	0	.500	311	301
Vikings	8	8	0	.500	316	328
Bucs	2	14	0	.125	241	380

Division scores

Packers 31, Bears 28
Bears 23, Packers 21
Lions 38, Packers 14
Lions 23, Packers 20
Vikings 20, Packers 17
Packers 29, Vikings 21
Vikings 23, Bears 14
Bears 19, Vikings 13
Vikings 20, Lions 17
Lions 13, Vikings 2

Lions 31, Bears 17
Lions 38, Bears 17
Lions 11, Bucs 0
Lions 23, Bucs 0
Packers 55, Bucs 14
Packers 12, Bucs 9 (OT)
Vikings 19, Bucs 16 (OT)
Bucs 17, Vikings 12
Bears 17, Bucs 10
Bears 27, Bucs 0

1984

	W	L	T	Pct.	Pts.	Opp.
Bears	10	6	0	.625	325	248
Packers	8	8	0	.500	390	309
Bucs	6	10	0	.375	335	380
Lions	4	11	1	.281	283	408
Vikings	3	13	0	.188	276	484

Division scores

Bears 16, Lions 14

Bears 30, Lions 13

Vikings 29, Lions 28

Lions 16, Vikings 14

Bears 16, Vikings 7

Bears 34, Vikings 3

Bears 34, Bucs 14

Bears 44, Bucs 9

Bucs 21, Lions 17

Lions 13, Bucs 7 (OT)

Packers 45, Vikings 17

Packers 38, Vikings 24

Bears 9, Packers 7

Packers 20, Bears 14

Packers 41, Lions 9

Lions 31, Packers 28

Bucs 30, Packers 27 (OT)

Packers 27, Bucs 14

Bucs 35, Vikings 31

Vikings 27, Bucs 24

1985

	W	L	T	Pct.	Pts.	Opp.
Bears	15	1	0	.938	456	198
Packers	8	8	0	.500	337	355
Vikings	7	9	0	.439	346	359
Lions	7	9	0	.439	307	366
Bucs	2	14	0	.125	294	448

Division scores

Bears 23, Packers 7

Bears 16, Packers 10

Vikings 16, Bears 13

Lions 41, Vikings 21

Packers 43, Lions 10

Packers 26, Lions 23

Bears 38, Bucs 17

Bears 27, Bucs 19

Bears 24, Lions 3
Bears 37, Lions 17
Packers 20, Vikings 17
Packers 27, Vikings 17
Bears 33, Vikings 24
Bears 27, Vikings 9

Vikings 31, Bucs 16
Vikings 26, Bucs 7
Lions 30, Bucs 9
Bucs 19, Lions 16 (OT)
Packers 21, Bucs 0
Packers 20, Bucs 17

1986

	W	L	T	Pct.	Pts.	Opp.
Bears	14	2	0	.875	352	187
Vikings	9	7	0	.563	398	273
Lions	5	11	0	.313	277	326
Packers	4	12	0	.250	254	418
Bucs	2	14	0	.125	239	473

Division scores
Bears 25, Packers 12
Bears 12, Packers 10
Lions 21, Packers 14
Packers 44, Lions 40
Vikings 42, Packers 7
Vikings 32, Packers 6
Bears 23, Vikings 0
Vikings 23, Bears 7
Bears 13, Lions 7
Bears 16, Lions 13

Lions 13, Vikings 10
Vikings 24, Lions 10
Vikings 23, Bucs 10
Vikings 45, Bucs 13
Bucs 24, Lions 20
Lions 38, Bucs 17
Bears 23, Bucs 3
Bears 48, Bucs 14
Packers 31, Bucs 7
Packers 21, Bucs 7

1987

	W	L	T	Pct.	Pts.	Opp.
Bears	11	4	0	.733	356	282
Vikings	8	7	0	533	336	335
Packers	5	9	1	367	255	300
Bucs	4	11	0	.267	286	360
Lions	4	11	0	.267	269	384

Division scores

Vikings 34, Lions 19	Lions 19, Packers 16
Vikings 17, Lions 14	Packers 34, Lions 33
Bears 30, Lions 10	Bears 20, Bucs 3
Bears 27, Vikings 7	Bears 27, Bucs 26
Bears 30, Vikings 24	Bucs 23, Packers 17
Packers 23, Vikings 16	Bucs 20, Vikings 10
Packers 16, Vikings 10	Vikings 23, Bucs 17
Bears 26, Packers 24	Bucs 31, Lions 27
Bears 23, Packers 10	Lions 20, Bucs 10

1988

	W	L	T	Pct.	Pts.	Opp.
Bears	12	4	0	.750	312	215
Vikings	11	5	0	.688	406	233
Bucs	5	11	0	.313	261	350
Lions	4	12	0	.250	220	313
Packers	4	12	0	.250	240	315

Division scores

Bears 24, Packers 6	Bears 24, Lions 7
Bears 16, Packers 0	Bears 13, Lions 12
Lions 19, Packers 9	Bucs 13, Packers 10
Lions 30, Packers 14	Bucs 27, Packers 24
Packers 34, Vikings 14	Vikings 14, Bucs 13
Packers 18, Vikings 6	Vikings 49, Bucs 20
Vikings 31, Bears 7	Bears 28, Bucs 10
Vikings 28, Bears 27	Bears 27, Bucs 15
Vikings 44, Lions 17	Bucs 23, Lions 20
Vikings 23, Lions 0	Bucs 21, Lions 10

1989

	W	L	T	Pct.	Pts.	Opp.
Vikings	10	6	0	.625	351	275
Packers	10	6	0	.625	362	356
Lions	7	9	0	.438	312	364
Bears	6	10	0	.375	358	377
Bucs	5	11	0	.313	320	419

Division scores

Bears 47, Lions 27
Lions 27, Bears 17
Vikings 24, Lions 17
Vikings 20, Lions 7
Bears 38, Vikings 7
Vikings 27, Bears 16
Vikings 26, Packers 14
Packers 20, Vikings 19
Packers 14, Bears 13
Packers 40, Bears 28

Packers 23, Lions 20
Lions 31, Packers 22
Bucs 23, Packers 21
Packers 17, Bucs 16
Vikings 17, Bucs 3
Vikings 24, Bucs 10
Bucs 42, Bears 35
Bucs 32, Bears 31
Lions 17, Bucs 16
Lions 33, Bucs 7

1990

	W	L	T	Pct.	Pts.	Opp.
Bears	11	5	0	.688	348	280
Bucs	6	10	0	.375	264	367
Lions	6	10	0	.375	373	413
Packers	6	10	0	.375	271	347
Vikings	6	10	0	.375	351	326

Division scores

Bears 31, Packers 13
Bears 27, Packers 13
Packers 24, Lions 21
Lions 24, Packers 17

Lions 34, Vikings 27
Vikings 17, Lions 7
Bucs 38, Lions 21
Bucs 23, Lions 20

Packers 24, Vikings 10

Vikings 23, Packers 7

Bears 19, Vikings 16

Vikings 41, Bears 13

Bears 23, Lions 21

Lions 38, Bears 21

Bucs 23, Vikings 20 (OT)

Bucs 26, Vikings 13

Bucs 26, Packers 14

Packers 20, Bucs 10

Bears 26, Bucs 6

Bears 27, Bucs 14

1991

	W	L	T	Pct.	Pts.	Opp.
Lions	12	4	0	.750	339	295
Bears	11	5	0	.688	299	269
Vikings	8	8	0	.500	301	306
Packers	4	12	0	.250	273	313
Bucs	3	13	0	.188	199	365

Division scores

Lions 24, Vikings 20

Lions 34, Vikings 14

Bears 20, Lions 10

Lions 16, Bears 6

Bears 10, Vikings 6

Bears 34, Vikings 17

Vikings 35, Packers 21

Packers 27, Vikings 7

Bears 10, Packers 0

Bears 27, Packers 13

Lions 23, Packers 14

Lions 21, Packers 17

Bears 21, Bucs 0

Bears 27, Bucs 0

Packers 15, Bucs 13

Packers 27, Bucs 0

Lions 31, Bucs 3

Bucs 30, Lions 21

Vikings 28, Bucs 13

Vikings 26, Bucs 24

1992

	W	L	T	Pct.	Pts.	Opp.
Vikings	11	5	0	.750	374	249
Packers	9	7	0	.688	276	296
Bucs	5	11	0	.313	267	365
Bears	5	11	0	.313	295	361
Lions	5	11	0	.313	273	332

Division scores

Bears 30, Packers 10
Packers 17, Bears 3
Packers 27, Lions 13
Packers 38, Lions 10
Vikings 23, Packers 20
Vikings 27, Packers 7
Vikings 21, Bears 20
Vikings 38, Bears 10
Bears 27, Lions 24
Lions 16, Bears 3

Lions 31, Vikings 17
Vikings 31, Lions 14
Bucs 31, Packers 3
Packers 19, Bucs 14
Vikings 26, Bucs 20
Vikings 35, Bucs 7
Bears 31, Bucs 14
Bucs 20, Bears 17
Bucs 27, Lions 23
Lions 38, Bucs 7

1993

	W	L	T	Pct.	Pts.	Opp.
Lions	10	6	0	.625	298	292
Vikings	9	7	0	.563	277	290
Packers	9	7	0	.563	340	282
Bears	7	9	0	.438	234	230
Bucs	5	11	0	.313	237	376

Division scores

Bears 10, Lions 6
Lions 20, Bears 14
Lions 30, Vikings 27
Vikings 13, Lions 0
Vikings 10, Bears 7
Vikings 19, Bears 12
Vikings 15, Packers 13
Vikings 21, Packers 17
Packers 17, Bears 3
Bears 30, Packers 17

Packers 26, Lions 17
Lions 30, Packers 20
Bears 47, Bucs 17
Bucs 13, Bears 10
Bucs 27, Lions 10
Lions 23, Bucs 0
Vikings 15, Bucs 0
Bucs 23, Vikings 10
Packers 37, Bucs 14
Packers 13, Bucs 10

1994

	W	L	T	Pct.	Pts.	Opp.
Vikings	10	6	0	.625	356	314
Packers	9	7	0	.563	382	287
Lions	9	7	0	.563	357	342
Bears	9	7	0	.563	295	361
Lions	6	10	0	.375	251	351

Division scores

Packers 33, Bears 6
Packers 40, Bears 3
Packers 38, Lions 30
Lions 34, Packers 31
Packers 16, Vikings 10
Vikings 13, Packers 10
Vikings 42, Bears 14
Vikings 33, Bears 27
Vikings 10, Lions 3
Lions 41, Vikings 19

Lions 21, Bears 16
Bears 20, Lions 10
Bears 21, Bucs 9
Bears 20, Bucs 6
Packers 30, Bucs 3
Packers 34, Bucs 19
Bucs 24, Lions 14
Lions 14, Bucs 9
Vikings 36, Bucs 13
Bucs 20, Vikings 17 (OT)

1995

	W	L	T	Pct.	Pts.	Opp.
Packers	11	5	0	.688	404	314
Lions	10	6	0	.625	436	336
Bears	9	7	0	.563	392	360
Vikings	8	8	0	.500	412	385
Bucs	7	9	0	.438	238	335

Division scores

Vikings 20, Lions 10
Lions 44, Vikings 38
Lions 24, Bears 17

Packers 30, Lions 21
Lions 24, Packers 16
Bears 25, Bucs 6

Lions 27, Bears 7

Packers 38, Vikings 21

Vikings 27, Packers 24

Bears 31, Vikings 14

Bears 14, Vikings 6

Packers 27, Bears 24

Packers 35, Bears 28

Bears 31, Bucs 10

Lions 27, Bucs 24

Lions 37, Bucs 10

Bucs 20, Vikings 17 (OT)

Vikings 31, Bucs 17

Packers 35, Bucs 13

Bucs 13, Packers 10 (OT)

1996

	W	L	T	Pct.	Pts.	Opp.
Packers	13	3	0	.813	456	210
Vikings	9	7	0	.563	298	315
Bears	7	9	0	.438	283	305
Bucs	6	10	0	.375	221	293
Lions	5	11	0	.313	302	368

Division scores

Packers 37, Bears 6

Packers 28, Bears 17

Packers 28, Lions 18

Packers 31, Lions 3

Vikings 30, Packers 21

Packers 38, Vikings 10

Vikings 20, Bears 14

Bears 15, Vikings 13

Lions 35, Bears 16

Bears 31, Lions 14

Vikings 17, Lions 13

Vikings 24, Lions 22

Packers 34, Bucs 3

Packers 13, Bucs 7

Lions 21, Bucs 6

Lions 27, Bucs 0

Bucs 24, Vikings 13

Vikings 21, Bucs 10

Bears 13, Bucs 10

Bucs 34, Bears 19

1997

	W	L	T	Pct.	Pts.	Opp.
Packers	13	3	0	.813	422	282
Bucs	10	6	0	.625	299	263
Lions	9	7	0	.563	379	306

Vikings	9	7	0	.563	354	359
Bears	4	12	0	.250	263	421

Division scores

Lions 38, Vikings 15	Lions 26, Packers 15
Lions 14, Vikings 13	Packers 20, Lions 10
Lions 32, Bears 7	Bucs 24, Lions 17
Lions 55, Bears 20	Lions 27, Bucs 9
Vikings 27, Bears 24	Bucs 28, Vikings 14
Vikings 29, Bears 22	Vikings 10, Bucs 6
Packers 38, Vikings 32	Packers 21, Bucs 16
Packers 27, Vikings 11	Packers 17, Bucs 6
Packers 38, Bears 24	Bears 13, Bucs 7
Packers 24, Bears 23	Bucs 31, Bears 15

1998

	W	L	T	Pct.	Pts.	Opp.
Vikings	15	1	0	.938	556	296
Packers	11	5	0	.688	408	319
Bucs	8	8	0	.500	314	295
Lions	5	11	0	.313	306	378
Bears	4	12	0	.250	276	368

Division scores

Packers 26, Bears 20	Vikings 29, Lions 6
Packers 16, Bears 13	Vikings 34, Lions 13
Packers 38, Lions 19	Vikings 31, Bucs 7
Lions 27, Packers 20	Bucs 27, Vikings 7
Vikings 37, Packers 24	Packers 23, Bucs 15
Vikings 28, Packers 14	Bucs 24, Packers 22
Vikings 31, Bears 28	Bucs 27, Bears 15
Vikings 48, Bears 22	Bucs 31, Bears 17
Bears 31, Lions 27	Lions 27, Bucs 6
Lions 26, Bears 3	Lions 28, Bucs 25

1999

	W	L	T	Pct.	Pts.	Opp.
Bucs	11	5	0	.688	270	235
Vikings	10	6	0	.625	399	335
Lions	8	8	0	.500	322	323
Packers	8	8	0	.500	357	341
Bears	6	10	0	.375	272	341

Division scores

Lions 25, Vikings 23

Vikings 24, Lions 17

Lions 21, Bears 17

Bears 28, Lions 10

Bears 24, Vikings 22

Vikings 27, Bears 24

Packers 23, Vikings 20

Vikings 24, Packers 20

Lions 23, Packers 15

Packers 26, Lions 17

Bears 14, Packers 13

Packers 35, Bears 19

Vikings 21, Bucs 14

Bucs 24, Vikings 16

Packers 26, Bucs 23

Bucs 29, Packers 10

Lions 20, Bucs 3

Bucs 23, Lions 17

Bucs 6, Bears 3

Bucs 20, Bears 3

2000

	W	L	T	Pct.	Pts.	Opp.
Vikings	11	5	0	.688	397	371
Bucs	10	6	0	.625	388	269
Packers	8	7	0	.563	353	323
Lions	9	7	0	.565	307	307
Bears	5	11	0	.313	216	355

Division scores

Bears 27, Packers 24

Packers 28, Bears 6

Lions 31, Packers 24

Packers 26, Lions 13

Vikings 31, Lions 24

Vikings 24, Lions 17

Bucs 41, Bears 0

Bears 13, Bucs 10

Packers 26, Vikings 20 (OT)

Packers 33, Vikings 28

Vikings 30, Bears 27

Vikings 28, Bears 16

Lions 21, Bears 14

Bears 23, Lions 20

Bucs 31, Lions 10

Lions 28, Bucs 14

Bucs 20, Packers 15

Packers 17, Bucs 14 (OT)

Vikings 30, Bucs 13

Bucs 41, Vikings 13

2001

	W	L	T	Pct.	Pts.	Opp.
Bears	13	3	0	.813	338	203
Packers	12	4	0	.750	390	266
Bucs	9	7	0	.563	324	280
Vikings	5	11	0	.313	290	390
Lions	2	14	0	.125	270	424

Division scores

Vikings 31, Lions 26

Lions 27, Vikings 24

Bears 13, Lions 10

Bears 24, Lions 0

Vikings 35, Packers 13

Packers 24, Vikings 13

Bears 17, Vikings 10

Bears 13, Vikings 6

Packers 28, Lions 6

Packers 29, Lions 27

Packers 20, Bears 12

Packers 17, Bears 7

Vikings 20, Bucs 14

Bucs 41, Vikings 14

Bucs 14, Packers 10

Packers 21, Bucs 20

Bucs 20, Lions 17

Bucs 15, Lions 12

Bears 27, Bucs 24

Bears 27, Bucs 3

2002

	W	L	T	Pct.	Pts.	Opp.
Packers	12	4	0	.750	398	328
Vikings	6	10	0	.375	390	442
Bear	4	12	0	.250	281	379
Lions	3	13	0	.188	306	451

Division scores

Packers 34, Bears 21   Bears 27, Vikings 23
Packers 30, Bears 20   Vikings 25, Bears 7
Packers 37, Lions 31   Vikings 31, Lions 24
Packers 40, Lions 14   Vikings 38, Lions 36
Vikings 31, Packers 21   Lions 23, Bears 20
Packers 26, Vikings 22   Bears 20, Lions 17

2003

	W	L	T	Pct.	Pts.	Opp.
Packers	10	6	0	.625	442	307
Vikings	9	7	0	.563	416	353
Bears	7	9	0	.438	283	346
Lions	5	11	0	.313	270	379

Division scores

Vikings 23, Lions 13   Vikings 30, Packers 25
Vikings 24, Lions 14   Packers 30, Vikings 27
Bears 24, Lions 16   Packers 31, Lions 6
Lions 12, Bears 10   Lions 22, Packers 14
Vikings 24, Bears 13   Packers 38, Bears 23
Bears 13, Vikings 10   Packers 34, Bears 21

2004

	W	L	T	Pct.	Pts.	Opp.
Packers	10	6	0	.625	424	380
Vikings	8	8	0	.500	405	395
Lions	6	10	0	.375	296	350
Bears	5	11	0	.313	231	331

Division scores

Bears 21, Packers 10

Packers 31, Bears 14

Packers 38, Lions 10

Packers 16, Lions 13

Packers 34, Vikings 31

Packers 34, Vikings 31

Bears 24, Vikings 21

Vikings 27, Bears 22

Lions 20, Bears 16

Lions 19, Bears 13

Vikings 22, Lions 10

Vikings 28, Lions 27

2005

	W	L	T	Pct.	Pts.	Opp.
Bears	11	5	0	.688	260	202
Vikings	9	7	0	.556	306	344
Lions	5	11	0	.313	245	345
Packers	4	12	0	.250	298	344

Division scores

Bears 19, Packers 7

Bears 24, Packers 17

Bears 38, Lions 6

Bears 19, Lions 13

Bears 28, Vikings 3

Vikings 34, Bears 10

Vikings 23, Packers 20

Vikings 20, Packers 17

Vikings 27, Lions 14

Vikings 21, Lions 16

Lions 17, Packers 3

Packers 16, Lions 13

2006

	W	L	T	Pct.	Pts.	Opp.
Bears	13	3	0	.688	427	255
Packers	8	8	0	.500	306	344
Vikings	6	10	0	.375	282	327
Lions	3	13	0	.188	305	398

Division scores

Bears 26, Packers 0　　　　Vikings 26, Lions 17
Packers 26, Bears 7　　　　Vikings 30, Lions 20
Bears 34, Lions 7　　　　　Packers 31, Lions 24
Bears 26, Lions 7　　　　　Packers 17, Lions 9
Bears 19, Vikings 16　　　　Packers 23, Vikings 17
Bears 23, Vikings 13　　　　Packers 9, Vikings 7

SHUTOUTS

A total of 23 shutouts have been posted in intradivisional games since 1967. The Vikings have the best record, posting eight and being held scoreless once. The Bears are 8-7 in shutout games, the Lions 6-6 and the Packers 1-9. Sixteen of the 23 shutouts occurred from 1967-80.

1968: Lions 42, Bears 0
1969: Vikings 27, Lions 0
1969: Vikings 31, Bears 0
1970: Lions 40, Packers 0
1970: Lions 20, Packers 0
1970: Vikings 24, Bears 0
1971: Vikings 3, Packers 0
1972: Lions 14, Bears 0
1973: Packers 21, Bears 0
1973: Lions 34, Packers 0
1974: Vikings 17, Bears 0

APPENDIX

1977: Bears 26, Packers 0
1978: Bears 14, Packers 0
1978: Bears 19, Lions 0
1979: Lions 20, Bears 0
1980: Vikings 34, Lions 0
1986: Bears 23, Vikings 0
1988: Bears 16, Packers 0
1988: Vikings 23, Lions 0
1991: Bears 10, Packers 0
1993: Vikings 13, Lions 0
2001: Bears 24, Lions 0
2006: Bears 26, Packers 0

INDEX

INDEX